THE LIFE *AND* POEMS *OF*
MIRABEAU B. LAMAR

From a daguerreotype

Mirabeau B. Lamar in 1845

COURTESY OF MR. LUCIUS Q. C. LAMAR, HAVANA

THE
LIFE *AND* POEMS
OF
MIRABEAU B. LAMAR

By

Philip Graham

———◆———

Chapel Hill

THE UNIVERSITY OF NORTH CAROLINA PRESS

1938

82819
811.39
L215g

This edition is limited to 1,000 numbered copies of which the first 350 are autographed. The type has been melted.

This is number. *927*. .

TO THE MEMORY OF

LORETTO EVALINA LAMAR CALDER,

*Of Whom, When She Was Five Years Old,
Lamar Wrote, "I Would Wish That My
Little Daughter May Acquire from
These Verses a Better Knowledge
of Her Father's Heart,"*

THIS VOLUME IS DEDICATED

PREFACE

THIS VOLUME presents Mirabeau B. Lamar's poems—many of them now published for the first time—against a background of personal and intimate biographical detail. Material has been gathered from many sources. These include the newspapers of Georgia, Alabama, and Texas; the albums, scrap-books, journals, and correspondence of Lamar and of the various branches of his family; and the slim volume of verses published by Lamar, now very rare. I have indicated in the fore-notes the source of each poem, as well as the circumstances of its composition. Immediately preceding each poem the date of composition appears on the left, the date of publication on the right.

In the biographical sketch I have intentionally emphasized the personal element, because Lamar's private life is the only proper setting for his poems. These verses must be associated, not with his public career, but with the emotions and intimate circumstances of his private life. It is only then that they take on their proper significance as a revelation of the man's character and personality. When viewed against such a background, these poems reveal much concerning not only the author, but also the section and time that produced them—the dramatic meeting of the Old South and the New West.

My obligations are as numerous as my sources. My sincerest gratitude is due Mrs. Henrietta Andrews (League City, Texas) for important and extensive manuscripts of Lamar and for use of the facsimile on page 98, to Miss Loretto L. Chappell (Columbus, Georgia) for Rebecca Ann Lamar's album of her father's poems, and to Mr. Lucius Q. C. Lamar (Havana, Cuba) for the daguerreotype of Lamar. For help generously given I wish to thank Mr. Oliver Orr (Macon, Georgia), Dr. John R. Long (Marion, Alabama), Judge A. W. Cozart (Columbus, Georgia), Mr. Douglas Goode (Montgomery, Alabama), Dr. Alex Dienst (Temple, Texas), Mr. Charles McDowell (Eufaula, Alabama) , Mr. W. D. Reid (Eatonton, Georgia), Mrs. Leila L. Sibley (Milledgeville, Georgia), Mrs. Walter D. Lamar (Macon, Georgia) , Mrs. Anne Brindley (Galveston, Texas), Mr. Peter A. Brannon (Montgomery, Alabama), Mr. Alva C. Smith (Columbus, Georgia), Mrs. J. L. Beeson (Milledgeville, Georgia) , Miss Ruth Blair (Atlanta, Georgia), and Miss Myra Black (Temple, Texas).

For courtesies extended I wish particularly to thank the Library of the University of Georgia (Athens, Georgia), The Washington Memorial Library (Macon, Georgia), *The Ledger-Enquirer* (Columbus, Georgia), The Rosenberg Library (Galveston, Texas) , The Houston (Texas) Public Library, The Library of the University of Texas (Austin), and the American Antiquarian Society (Worcester, Massachusetts).

PHILIP GRAHAM.

The University of Texas
April 21, 1937

CONTENTS

CONTENTS

CONTENTS

PART I

The Personal Incidents of Lamar's Life

I

A SON OF THE SOUTH

——◆·◆——

NOT MANY knew Mirabeau Lamar, the public official of
Texas, for he was not an easy person to get acquainted with.
Fewer still knew Lamar, the man—sociable among friends,
loyal, generous, home-loving, and affectionate. More than
most men, he lived simultaneously two lives, his public
career and his private life. Before the eyes of the public this
ambitious, courageous, and sternly duty-bound individual
seemed to have a particular gift for riding the very crest of
the highest waves of romantic adventure of his day. The
most exciting moments in Georgia history of the 1820's
and 1830's and the most dramatic years of the Texas story
cannot, any of them, be told without Lamar's name.

The brilliance of the man's public career has blinded
biographers to the other side of his life. The rather formal
bulwark of reserve which he unconsciously placed between
himself and the public, while it prevented his ever being a
politician, made more imperative for him a small circle of
intimate acquaintances with whom there was no reserve.
And these—both men and women—responded generously
to the needs of his affectionate nature with a loyalty and

3

love seldom given to men of more popular bent. These close friends, kinsfolk, and family relations form the personal background of his verse.

The pattern of the family character—these retiring men of strong feelings, with their sense of justice and their tenacity of opinion—had been forming in America for five generations before the birth of Mirabeau Lamar. Tradition has it that four brothers as early as the 1660's settled in Maryland and Virginia, Huguenots fleeing from religious persecution in France.[1] Here they and their descendants lived for almost a century on plantations with such alluring names as Valentine's Garden, Wilson's Delay, Conclusion, and Robert's Delight, until the spirit of adventure drew a group of the brothers down into South Carolina and Georgia. John Lamar settled on Beach Island in the Savannah River.

The grandson of this early settler in Georgia, another John Lamar (born in 1769), married Rebecca Lamar, his first cousin, and established himself on a plantation in Jefferson County (organized out of Warren and Burke Counties), near Louisville, then the capital of Georgia. Here Mirabeau was born August 16, 1798, the second child in a family that later was to include four sons and five daughters.

The new son was christened Mirabeau Buonaparte—a name which the Texans of the next generation could neither spell nor pronounce [2]—by an eccentric bachelor uncle, Zachariah Lamar, who was at the time living with

1 William H. Lamar, "Thomas Lamar . . . Descendants," *Publications* of the Southern Historical Association, I (July, 1897), 203-10; *Baltimore Sun*, Oct. 29, 1905; Edward Mayes, *Lucius Q. C. Lamar*, p. 13; W. A. Cate, *Lucius Q. C. Lamar*, pp. 8-15.

2 Texans usually pronounced it either *My-ree-bo* or *Mee-ry-bo*. Because Lamar never signed his middle name in full—only Mirabeau B. Lamar— a legend sprang up in Texas that he repudiated the *Buonaparte*.

4

the family. This self-taught man, in his delving into the past, had come to venerate the celebrities of history and literature, and, as his infant nephews arrived, he claimed the privilege of christening them, bestowing upon each the names of his favorites of the moment. His multiple selections—Lucius Quintus Cincinnatus, Mirabeau Buonaparte, Thomas Randolph, Jefferson Jackson, and Lavoisier Legrande (a grandson)—suggest not only the trends of Zachariah's reading, but also an uneasy fear that there might not be enough sons to take care of all his favorites.[3]

John Lamar found by 1808 that his family was growing faster than his fortune. The aroma of prosperity that had attracted him to the section was no longer in his nostrils, for the soil of Jefferson County was poor, and John Lamar was too thrifty to reside on a plantation not supporting his household. Furthermore, the state capital had been moved from Louisville to Milledgeville, and with it had gone much of the prosperity of the region. After two years of prospecting, he moved his entire establishment westward half across the state, to set up a new plantation in the bend of Little River, only fifteen miles northwest of the new capital at Milledgeville and only nine miles south of fast-growing Eatonton. "Little River John," as he was now styled, christened his new home Fairfield, and built a commodious, old-fashioned, two-story house, constructed after the enduring models of the day, with white-columned front and wide gallery. In front he thinned the old oaks into stately groups and planted long rows of Lombardy poplars; in the rear he dotted his Negro cabins over the half-wooded plain that shelved gradually down to the river. On one side

---

[3] After Zachariah's marriage he gave to his own children, strangely enough, the simple names of Mary Ann (later Mrs. Howell Cobb) and John Basil, family possessions since the French exodus.

he planted the orchard trees and marked out the garden, and on the other cultivated more than a thousand rolling acres.

Here at Fairfield, beautiful in its bountiful comfort, the children of the Lamar home grew to maturity. The house was a relay for the stage, and each day at noon Mirabeau saw coming up the red lane the lumbering coach and four, to empty its crowd of bustling, hungry, and usually talkative passengers for the midday meal. That stage must have seemed to the imaginative boy a messenger from the world of adventure.[4]

Most of the farm labor on the plantation was performed by slaves, though the four brothers—Lucius, Mirabeau, Thomas, and Jefferson—occasionally took turns as overseer. Mirabeau became especially fond of riding and fencing, and there were long boat-excursions up the Oconee and frequent stage journeys to Macon. His education, in the sense of formal schooling, was desultory. John and Rebecca Lamar, though not wealthy, were well-to-do, and would gladly have sent their son to Princeton. But from early childhood his nervous, impetuous temperament, much to his parents' distress, rendered unbearable the routine of school, and the restlessness apparent throughout his life made doubly hard any regular academic course. For a short period he attended the academy at Milledgeville, and when in 1816 the Eatonton Academy (supported by lottery) was chartered, with Dr. Alonza Church as principal, he enrolled there. But even the steady eye of this Presbyterian Vermonter could not cure Mirabeau's incorrigible aversion to study. Here he learned a little Latin and was en-

---

[4] *The Houston Chronicle,* Jan. 27, 1929, carries a picture of Fairfield. The old homestead, the house still unchanged, is now the property of the Georgia Power Company.

couraged to continue his reading of history and literature, channels into which his Uncle Zachariah had long before guided him. Some of his favorites, now and later, were Thomas Moore, Byron, Churchill, Dryden, Pope, Gibbon, and Scott. He was especially fond of ancient history, seeing in the inflexible integrity of the old heroes models after which he desired to shape his own character. At one public exhibition at the academy he took the rôle of Brutus in *Julius Caesar* with such spirit as almost entirely to lose his own identity in portraying the motives that prompted the noble Roman to slay his friend for his country's good. His reading, wide though unsystematic and independent of academic walls, was responsible for Lamar's large fund of varied information, as well as for his ready allusion and his polished literary style, which years later were to stamp him, in the eyes of the Texan frontiersmen, as "highly cultured." As he looked back over his school years, in spite of his enthusiastic reading he could say with a rather painful degree of truth, "It has not been my good fortune to wander far in the labyrinth of letters." [5]

As the boys grew to manhood they found social doors swung wide for them throughout more than five counties, from Sparta to Monticello, from Eatonton to Macon. They represented a social force not to be ignored in those antebellum days in Georgia. They represented also a physical force which no rustic bully cared to encounter, for if ever there lived men insensible to fear and superior to corruption, they were the four brothers Lamar.[6] Mirabeau was sketching from life when he wrote:

[5] Charles Gulick, Winnie Allen, and Harriet Smither, eds., *The Papers of Mirabeau Buonaparte Lamar* (hereafter cited as *Lamar Papers*), Nos. 85 (V, 41) and 88 (V, 44); W. H. Sparks, *The Memories of Fifty Years*, pp. 170-72.

[6] Sparks, *op. cit.*, p. 172.

Now pause we here a while to tell
What at a country dance befell,
In Christmas times, at father Grumpus'
Where they cut a dreadful rumpus.
He lives three miles from Doctor Sneak,
On what is called the Rackoon Creek,
In cabin built of swamp oak strong,
Twenty feet wide and thirty long,
The chinks well daub'd with straw and clay
That ne'er admits the solar ray;
A cyprus roof and puncheon floor,
A four square window and a door,
Screaking on new hickory hinges,
At which your very bosom scringes.
A bed, a barrel and a broom
Grac'd south-east corner of the room.
Another held a cross'd leg'd table,
A tripod, bench, and rocking cradle;
In the third lay pots and griddles,
The fourth cleared out for him that fiddles,
Whilst round the walls in gay festoons
Swung petticoats and pantaloons.
Such is the spacious drawing-hall
In which was held our lively ball.[7]

Dr. Horace Shaw's store, half-way between Eatonton and the plantation, became a popular meeting place for the young people of the vicinity. It was here that Mirabeau met Sarah Gordon ("Sally Riley"), his first sweetheart, the youngest daughter of Charles P. Gordon, a lawyer of Eatonton. It was on the altar of her golden beauty—"the morn-

[7] See p. 112.

ing's glory and the bloom of spring"—that the youthful lover intermittently poured his devotion for almost two years.[8] But even Sarah had her rivals, for Mirabeau was addressing poems to Martha Fannin (the niece of James Fannin), Laura Dent, Eliza Moore, Nancy Mason (all of Eatonton), Eliza Springer (of Sparta), and a certain "village coquette" of Monticello.

Of the four Lamar brothers only Lucius could be called handsome, with slightly curled hair brushed forward at the sides, mouth tilted delightfully upward at the corners, and daring eyes rakishly prominent. Thomas, later known as "the good physician," was liked for his sweet disposition, and Jefferson for his unobtrusive quietness. Mirabeau affected a plainness in striking contrast with the cavalier Lucius. He was below medium height, but stout and muscular. His hair was black and straight, his face was oval, and his blue eyes—exceedingly soft and tender except when aroused by excitement—had the trick of varying in their expression to reflect every thought in his mind. The quizzically up-turned corners of the mouth softened an expression otherwise stern, but could not hide a distinct tendency toward melancholia. His apparently natural chivalry sometimes gave way to a playful satire. Usually diffident and retiring, when aroused he was impetuous and startling.[9]

The last five children born to John and Rebecca Lamar were daughters. Louisa, Amelia, Mary Ann, and Evalina had followed the boys in quick succession. It was a wholesome group, bound by unusual loyalty. Even before the congenial circle had been completed by the birth of Loretto

[8] "Sally Riley," "Anacreontic," and "No Girl Can Win My Stubborn Breast" were all addressed to Sarah Gordon.
[9] Sparks, *op. cit.*, pp. 169-72.

9

Rebecca, the youngest, it had already been broken.[10]
Lucius, after working as a salesman in Eatonton, in 1816
began the study of law in the office of Joel Crawford at
Milledgeville, and a year later left for the celebrated law
school in Litchfield, Connecticut. Jefferson was planning
to be a planter, and Thomas had already decided on medi-
cine as a profession. Mirabeau was the most ambitious of
the four boys, yet he dreaded the strict confinement of the
law as much as the monotony of the plantation. Fame apparently was his goal, though his interpretation of it reached
higher than mere conspicuousness. He hoped, rather, to be
able to accomplish something that would embalm his memory in men's minds. Never very practical, and always remarkable among his friends for his indifference to money,
he had conceived his purpose and result without much
thought to the means at hand. Perhaps a commission in
King Arthur's court would have enabled him to realize
his aims better than any vocation available in Georgia. His
hope was that some star might rise out of the West.

When in 1819 Willis Roberts, long a friend of the family
at Eatonton, set out to try his fortune in newly admitted
Alabama, Mirabeau gladly joined him. Here was the lure
of the frontier, with the action and promise of adventure in
a new country. Here perhaps Mirabeau would meet with
those great deeds which he had dreamed of since childhood.
Cahawba, in Dallas County at the junction of the Cahawba
and Alabama rivers, had the year before been named the
capital of the new state, and the two friends decided to

[10] Louisa later married Abner McGehee; Amelia, John S. Randle; Mary
Ann, Joseph Moreland; Evalina, a Mr. Harvey; Loretto Rebecca, Absalom
Chappell.

establish here a general mercantile business. They arrived in time for the auction of the lots in May, 1819.[11]

For the next year Mirabeau became a member of the Roberts household.[12] He found the large family almost a replica of his own at Fairfield. This father and the three sons (Samuel, Joel, and Reuben) were the men to whom twenty years later Lamar was to give a total of five Texas offices. Olivia was his choice among the daughters (Olivia, Sophia, Laura). To Mirabeau this latter attachment remained throughout life one of his closest friendships; with Olivia it was recurrently bursting into a more ardent feeling.

But the mercantile business did not thrive. Such heavily capitalized firms as Cocheran and Perine had set a standard far beyond the reach of the rather meager means of Roberts and Lamar. Mirabeau, under no circumstances, could have been a good shopkeeper, and he was soon glad to sell out to his genial partner, Dr. Roberts.[13] But Lamar found himself loath to leave Cahawba.[14] There was not another community more representative of the South's best culture than this new capital. No people in all America sat down to more bounteous dinners, served by better servants on richer mahogany. No people rode better groomed horses, or spoke their vernacular with gentler accents. Such plantations as those of James B. Clarke, James

[11] Thomas M. Own, *History of Alabama* (Chicago, 1921), II, 186; A. M. G. Fry, *Memories of Old Cahaba,* pp. 3-12.

[12] *Lamar Papers,* No. 827 (V, 200).

[13] Francis Copcutt, "Mirabeau B. Lamar," *The Knickerbocker,* XXV (May, 1845), 379.

[14] Fifteen years later Lamar remembered Cahawba as "the theater of my first adventures, associated with some of the most pleasing recollections of my life."—Lamar's manuscript, "Journal of My Travels," p. 20.

Craig, and A. J. Safford radiated out into the rich bottom lands like the spokes of a wheel, and Cahawba was the hub. Lamar's cavalier manner and his sincerity of address made him a welcome visitor at manor houses that must have reminded him of his mediaeval history. Instead of the military adventure that he had expected, he found himself in a social culture and a wealth far surpassing any that he had known. He was at ease in the society, but as to wealth— he did not have enough to pay his board bill at Curtis Bell's hotel, where he roomed with Hewes the tailor after the departure of the Roberts family.[15]

In order to support himself in surroundings altogether congenial, he joined William Allen in the publication of the *Cahawba Press,* one of the two weekly newspapers in the town.[16] His duties as co-publisher and probably editor were not onerous, for he made frequent visits to the new town of Montgomery and to Mobile, and began practicing political speech-making on tours that carried him over most of Alabama and Georgia.[17] He found time, too, for considerable scribbling. Early in 1821 he announced his purpose of publishing the *Village Miscellany,* a humorous paper to be issued "by Mr. Lanthernbalvon, Batchelor of mericles, and late from the court of fashionable folly." The periodical was to be supported by "several young men whose names it will be vain to enquire after," and two sets of

---

[15] *Lamar Papers,* No. 2551 (VI, 351). Cahawba, like its glories, has passed away. Bounded on three sides by rivers, it fell a victim to floods in 1825 and again in 1833. The capital was removed in 1826, and the Civil War swept away the little that remained. In 1919 a centennial stone was erected to mark the site of its prosperity.—Fry, *op. cit.,* p. 13.

[16] The issue for July 15, 1820 (now in the possession of the American Antiquarian Society, Worcester, Mass.) carries the statement that the paper is published by Allen and Lamar. See also Copcutt, "Mirabeau B. Lamar," *The Knickerbocker,* XXV (May, 1845), 379.

[17] Lamar's "Journal of My Travels," pp. 8, 24, 32.

each issue were promised—one for the ladies and one for the gentlemen. Though the public was facetiously assured that Mr. Lanthernbalvon was capable of producing something that "will roll down the gutters of time to the latest posterity," probably no issue of the magazine was ever published.[18]

Lamar's last contribution to the *Cahawba Press,* a rhymed New-Year's address to the patrons, appeared in the issue for January 1, 1822.[19] Newspaper work had proved no more lucrative for him than the mercantile business. It had, however, furnished him a congenial occupation and probably awakened his political aspirations. It helped him to a new interpretation of adventure, this time in terms of politics. And the political battlefield of Georgia at this time held bright promise of excitement. On the back of a copy of the "Address" sent to brother Lucius, Mirabeau wrote a hasty note: "I am here in Cahaba, without any business, or liklyhood to obtain any shortly— You need not be disappointed if you see me back in Geo. again in a few weeks." [20]

Meanwhile brother Lucius had returned from law school, to become the partner of Joel Crawford in Milledgeville. Mirabeau could not have decided to enter Georgia politics at a more opportune moment. For four years the John Clarke and the William Crawford factions had waged bitter battle throughout the state, with the Clarke forces victorious by a narrow margin. The election for governor in 1823 found the old feud renewed, the Clarke forces represented by Matthew Talbot, the opposing group by George M. Troup.

[18] *Lamar Papers,* No. 34 (V, 7).
[19] The "Address" appears on p. 112.
[20] *Lamar Papers,* No. 44 (V, 19).

Mirabeau returned to Georgia in time to witness the most exciting election recorded in the annals of the state. When it became apparent that the voting, which was carried on by the legislators, had resulted in the election of Troup by a majority of two, the excitement was unbounded. "One wild shout seemed to lift the ceiling . . . ," a witness wrote. "The lobby and the galleries joined in. Members and spectators rushed into each other's arms, kissed each other, wept, shouted, kicked over the desks, tumbled on the floor." When the first outburst had subsided, an Irish minister in the chamber ejaculated, "O Lord, we thank Thee! The State is redeemed from the rule of the Devil and John Clarke." [21]

The Crawfords and the Lamars had been loyal supporters of the new governor, and scarcely had Troup dusted his gubernatorial desk in the old Milledgeville capitol when Mirabeau presented himself at the door. He carried this explanatory note from Joel Crawford, brother Lucius' partner:

Permit me to recommend to your confidence and patronage, my young friend Mirabeau Lamar. He is a gentleman not more distinguished by the loftiest sentiments of honor than by mental superiority and devotion to republican politics—Mr. Lamar asks the appointment of Secretary to the Executive Department. . . .[22]

Governor Troup not only made Mirabeau his private secretary, but also took him into his home, giving him unbounded trust and ardent friendship—a relation that continued throughout the three years of Troup's first term.

[21] Sparks, *op. cit.*, pp. 129-30; Edward J. Harden, *The Life of George M. Troup*, p. 170.

[22] *Lamar Papers*, No. 50 (I, 54).

As a member of the governor's household, the young politician mixed with the social cream of Georgia, and at the State House, intimately associated with such men as Seaborn Jones and David Blackshear,[23] he became thoroughly conversant with the political issues of the day. In the Troup camp there was only one religion, and that was State Rights. In the dispute over the Indian lands Lamar saw "the mad Governor of Georgia" openly defy the federal government and make good that defiance. From the whole episode Lamar carried away a feeling of increased hostility toward Indians, and strengthened faith in the doctrine of State Rights. Governor Troup, a man of lofty but stern ideals, exerted also a personal influence on Lamar hardly to be estimated.

There was glamor as well as politics in this business of being Secretary to the Governor. General Lafayette on his visit to America in 1825 became the guest of Georgia when, March 19, Governor Troup and his staff welcomed him at Savannah. On this occasion Lamar wore his first sword, and was so deeply impressed by the whole ceremony that more than twenty years later he still attached a special significance to the cherished weapon because, he said, "I placed it at my side for the first time when voluntarily called upon to command a corps on the memorable occasion of giving welcome to the glorious La Fayette. . . . "[24] The escort, with Lamar at its head, interpreted military style with a strong Southern cavalier accent, and thus accompanied the old patriot on to Milledgeville. Here a banquet was spread in the State House, an occasion made memorable by the gorgeous ceremonial of the parade,

---

[23] For a short period Lamar served as secretary also to General David Blackshear (S. F. Miller, *The Bench and Bar of Georgia*, I, 480).
[24] *Lamar Papers*, No. 2212 (VI, 16).

and the grace of the toastmaster, Seaborn Jones, as well as the highly appropriate speech of Lafayette himself. The guests of honor were then conducted on a tour of the Creek Nation in Georgia, for the Frenchmen were very curious about the Indians.[25]

As Lamar's secretariate drew to a close in November of 1825, the young cavalier found himself in most favored circumstances. His alignment with the State Rights cause promised a bright political future. He was twenty-seven years old, of a good family, cultured and well-versed in the social graces, and he knew how to wear a sword. His circle of acquaintances widened rapidly. He often visited his old friends, the Roberts family at Mobile, and at Macon he listened "at Lanier's" to the songs of Irene Nisbet, the "Jenny Lind of Georgia." She lived in Macon, but fortunately had country cousins in Eatonton. He strolled along the banks of the Oconee with "lovely Anna Cowles" (daughter of Macon's railway pioneer), the one "of all the gay, enchanting throng" that Mirabeau best remembered in after years.[26] In Milledgeville Miss Sarah H. Rossetter occupied most of his softer moments. The first canto of "Sally Riley," which years before he had begun in praise of Sarah Gordon, he now finished in praise of Sarah Rossetter, "well worthy," he remarked, "of all that had been said" of the former idol. The acrostic "Sonnet to Solitude" Lamar wrote in Miss Rossetter's album, and to her little sister, Susannah, who had just reached the troublesome age, he wrote the playful "To Susannah," the most delightfully fresh of all his early verses.

25 A. Levasseur (Lafayette's secretary), *Lafayette En Amerique*, II, 155-87; Harden, *op. cit.*, p. 292; Lucian L. Knight, *Georgia's Landmarks, Memorials, and Legends*, II, 401, 574.

26 See poems to Irene Nisbet and Anna Cowles, pp. 219 and 222.

One affair of the heart was beginning to take on great seriousness for Lamar. Many legends surround his meeting Miss Tabitha Jordan. She may have been the "Miss Tab" of his Cahawba days.[27] Local tradition, in the best melodramatic manner of the day, tells the story of his courtship:

In 1821 he accidentally met the being who was to have a powerful influence over his future life. He saw the face but a moment, and it was that of a mere girl, upon whose cheeks some fourteen summers had scattered their roses. He knew neither her name nor residence, nor did he endeavor to discover them until it was too late, but the memory of that face haunted him like a pleasant dream.

At a social gathering at Eatonton in the spring of 1824, the legend continues, Lamar was much surprised upon entering the gay saloon to behold the girl whom he had met three years before, now grown to womanhood. Before the evening was over he proposed and was as promptly refused. Then one day he was startled at seeing her in a carriage, this time in Milledgeville, on her way to Alabama to settle with her brother-in-law. Lamar followed her to a hotel, and "in a burst of passionate eloquence begged her to reverse her cruel decision; and the lady, softened by his enthusiasm, gave him some words of encouragement." [28]

Stripped of legendary frills, the facts seem to be that on a speaking tour in Georgia about 1821 Lamar met Tabitha Jordan in Twiggs County, where her parents, Burwell and Ann Dupree Jordan, lived on a plantation. It is altogether

[27] Lamar's "Address to the Patrons . . .," p. 127; the year of Tabitha's birth (1809) precludes any idea of a love affair earlier.

[28] Copcutt, "Mirabeau B. Lamar," *The Knickerbocker,* XXV (May, 1845), 379-80.

probable that Lamar met her again at Eatonton, as he was a frequent visitor there during his secretariate with Governor Troup, and the enthusiastic proposal is entirely in keeping with Lamar's impulsive nature. After her father's death in 1825 Tabitha went to Alabama to live with her sister Rebecca, and, as she passed through Milledgeville en route, Lamar could easily have found opportunity to renew their acquaintance.[29]

Certain it is that by December of 1825 Tabitha was in Alabama and Mirabeau, busy in Milledgeville, was uneasy about the progress of his suit. From the executive office, December 3, 1825, he wrote to her:

Dear Tabitha,

I should have written to you, in compliance with my promise, long before this, but I have been ever since my arrival at home in the daily expectation of returning to Alabama in anxious solicitude to see you. Business, however, has so accumulated in this office since the Session has commenced, that my services cannot be dispensed with . . . I am therefore compel'd, certainly much against desire, to delay my return until the adjournment of the Legislature. So soon as it rises you may expect to see me again, with feelings of affection considerably augmented by absence.

But Tabitha, I cannot conceal from you an uneasy apprehension which I feel, arising from the information received a short time since that I am likely to experience, in ——, [30]

29 Tabitha was the fourth of five daughters of the Jordan family: Rebecca (Mrs. Jabez Curry of Perry County, Alabama), Sarah (Mrs. Crocker of Lincoln County, Ga.), Caroline (Mrs. Steele of Louisville, Ky.), Tabitha, and Jane Ann (Mrs. Walker of Faunsdale, Marengo County, Ala.). The mother, who later married a Mr. Worthy, is buried on the Curry plantation, seven miles northwest of Marion, Ala. (Letters and scrap-book now in the possession of the Curry family.)

30 The name has been carefully blotted out—I suspect by Tabitha herself—with an ink different from that of the letter.

a formidable rival. My brother met him going to Alabama, with a view to renew his addresses to you . . . and I have very lately heard that his hopes of success are flattering . . . I hope for the best. I am unwilling to harbour a belief that you are capable of a dereliction of plighted faith. My anxious uneasiness arises, not from a want of confidence in her who has my highest esteem, but from a natural jealousy inseparable from all who love with much devotedness. All who love sincerely are easily alarmed by a rival, and if my fears are groundless upon this score, I hope you will forgive a weakness which I cannot control and which I flatter myself is not allied to badness of heart . . . I pray you to write if it be only three lines giving the state of your health.

Give my respects to your Brother and Sister,
And accept the same.

Mirabeau B. Lamar.[31]

Tabitha's reply must have been satisfactory enough to stimulate eager interest, for less than a month later (January 1, 1826) Lamar married her, probably at the home of her sister Rebecca in Perry County, Alabama.[32] At the time of the marriage Lamar was twenty-eight, Tabitha seventeen. Strangely enough, no verses relating to the courtship have been preserved.

Lamar was journeying with his bride back toward Putnam County when an accident came near wrecking his new-found happiness. While passing through the Indian country, he left the carriage for a moment in charge of the Negroes. The horses took fright, the carriage was splintered against a tree, and Tabitha was thrown on the rocks. Lamar rushed to the spot, to find her face laid open to the

[31] This is the only extant letter from Lamar to his first wife.

[32] See also *Lamar Papers*, No. 885 (V, 216); Asa K. Christian, *Mirabeau Buonaparte Lamar*, p. 3. Destruction of the Perry County records during the Civil War renders official verification impossible.

bone. In a nearby Indian hut she recovered consciousness, and, according to the legend, said to her husband, "You loved me for my beauty—it is gone forever." He placed her head upon his knee, trimmed the ragged edges of the wound with his razor, and with a common needle-and-thread sewed the severed parts together.[33]

[33] Copcutt, "Mirabeau B. Lamar," *The Knickerbocker,* XXV (May, 1845), 380-81.

II

ON THE BANKS OF THE
CHATTAHOOCHEE

———•—•———

LAMAR resigned his position with Governor Troup to
nurse his bride back to health. The wound healed rapidly,
leaving only a small white line, hardly perceptible, which
did not in the least mar her beauty. But the shock had been
too severe, and in her weakened condition she contracted
tuberculosis. Unsuspecting the presence of the insidious
disease, the bride and groom visited back and forth in
Georgia and Alabama. The Jordan estate was settled, Mirabeau and Tabitha receiving in the proceedings three hundred and fifty acres of land in Twiggs County, five slaves,
and considerable personal property.[1] On November 7, 1827
a daughter was born, named Rebecca Ann, after her two
grandmothers.[2]

During the two years immediately following his marriage
Lamar probably did not entertain any idea of settling upon

[1] The original probate papers are in the possession of Mirabeau Lamar's
grand-children, though all official records of Twiggs County were destroyed by fire in 1901.

[2] The date is taken from the inscription in Rose Hill Cemetery, Macon,
Ga. Sam H. Dixon and Louis W. Kemp (*Heroes of San Jacinto*, p. 299)
erroneously give 1829 as the date of her birth.

a plantation. The farm in Twiggs County did not actually come into his possession until late in 1829, and the plantation seven miles northwest of Marion, in Perry County, Alabama, with which his name is sometimes associated,[3] was owned and operated by Jabez Curry, Tabitha's brother-in-law. Lamar felt that through a public career he might better realize those ideals cherished since boyhood.

His opportunity came with the opening of the Indian lands in Muscogee County. The Georgia Legislature of 1827 passed "An Act to Lay Out a Trading Town on the Chattahoochee River," and the duly appointed commissioners laid out Columbus, cutting the site into six hundred and thirty-two half-acre lots. The surveyors had not driven their last stakes before Lamar was on the ground, planning to establish a newspaper. The new country had a rich natural scenery and a highly romantic background of legend.[4] Here were possibilities, too, of carrying his cherished State Rights principles into new territory in the congenial capacity of editor; and, best of all, here was promise of the modest but happy home for Tabitha and Rebecca Ann that his affectionate, domestic nature demanded.

The first issue of *The Columbus Enquirer* appeared May 29, 1828.[5] In politics the paper was frankly attached to the Republican creed "as exemplified in the administration of Thomas Jefferson," and to the principles "that characterized the late able administration of Governor Troup." The editor was resolved "to adhere to truth and justice in his matter, and if possible to moderation in his manner." Here Lamar, with the minds of the nation's political fathers back

[3] Christian, *op. cit.*, p. 3.

[4] John H. Martin, *Columbus, Georgia*, pp. 5-123 (history), pp. 190-96 (legend).

[5] Eugene Barker, "Mirabeau Bonaparte Lamar," The University of Texas *Record*, V, No. 2 (Aug., 1903), 148.

of him, was to pen some of the strongest arguments in the entire South for the doctrine of State Rights. Politics was not to be, however, the only concern of the *Enquirer,* for it was to publish also "such miscellaneous selections as are calculated to please and instruct; to gratify fancy and to increase knowledge—making it a literary as well as a political paper." [6] Each issue during Lamar's editorship contained at least one poem, and some issues as many as four. He was finding an outlet for his literary productions accumulated since his Cahawba days.

The life of the editor was not easy in a frontier town which was trying to lure commerce up the river and attract new settlers, and at the same time to establish order in a community in which squads of vagabond, thieving Indians daily lounged about its streets, and where—worst of all—local politics tended toward bitter personal feeling and resulted in almost weekly duels. The columns of the *Enquirer* bristle with reports of duels and dueling correspondence. Lamar was thinking of these early days in Columbus when in later years he wrote to a friend who had turned editor: "I have had some experience in editing a paper and can sympathize with you in the troubles and vexations . . . The best counsel that I can give you is to use the *strongest arguments* and the *blandest words;* which was my device when I played the rôle of editor." [7]

Columbus was growing rapidly. Before the *Enquirer* was a year old its editor could write:

Building is carried on in a style that would do honor to our populous cities . . . We frequently find large two-story houses and well cleaned gardens in various parts of the town where but a short time previously we were rambling for game.

6 The Prospectus, *Lamar Papers,* No. 73 (V, 29).
7 *Lamar Papers,* No. 2635 (VI, 378).

Hunters are not infrequently surprised at finding their hunting grounds suddenly converted from a wilderness into cultivated fields or adorned by the architect and enlivened by traffic.[8]

Stores, two hotels, a theater, a bank, a lumber mill, and a bridge over the Chattahoochee were fast converting the settlement on the reserve into a young city. It could boast even a temperance society, with James W. Fannin the first recording secretary.[9] Lamar had bought one of the lots sold at the original auction and had built a wide one-story wooden cottage, with low windows, approximately on what is now Number 1321 Third Avenue. The first office of the *Enquirer* was probably on the same lot, though it was later moved to Randolph and Oglethorpe streets. The home was not far from the Chattahoochee, and on many evenings Lamar, Tabitha, and Rebecca Ann strolled along the wide promenade between the town and the river, which the *Enquirer* declared would some day become "the handsomest and most romantic walk in the State." [10] The whole scene—the Coweta Falls below, the gushing springs of the opposite bank, and the rich forest behind—became in later years the background of Lamar's fondest memories.[11] Seated here on summer evenings he composed his songs

> To one whose smiles and tears proclaimed
> The triumph of [his] art
> And plainly told, the minstrel reigned
> The monarch of her heart.[12]

Not one of the songs then written has survived.

[8] *The Columbus Enquirer,* Feb. 14, 1829.
[9] Martin, *op. cit.,* p. 20.
[10] *The Columbus Enquirer,* Aug. 9, 1828.
[11] Martin, *op. cit.,* pp. 7, 22.
[12] "On the Banks of the Chattahoochee."

At the time of the incorporation of Columbus (1829) Lamar declined nomination as one of the six commissioners.[13] Up to this point he had refused to become a candidate for any office, feeling that such a course strengthened the political power of the *Enquirer*. In the summer of 1829, however, he announced for state senator from Muscogee County against Sowell Woolfolk, a Columbus merchant who had already served one term in the office. The columns of the *Enquirer* and Lamar's command over language brought him a sweeping victory in the October election.[14] He sold half interest in his paper to Richard T. Marks, and during the following year was both editor and senator. The next summer found him a candidate for a second term in the state senate. The *Enquirer* reported that "July Fourth was celebrated with becoming spirit . . . the oration, delivered by M. B. Lamar, was followed by the usual dinner at Howard's Hotel, a feast of good things, including patriotism and hilarity." Just as a repetition of the success of the year before seemed certain, a blow fell upon Lamar from which he was never fully to recover.

Tabitha died August 20, 1830,[15] at the age of twenty-one. The event could not have been altogether unexpected, for "the disease which removed her hence," recorded her sister, "was protracted and severe";[16] yet the emotional shock to

13 Martin, *op. cit.*, p. 17.

14 Martin, *op. cit.*, pp. 15, 16, 20.

15 The date is taken from *The Columbus Enquirer* (Martin, *op. cit.*, p. 21) and the scrap-book of Rebecca Curry, Tabitha's sister. H. P. Gambrell (*Mirabeau Buonaparte Lamar*, p. 52) incorrectly gives 1833 as the date of Tabitha's death, probably following Christian (*op. cit.*, p. 5). The fire which destroyed the Muscogee County Records in 1839 cut off official information.

16 Obituary preserved in the Rebecca Curry scrap-book. The Negro Primus, a house boy in the Lamar home at Columbus, also died of tuberculosis seven years later.—*Lamar Papers*, No. 585 (V, 152).

Lamar was great. He immediately withdrew from the senatorial race, and disposed of his remaining interest in the *Enquirer*.[17] Closing his cottage in Columbus and leaving Rebecca Ann in the care of his mother at Fairfield, he gave himself up to his grief.[18] Like his brother Lucius, he had from boyhood been too much inclined toward melancholia, and it was feared for a time that he could never rise from the despair into which he sank. Always able to share good fortune with those around him, he could never share his troubles with any one; rather, he drew within himself to coddle his grief. He even destroyed the verse which he had written to Tabitha, feeling that any reminder of her only renewed his sorrow. His later lines,

> When she died and left me here—
> My soul in desolation—
> I broke the shell she loved so well,
> Destroyed the songs I wrought her,

are to be taken literally.[19] For these songs recording his former happiness he substituted two elegies to Tabitha, "Thou Idol of My Soul," and "At Evening on the Banks of the Chattahoochee," the first written at her grave, and the second composed on the beautiful river bank which had been their favorite promenade. Peculiarly without the ordinary ambitions for wealth and power, he had found in Tabitha a sufficient motive for the struggle of living. Her death meant to him the loss of the goal of all his labors.

[17] Martin, *op. cit.*, p. 16.
[18] A son, born after Rebecca Ann, survived its mother only a short time. Tabitha's obituary (Rebecca Curry's scrap-book) lists as her survivors "a fond husband and two children, one an infant."
[19] "To My Daughter," p. 214.

26

The next two years Lamar spent in travel. He had become restless and considered change necessary for the restoring of his impaired health. He renewed political acquaintances, and as early as March, 1832, he announced for Congress. *The Columbus Enquirer* championed him as a "States-rights man of sound intellect, finely cultivated taste, and the most uncompromising political integrity . . . well fitted to represent the western section of the state." [20] When the caucus did not give party sanction to his candidacy, however, he ran on an independent ticket, waging a vigorous campaign against the caucus system then in vogue. "If my political bark cannot sail upon the sea of correct principles," he declared, "it shall never float upon the waves of triumphant error." [21] Political machinery was stronger in Georgia in 1832, it appears, than political principle, and Lamar, with both party systems arrayed against him, was defeated.

The next year he became one of the moving spirits at the birth of the new State Rights Party, and announced again as a candidate for Congress, this time with nullification as the main plank in his platform. For years he had been reading law, and was admitted to the Georgia bar in preparation for this second campaign.[22] He was living once more in Columbus, but preferred to stay at the Montague and Pomeroy Hotel rather than open up the cottage with its intimate associations of the past.[23] He bought back half interest in the *Enquirer*, and became again its editor, with

[20] *The Columbus Enquirer*, March 31 and April 7, 1832.

[21] *Lamar Papers*, No. 168 (I, 148).

[22] The license, dated April, 1833, is now in the possession of the Lamar family. Lamar probably never practiced, and always evinced a contempt for an incompetent lawyer (*Lamar Papers*, No. 55 (V, 19); also "New-Year's Address," p. 112).

[23] *Lamar Papers*, No. 1266 (V, 283).

the avowed policy "to awaken the people from their criminal supineness into a bold and determined effort to avert that degradation and servitude to which they" were about to be reduced by the strong arm of the federal power.[24] Exciting days followed, filled with oratory and editorial controversy. More than a decade later, in recalling the stirring days of this campaign, Sol Smith, the actor, wrote to Lamar: "You were a candidate for Congress on your own hook, and I a leader of a chosen band of Thespians—when you, in search of excitement, delivered speeches on the then all-absorbing subject of nullification, and I, in search of the dimes, acted plays in newly built theatres." Years afterward the strolling actor remembered Lamar's good face and person, his ready fencing sword, his easy quoting of Shakespeare, and his love of a good joke and a substantial dinner.[25]

Though Lamar steered clear of complications during the campaign, he saw one of his opponents, John Milton, shoot down a political enemy on the streets of Columbus. His other opponent, Seaborn Jones, the same shrewd lawyer with whom Lamar had served on Governor Troup's staff in Milledgeville, won the race by a handsome majority, and Lamar found himself again defeated.[26] He sold his remaining interest in the *Enquirer,* as if to write finis to his political career.

24 *The Columbus Enquirer,* Feb. 8, 1834.

25 Sol Smith, *The Theatrical Apprenticeship and Anecdotical Recollections of,* dedication to Lamar. Sol Smith and his troupe were playing in his own theater, which he had built of logs in three days, in Columbus in 1833 (Martin, *op. cit.,* p. 44; Sol Smith, *Theatrical Management,* p. 79). See also Smith's *Theatrical Journey-Work* and Rutland's "The Artistic Side of Lamar," *Dallas News,* Nov. 26, 1933.

26 Barker, "Mirabeau Bonaparte Lamar," University of Texas *Record,* V, No. 2 (Aug., 1903), 148-49.

Meanwhile heavy personal afflictions had visited the Lamar family. Mirabeau's sister, Evalina (Mrs. Harvey), died April 29, 1833.[27] She was buried in the garden at Fairfield. The next summer the father, John Lamar, died, and was also laid to rest in the quiet garden. His sons placed a marble slab over the grave and Mirabeau wrote on it:

In memory of John Lamar, who died August 3, 1833, aged sixty-four years. He was a man of unblemished honor, of pure and exalted benevolence . . . thus leaving behind him, as the best legacy to his children, a noble example of consistent virtue. In his domestic relations he was extremely blest, receiving from every member of a large family unremitting demonstrations of respect, love, and obedience.[28]

But the heaviest loss since Tabitha's death came to Mirabeau when his favorite brother, Lucius, committed suicide (July 4, 1834), a victim of melancholia.[29] The two brothers had from early boyhood been great admirers of each other, and in emotional nature had much in common. Mirabeau must have realized that he himself had narrowly escaped the same fate four years earlier. So poignant was his sorrow that for years afterward he could not bear the mention of Lucius' name.

[27] Letters to Mirabeau from both Mary Ann and Lucius announcing her death are among the private letters now in the possession of the Lamar family.

[28] Knight, *op. cit.*, II, 943.

[29] Lucius was buried in Town Cemetery, Milledgeville, Ga. (*ibid.*, p. 349). He was father of Lucius Q. C. Lamar, Jr., in whom Mirabeau always took a very intimate interest, and who later became one of the South's most celebrated statesmen. The distinct strain of melancholia apparent in both Lucius and Mirabeau suggests an unwholesome effect of the marriage of cousins, though the practice was rather common among the Lamars.

Defeated in politics, suffering from failing health (which he believed rendered travel necessary), and stricken to the heart with personal griefs, he turned his back on the scene of his troubles. To one of his sensitive and introspective nature a change was essential. His leaving Georgia in 1835 was his half nonchalant, half bitter gesture against what seemed to him the decrees of fate.

The *Enquirer* had with increasing frequency been publishing glowing accounts of Texas. Lamar's intimate friend, James W. Fannin, had already left Columbus for that land of new fortunes, and Mirabeau was cavalier enough to wish to go adventuring. Certainly there was little left in Georgia to hold him in the regular channels of living, and perhaps in that far western region he might stumble upon the fulfilment of some of his early dreams of accomplishing that which would attach lasting significance to his name. He may have had, too, a half-formed purpose of collecting material for a history of Texas.[30] And such a journey would certainly furnish the required "continued exercise and the excitement of travel." Writing over Tabitha's grave, as a final pledge of devotion, the pathetic inscription,

> Erected by Mirabeau B. Lamar in memory of
> his wife whose death has left him no other
> happiness than the remembrance of her virtues,

he turned his face toward Texas.[31]

[30] The reason assigned in the *Nacogdoches Chronicle* account, quoted in *The Telegraph and Texas Register* (Houston), April 14, June 23, 1838.

[31] This severely simple obelisk of white marble now stands on the W. L. Jeter lot in Linnwood Cemetery, Columbus, Ga. It was originally erected in the St. Luke's Methodist Churchyard (Columbus), where Tabitha was first buried.

III

A SOLDIER BEYOND THE SABINE

———•———

"Miserably dyspeptic and melancholy," Lamar took his seat at Columbus in the Montgomery stage on the 15th of June, 1835, about ten o'clock at night, "in company," he wrote, "with three other passengers, who, soon falling asleep, snored away at the comfortable rate of ten knots an hour, interrupted occasionally by violent collision of skulls which only made them 'swear a prayer or two and sleep again.' " [1] When they reached Uchee Creek, thirteen miles from Columbus, the unmanageable horses missed the bridge, almost upsetting the stage. As the driver attempted the bridge the second time, Lamar found himself the only occupant of the careening vehicle. Though entreated by fellow-passengers to walk, he preferred "the peril to the disagreeableness of getting out and trudging through the mud." At Montgomery he was disappointed to find, in-

[1] The sections concerning Lamar's first trip to Texas are drawn from his "Journal of My Travels," a sixty-eight-page manuscript descriptive of his journey from Columbus, Ga. to Nacogdoches, Texas. Portions of the story (edited by Philip Graham) were published in *The Southwest Review*, XXI (1936), 369-89, under the title, "Mirabeau Lamar's First Trip to Texas."

stead of the hospitable village he had known in his Cahawba days, a thriving city, "with the better impulses of the heart perished in prosperity." After three days "with a landlord whose punch was preferable to his principles," Lamar took passage on the "Little Rock," down the Alabama River to Mobile.

Stopping at Cahawba only long enough to renew memories of this theater of his first adventures, he arrived in Mobile to find the little dirty town that he had known a few years before grown into "a populous city, reared up as if by fairy magic, with beauty unrivalled and wealth unbounded." Here he was a guest of the Franklin Society, a philosophical group lately organized. His visit to the cemetery is explained by his statement, "I never pass by a graveyard without stopping to peruse these pathetic records of bereaved friendship and affection." He had nursed his own sorrows until they had become a source of a strangely melancholy joy. "I never read upon the marble tablet," he wrote,

of a young and beautiful wife . . . fading into dust like a drooping rose in the bloom of loveliness, but what I mourn afresh the loss of my own sweet flower. . . . My gifted sister, my noble-hearted father, my unsullied brother all rise to view and awaken a train of reflections which, though sad and melancholy, are still fraught with consolation and peace. It is true their memory makes me weep, but there is bliss in tears shed for the loved. To forget is guilt, and not to weep is worse than ingratitude.

At New Orleans he was disappointed that all the theaters were closed except the French, and in this he was surprised at "the dearth of beauty in the boxes." In a Meth-

odist book store he purchased one of "Mr. Maffitt's ser-
mons"—the same John Newland Maffitt whose daughter
Lamar was to marry almost twenty years later. He took passage up the Mississippi on the "Romeo" for Natchitoches.
Here he found "many of the citizens drunk as deacons and
as funny as fiddlers," and the town in a wild uproar—a
condition explained by the date, the Fourth of July. His
stay at Natchitoches was longer than Lamar had planned,
for he contracted a fever, probably malaria. Neglected by a
selfish landlord and swindled by a sottish physician, he en-
dured a most uncomfortable week.

Three days' riding brought his first glimpse of the Texas
landscape. A rattlesnake! A family of twenty-five children!
One night rations for the mare so short as to bring forth
Lamar's resentment, and the next so generous as to bid fair
to founder her! A camp meeting in full blast! This was
Texas! Upon his arrival at Nacogdoches (July 22, 1835) he
marked a political restlessness among the people, whom he
found strangely reticent as to governmental matters.[2]

He proceeded to Coles' settlement (now Independence,
Washington County), and found this section so much to his
liking that he quickly determined to change his visit to
Texas into permanent settlement. He employed Horatio
Chriesman to survey a headright near that of John Coles,
but when he went to San Felipe to get title he found the
land office closed. When asked to speak at a meeting in
Washington, he was the first to declare publicly in favor of
the independence of Texas.[3] At Brazoria he met the editor
of *The Texas Republican*, and contributed to that paper

[2] Lamar's "Journal" ends at this point.
[3] *Galveston News*, Jan. 30, 1879. For Lamar's statement of his itinerary
in 1835 see *The Telegraph and Texas Register* (Houston), June 23, 1838.

three poems: "Song" ("Arm For Your Injured Land"), a Texas adaptation of "Arm For the Southern Land," which he had published two years before in Georgia; "Give to the Poet His Well-Earned Praise," probably his first poem composed on Texas soil; and "At Evening on the Banks of the Chattahoochee," the elegy to Tabitha.[4] At Velasco he helped build a fort, and, incidentally, met Mrs. Jane Long, to whom he lent money.[5]

Meanwhile the family in Georgia was becoming more and more uneasy as to Mirabeau's safety. Brother Thomas wrote from Macon on October 25, 1835, "I beseech, entreat, implore and conjure you by all that's near and dear delay not a moment longer in writing to us." Lamar, always a negligent correspondent, did not answer the letter, but a month later, with Austin's assurance that he ran no risk of forfeiting his Texas rights, he embarked for Georgia to make final arrangements for his removal to Texas.

Scarcely had he reached his destination when he heard of alarming developments in the West. The Alamo had fallen, and Fannin and his comrades had been murdered at Goliad. Without settling his affairs Lamar began a hurried return to Texas, to battle for a cause fast falling into desperate straits. He spent only one night in Montgomery, the guest of Judge Samuel W. Goode. When Miss Emily Goode, one of the four daughters, asked Lamar to write in her album, he found that John Howard Payne, the minstrel author of "Home Sweet Home," had immediately preceded him with the verse:

[4] *The Texas Republican* (Brazoria), Oct. 10 and Oct. 24, 1835. All are signed "Z." Two of Lamar's poems had already appeared in this paper— "Beauty" (July 4, 1835) and "To Susannah" (May 2, 1835)—both probably brought to Texas in newspaper form by Lamar's friends.

[5] *The Telegraph* (Houston), June 23, 1838.

Lady, your name, if understood,
  Explains your nature to a letter;
And may you never change from *Goode,*
  Unless, if possible, to *better.*

J. H. Payne

Lamar wrote this felicitous rejoinder:

I am content with being *Goode,*
  To aim at *better* might be vain;
But if I do, it's understood,
  Whate'er the cause, it is not *Payne.*

Mirabeau B. Lamar [6]

Hurrying on to Mobile, he heard news which convinced him that "Texas was on the eve of a dreadful revolution, with bigotry and despotism on one side and civil and religious liberty on the other." [7]

He arrived at Velasco, Texas, in early April, 1836, and immediately set out on foot for the army. He found the country in a state of near-panic, with an exodus of settlers in a mad rush toward the eastern frontier. [8] From Harrisburg Mirabeau wrote to brother Jefferson:

A dreadful battle is to be fought in three or four days on the Brazos, decisive of the fate of Texas; I shall of course have to be in it. . . . Texas is in a dreadful state of confusion. . . . Almost the whole of the Americans from Georgia and Ala-

[6] Scrap-book in the possession of the descendants of Mrs. Emily Goode Finley, Atlanta, Ga.

[7] Lamar's reply to Willis Roberts when his old friend invited him to remain in Mobile to assist in editing *The Mobile Chronicle* (*The Telegraph and Texas Register,* June 23, 1838).

[8] "The Reminiscences of Mrs. Dilue Harris," *Quarterly* of the Texas State Historical Association, IV (Jan., 1901), 163; *The Telegraph* (Houston), Sept. 26, 1836.

35

bama have perished. The citizens of Texas are flying in every direction. I shall reach [Sam] Houston day after tomorrow. In the event of my falling in Battle, you will find my trunks, papers, etc. in the possession of Mrs. Jane Long. The money brought by me to be laid out in lands I have of course, in the present confused state of things, not been able to lay out. . . . I have placed it in the hands of Lorenzo Zavala, the Vice-President of the Government, the most responsible and probably the most honest among them. . . .

If I fall I shall leave . . . something in the shape of a will either with Zavala or Mrs. Long.

My health at present is good. I feel much solicitude for my mother— Tell Rebecca Ann that she must learn to write, read, and spell well, and that is the best education.[9]

Lamar joined the retreating Texas army at Groce's Settlement, as a private, and a few days later arrived with it at what was to be the battleground of San Jacinto. The story of his conduct on that historic field reads more like a romance of the knights of old than anything else recorded in modern times. On the afternoon of April 20 during skirmishes by the Texas cavalry Lamar rushed to the rescue of Walter P. Lane and Thomas J. Rusk, who had been surrounded by the enemy. Killing one Mexican lancer, and putting the others to flight, Lamar extricated his comrades-in-arms. Legend adds that he then coolly rode in front of the Mexican lines back to his own squad, the enemy acknowledging their admiration by a volley as he passed, and he reining in his horse and bowing in reply.[10] It was a deed

9 *Lamar Papers,* No. 351 (I, 350).
10 *Galveston Weekly News,* Dec. 27, 1859; *The Telegraph* (Houston), April 14, 1838; *Colorado Tribune,* Nov. 12, 1849; *The Texas Almanac,* 1858, p. 110; *The Northern Standard,* Jan. 14, 1860. For Lane's none too gracious account of his own rescue, see Walter P. Lane, *Adventures and Recollections,* pp. 12-13.

the Black Prince would have envied. The next morning Lamar was acclaimed commander of the cavalry, but he refused the post out of consideration for the regular officers. These very officers, however, after Colonel Rusk had invited him to his staff, added their insistence to that of the men, and Lamar took command of the cavalry corps.[11] As the main Texas army advanced to the fife and drum music of "Come to the Bower I Have Shaded For You," Lamar and his sixty cavalrymen swept forward on the right wing like an avenging fury.[12]

Lamar's recent bereavements had rendered him careless of all physical danger, and furthermore the swelling yell of "Remember the Alamo! Remember Goliad!" fast rippling up and down the Texas lines held for him a special significance—the bitter loss of Fannin and other friends. Like many another Texan on the field of San Jacinto, he fought savagely, pursuing fugitive Mexicans with his cavalry until nightfall, killing many, capturing few.[13] As a climax to the battle, Lamar witnessed the captured Santa Anna brought into the Texas camp next morning, and his dramatic identification by the Mexican soldiers.

From that point Lamar's rise was meteoric. Within ten days he was appointed Secretary of War, in which capacity he bitterly opposed any compromise with Santa Anna, insisting that "view the matter in every possible light, and Santa Anna is still a murderer." By negotiating with the Mexican captive, Texans, he argued, published to the

[11] *Galveston News,* Jan. 30, 1879.

[12] William Kennedy, *Texas,* II, 227; Alex W. Terrell, *Library of Southern Literature,* VII, 2989; the music is preserved among the Dienst Collection. Lane (*op. cit.,* p. 14) errs in stating that the tune was "The Girl I Left Behind Me."

[13] Eugene Barker, "The San Jacinto Campaign," *The Quarterly* of the Texas State Historical Association, IV (April, 1901), 237 ff.

world their desire to subordinate justice to political interest. His policy—for once—accorded with the popular view; and, though the Cabinet overruled him, his able advocacy of his opinions before that body certainly lost him no friends. Throughout Georgia, Alabama, and Louisiana (the home states of the Alamo and Goliad victims) he was considered the advocate of the martyred dead.[14]

Within four weeks after San Jacinto, Lamar was appointed commander-in-chief of the army. He designated Robert E. Handy as his aide, and for at least one day issued orders. Upon joining the army he found considerable feeling against him. The sentiment took the form both of personal jealousy, and of resentment that the Cabinet, without consulting the volunteers, had presumed to appoint a commander. When the poll went against him, Lamar resigned.[15]

Four months after San Jacinto Lamar was elected to the Vice-Presidency and inaugurated, along with President Houston, at Columbia, October 22, 1836. The Vice-President's address turned generously to the praise of his predecessor in office, Lorenzo de Zavala, "the unwavering and consistent friend of liberal principles and free government," "the gentleman, the scholar, and the patriot." Within the same year Lamar penned a final tribute to a still greater Texas hero, Stephen F. Austin, the "first of patriots and the best of men." [16]

The duties of the Vice-President were not onerous, and

[14] *Lamar Papers*, No. 362 (I, 370). Among the other heroes of San Jacinto, William H. Jack was especially ardent in his support of Lamar's view concerning Santa Anna.

[15] *Lamar Papers*, No. 361 (I, 370); *The Telegraph* (Houston), Dec. 6, 1836.

[16] Reprinted in John H. Brown, *History of Texas*, II, 107 (Zavala); Kennedy, *op. cit.*, III, 272 (Austin).

Lamar devoted the early months of 1837 to collecting historical material. His headquarters were at Brazoria, where he boarded with Mrs. Jane Long.[17] He advertised in the Houston *Telegraph* for the Stephen F. Austin papers, and began extensive biographies of Gutierrez, Long, and other filibusters. For an ambitious account of Santa Anna, to be done in Spanish, he seriously applied himself to a study of that language, which he learned to write with a fair degree of facility. During the remainder of his life he was busy collecting historical matter, always intending some day to write an extensive and accurate history of Texas.[18]

Lamar's personal affections were still in Georgia with his little daughter (Rebecca Ann), his mother, and his brothers and sisters. Since news of the Battle of San Jacinto had got abroad, letters of congratulation had been pouring in upon him. His old friend, W. Porter of Eatonton, Georgia, had written: "All your life, Mirabeau, you have bemoaned the quiet spirit of our age and seemed to have renounced all hope of jostling your way up fame's proud summit. But there you are." [19] And even the advice-giving, envious, financially-gifted Gazaway Bugg Lamar condescended to write to his Texas-hero cousin:

We have all seen with just admiration and delight your brilliant career in Texas, by which you have illustrated the name even in modern times to something more than its ancient glory. We are proud of your success. . . . I have just returned from a visit to Europe where your fame had preceded

[17] Francis R. Lubbock, *Six Decades in Texas*, p. 43.

[18] *The Telegraph and Texas Register*, Jan. 21 and Feb. 3, 1837; Barker, "Mirabeau Bonaparte Lamar," University of Texas *Record*, V, No. 2 (Aug., 1903), 152; Christian, *op. cit.*, p. 15. Much of this material is preserved in the published *Lamar Papers*.

[19] *Lamar Papers*, No. 413 (V, 104).

me. . . . I hope your health will be so improved as to enable you long to enjoy your well carried laurels and that you may, unlike most modern heroes, learn to wear them without ostentation and vain glory.[20]

His immediate family was deeply concerned for his safety. His sister Mary Ann wrote to him from Eatonton:

My dear Mother's greatest source of uneasiness is about yourself, but we all do every thing we can to mitigate her fears, and frequently tell her that her prophetic feelings of never seeing you again have so often proven false that she ought not to let them render her unhappy now. And I have repeated *this* to her so often that at times I almost persuade myself into the belief that there can be no doubt of your safe return home; but when I return to my reason, I know that it is all sophistry and that my brother is no more immortal than other men, and then I only pray that it *may* turn out as I wish. . . .

I hope you will neglect no opportunity of letting us hear from you; it is a duty to save our dear Mother all the unhappiness you possibly can, and I assure you it would be a great alleviation to her feelings to hear from you more directly than by flying reports of other people. But oh! how much more rejoiced she would be . . . to know that you would come home, and remain amid scenes of danger and hardship no longer; and if I thought any persuasion could induce you to leave Texas for home, I would write till tomorrow morning urging them upon you. . . .

All send their love to you, and Rebecca Ann says you may look for a letter from her. . . .[21]

It was in response to such appeals that Lamar, with the

[20] Unpublished letter, Dec. 13, 1836.
[21] Unpublished letter, May 30, 1836.

consent of the Senate, over which he presided, set out for Georgia in April, 1837. Personal business, too, demanded his presence in that state, as his hurried return to Texas in 1836 had precluded any final settlement of his affairs. He was undoubtedly influenced also by the very human desire to return to that section from which he had gone forth under the shadows of personal grief and political defeat. If he had won laurels in Texas, certainly Georgia was the place where he wished to wear them, triumphantly but gracefully.

As he left Texas, he cut a striking figure: medium in height, with dark skin, long black hair inclined to curl, and blue eyes that often took on glints of gray. He was probably the only man in Texas of that day who wore the old-style, very baggy trousers, with large pleats; his whole attire gave one the feeling of odd looseness. In public he was reserved, but among intimate friends he was quite companionable.[22] His feelings on the eve of his departure he reproduced in his sentimental short-story, "The Parting Kiss," which begins:

The driver sounded his horn, and in one hour more, I was to depart in the stage for my native state. The idea of revisiting the home of my childhood—of meeting my brothers and sisters, and beholding once more my aged parents . . . filled me with rapture which I had never experienced before. Already transported in imagination over the long journey, I received the joyous welcome of the happy family . . . My mother, now feeble with years and trembling with affection, tottered half way down the steps to grasp my hand, and unable to restrain her feelings, burst into tears . . . and there was a joy—aye a

22 Lubbock, *op. cit.*, p. 43.

rapture, even in the reverie of imagination, which I would not barter for a world's wealth and all its honors besides.[23]

Such must have been his anticipations of personal pleasure as he took boat at Velasco.

His journey was punctuated by public dinners and military receptions. He found himself the symbol of that Texas liberty for which the sons of Georgia and Alabama had died. Marion and Irwinton, Alabama, and Milledgeville and Macon, Georgia, vied with each other in fêting him.[24] The climax to his visit came at Columbus, on the occasion of a Fourth-of-July public dinner in his honor. The main toast was, "To our esteemed friend and distinguished guest, General M. B. Lamar: the pride of his native state, the boast of his adopted country, endeared to both by the purity of his character, and his chivalrous and enthusiastic devotion to the cause of freedom."

Lamar responded in a speech extolled by the journals of Georgia for its vivid descriptive eloquence, poetic energy, and patriotic sentiment: "You have known me long enough," he told them, "to know that gold with me is lighter than a cricket's bones when weighed against the durable affections of a virtuous mind . . . for myself I ask no treasure but a quiet conscience, no fame but the smiles of affection from the friends I love."

Then he painted a glowing picture of Texas, that boundless garden. "When I stand upon the mountains of San Saba"—Lamar was speaking in his best manner to the two

[23] "The Parting Kiss," with sub-title "From a Lady's Album," a three-thousand-word prose story, preserved in Lamar's manuscript album, was published in *The Telegraph* (Houston), Feb. 17, 1838, and in *The Columbus* (Ga.) *Enquirer*, Nov. 10, 1841.

[24] *The Columbus Enquirer*, June 1, 1837; *Lamar Papers*, No. 572 (V, 146).

hundred enthusiastic listeners gathered around the improvised tables,

and cast my eyes over the surrounding country, where the lily and the rose and every flower of Tyrian dyes are spreading their beauty, where birds of the brightest plumage are pouring out their melody to the music of the waters, . . . where the buffalo darken the distant horizon with their numbers, and the fiery mustangs toss their manes to the wind and make the earth tremble beneath their wild stampede, I cannot refrain from baring my head to the Great Being of Benevolence.

The body of the speech became a résumé of the Texas Revolution, followed by a eulogy of the sons of Georgia who had died on Texas soil. And then the hero of San Jacinto proposed the toast, "The blood of Goliad and the Alamo—the hand that spilt it wrote *Tekol* on the walls of Mexico." [25]

Lamar had said, most tactfully and appropriately, as well as truthfully, exactly what people wanted said, and his popularity in Georgia knew no bounds. Already his name was on Texas tongues as a possibility for the next president of the Republic. Friends in his adopted country were therefore urging his immediate return. October consequently found him en route to resume his official responsibilities. At Mobile there was another public dinner, which turned out to be the manifestation of Alabama good feeling and sympathy for Texas.[26] Here, too, Lamar renewed his acquaintance with his old friends, the Roberts family, to find that his former sweetheart, Olivia, had become a widow—

[25] *The Columbus Enquirer,* July 6, 1837; *The Telegraph* (Houston), Oct. 11, 1837; *Lamar Papers,* No. 566 (V. 137); Martin, *op. cit.,* p. 86.

[26] *The Morning Chronicle* (Mobile), Oct. 8, 1837; *Lamar Papers,* Nos. 599 (V, 158) and 609 (I, 576).

she to whom he had written "Grieve Not, Sweet Flower."
The old love, smouldering since the Cahawba days, leaped
again into full flame in Olivia's breast, and for the rest of
her life she remained Lamar's ardent worshipper, willing
to endure Texas hardships and the forked tongues of
frontier gossips to be near him. After his departure for New
Orleans, she wrote after him, hysterically pleading for his
return:

My earliest and best loved friend:

Come back to us instantly, come back. I learned late last
night that you had missed the boat for Texas and was still at
the Lake House. Your death is talked of here as an event that
must soon take place—they say you can not escape should you
attempt the Red River route as we fear you will do.

I am so much alarmed that I have lost the powers—to think
about it almost—and can only repeat—*come back*—come at
once and you will yet be in time for the Brig which goes in two
or three or four days at the latest—a large party I believe dine
with us tomorrow who are going with her. Brother is all ready
and intends to pack up tomorrow. Come and go with them and
all may yet go well. . . .

Yours—Affectionate friend Olivia [27]

But Lamar did not turn back, and by November the
Vice-President was in Texas, assuring the senate that "our
valor is famed throughout all civilized nations, and it is
now in our power by a course of high integrity to prove to
the world that we are as inflexible in virtue as we are in-
vincible in arms." [28]

During his visit Lamar had renewed another friendship.
Even before his arrival in Georgia he received from his old

[27] *Lamar Papers,* No. 607 (I, 575).
[28] The entire address is printed in *The Telegraph* (Houston) Nov. 18,
1837.

44

friend William Redd news of one in Columbus who appeared to languish "like a prophet who wants the inspiration of his god." [29] This "most magnificent of inquirers" after Lamar was Mrs. Mary Ann Jeter. Mirabeau had known her as Mary Ann Gartrell before her marriage to Oliver Jeter, and after her husband's death had addressed "To a Lady" to her (1834). In 1837 she was evidently eagerly awaiting his visit to Georgia. His feeling for her remained, however, only a sympathetic, affectionate friendship, and, in spite of rumors that he had been bound by "the silken chain of Hymen," [30] he returned to Texas alone. Only one of her letters has been preserved. On October 31, 1837, she wrote to "Mr. Lamar":—

I am tired of the place [Columbus] and would gladly leave it forever if I could. I expect that you will wonder why it is, and as I have no particular reason to alledge for the assursion you must look over this with the rest of my many faults. . . . I think there is scarcely any pleasure on earth that is eaqual to that of hearing from absent *friends.*

Mr. Lamar, before I sit down to write I think I have a greate deale to write about, but when I commence I can think of nothing. . . . I know that you must get very tired of reading my foolish letters, and I sometimes think that I never will trouble you with any more of my foolishness. And would not if it was not for the reason of receiving a letter from you. See how selfish I am. . . .

The idea of ever seeing you again is altogether banished, but I hope to hear from you often.

Your affectionate friend
Mary Ann [31]

Do not forget to write often.

[29] *Lamar Papers,* No. 503 (V, 514).

[30] *Ibid.,* Nos. 542 (V, 134) and 552 (I, 551).

[31] The letter is preserved among the unpublished Lamar papers (State Library Archives, Austin, Texas).

From Velasco, Lamar wrote her a poem, "To Mary Ann," in which he assured her,

> Thou must not deem thyself forgot,
>   Or less beloved by me.
> . . . the flowers
>   Are bright in Texan dells
> And brighter still the sparkling eyes
>   Of Texas sprightly belles;
> Yet in this land of light and love,
>   All beautiful—divine—
> There is no flower or living thing
>   Whose charms can equal thine.

But his aversion to letter-writing and his long absence from Georgia put an end to the friendship.

IV

PRESIDENT OF A NEW REPUBLIC

FOR SEVERAL weeks after his return to the Republic, Lamar's plans seemed uncertain. He had already contemplated establishment of a printing press at Houston, and now he considered setting up a newspaper business at Nacogdoches. He conceived the project, also, of cutting up a tract of land into lots and establishing a townsite—to be called Lamar—on Aransas Bay.[1] All these projects were brushed aside, however, when political friends petitioned him to become a candidate for the presidency.[2]

From the very outset, he was assured of success. A serious handicap, however, was his lack of adequate funds. Loyal friends came to his assistance, among them Robert Handy, who wrote: "I am as usual badly off for money, but send you fifty dollars and regret 'tis not as many thousand—I have settled your stage fare." [3] *The Civilian* (Gal-

---

[1] *Lamar Papers*, Nos. 542 (V, 134) and 612 (V, 161); Kennedy, *op. cit.*, III, 411; Decca Lamar West, "Mirabeau B. Lamar," *Houston Chronicle*, Jan. 27, 1928. The present town of Lamar is on Aransas Bay, on Highway 35, 180 miles southwest of Galveston.

[2] *The Telegraph* (Houston), Dec. 9, 1837; Rusk's and Lamar's letters, *ibid.*, June 2, 1838; *Lamar Papers*, No. 666 (II, 29).

[3] *Lamar Papers*, No. 765 (V, 191).

47

veston), probably seeking a challenge, was bitter in its opposition, but Lamar, realizing his constitutional irritability when wantonly attacked, wisely refrained from reply.[4] At the climax of the campaign the two principal opposing candidates, P. W. Grayson and James Collingsworth, both committed suicide. Lamar's majority over the remaining opponent, Robert Wilson, was almost thirty to one.

Before his inauguration Lamar enjoyed a pleasure that meant much to him—his little daughter's first visit to Texas. Rebecca Ann, since her mother's death in 1830, had been living in the homes of various aunts and uncles in Georgia and Alabama. All loved her; and yet the "dear aunts," as Rebecca Ann called them, seemed implacably bent on the improving of her mind. In 1838 she was eleven years old, frail, and very conscious of her "dear papa's" high position. The whole family felt obligated to look after her welfare. During June and July (1838) Thomas (Mirabeau's physician brother at Macon), Mary Ann (the sister at Irwinton, Alabama), and Jefferson (the brother at Lumpkin) all wrote letters inquiring the exact time when Lamar wished Rebecca Ann accompanied to Texas.[5]

Mirabeau's reply can be guessed from the first entry in Rebecca Ann's diary—which she began at the suggestion of Aunt Loretto for the purpose of "improving her writing and composing." "I left home [Lumpkin, near Columbus]," she wrote, "the 22 of July in company with my Uncle [John] and Aunt [Amelia] Randle." The travelers journeyed through Montgomery, Mobile, and New Orleans, and on the third of August reached Galveston, and the next day, Houston—only after overhanging trees had raked

---

4 *Ibid.*, No. 756 (II, 177); *The Telegraph* (Houston), Aug. 4, 1838.
5 Letters to Lamar, dated June 13 and July 6, 1838, among the private Lamar papers, now in the possession of the grandchildren.

both the smoke-stack and the captain into the bayou.
"When I landed in Houston," Rebecca Ann wrote,

I was very impatient to see my Papa, and I got my Uncle to
go up town and see if he could hire some one to go after him.
When my Father came in town means of conveyance were
then procured to carry us out to Oak Grove where he resides,
and there we found Mrs. Wilkins [the house-keeper]. . . . The
place where papa lives is beautiful, it has a great many shady
trees in the yard and you can see for two miles all around you.
My papa receives a great deal of company at Oak Grove.
Among them was Major Cocke, who had a beautiful little
pony. I liked it so much that he presented it to me. . . . I have
been very lucky in getting presents.

"Dear Papa" and his friends and the pony entertained
the little guest royally. There was a ride "nearly every
evening in company with Mrs. Wilkins and her little
daughter." There was also a visit to the San Jacinto battle-
field, followed by a pleasure-trip to Galveston and an expedition to Bolivar Point, where, Rebecca Ann remarked,
"all the ladies went on shore to the ball except my Aunt
and myself; she being a member of the Methodist Church
did not attend such places, and I was not willing to go
without her." These days in Texas gave a breath of fresh
air to the slim little girl, already in the grip of tuberculosis.
There was some talk of her remaining, and one gentleman,
too weak to walk out to Oak Grove, Lamar's home, applied
for the position of tutor.[6] But the educational opportunities
in Texas seemed too meager for the eleven-year-old child
who had felt duty-bound during her visit to read each day
a portion of "Queen Elizabeth's Reighn," and on October
fourth—six days before Lamar's inauguration—she wrote

6 *Lamar Papers,* No. 824 (V, 199).

49

in her diary: "Passed the day in arranging my clothes, talking to my dear Father, and taking leave of my friends, as Uncle Randle, Aunt Amelia, and myself will leave tomorrow for the United States. I cannot express the sorrow I feel at having again to be separated from my beloved parent." After "twenty-three days of tedious ride" she reached Lumpkin safely.

The new President was inaugurated December 10, 1838, in Houston in front of the Capitol where now stands the Rice Hotel. There is a legend that Sam Houston, the retiring President, knowing that the crowd was expecting an unusual speech from Lamar, and knowing, too, that Lamar became impatient and nervous under delay, deliberately planned a tediously long speech; Lamar consequently turned his manuscript over to his secretary, Algernon Thompson, to be read to an exhausted and disappointed audience.[7] *The Telegraph* (Houston) does not mention these circumstances, but remarks of the inauguration: "It was pleasing to notice the remarkable degree of confidence and esteem that was everywhere manifested toward Pres. Lamar. He is almost universally regarded as the pride and ornament of his country." [8] The inaugural address sounds the note of Lamar's general policy: "To awaken into vigorous activity the wealth, talent and enterprise of the country, and at the same time to lay the foundation of those higher institutions for moral and mental culture, without which no government on democratic principles can prosper, nor the people long preserve their liberties."

For a year the government and President Lamar re-

7 William S. Red, "Allen's Reminiscences," *Southwestern Historical Quarterly*, XVII (Jan., 1913), 295; Lubbock, *op. cit.*, p. 92; Brown, *op. cit.*, II, 147; Kennedy, *op. cit.*, III, 320.

8 *The Telegraph* (Houston), December 12, 1838.

mained in Houston, then a village less than two years old, of only fifteen hundred souls. All the two hundred houses were of wood, many of them built of rough-hewn logs. Great pines were still standing in the ill-defined streets. Newcomers arrived on horseback, wrote a French visitor in 1838, and were "armed with the famous bowie-knife and an excessively long rifle." Even the congressmen turned their horses out on the prairie to graze.[9] But the government was made comfortable in two large temporary wooden structures, and Lamar continued to reside at the site of the present Lamar Park (Hyde Park Boulevard and Commonwealth),[10] though for a short time the official White House was at the corner of Main and Preston.

The situation at the beginning of Lamar's administration was difficult. The white population of the country was scarcely thirty thousand, and Indians occupied four-fifths of the territory. By his procrastination Houston had merely shifted the problems of his administration on to his successor. With the Treasury empty, with the paper money worth only forty cents on the dollar, with no public credit and no recognition, the national prospects were dark. To make matters worse, Mexico, temporarily relieved of French invasion, was contemplating renewed Texas activities, while an Indian war seemed about to burst upon the country.

Lamar's idealism was the answer to the problem. It enabled him to see the future greatness of the country in spite of seeming facts, and this vision inspired him to build where apparently there was nothing on which to build. His

[9] Frederick Leclerc, *Le Texas et sa Revolution*, pp. 3-7; *The Telegraph* (Houston), Oct. 25, 1836; Lubbock, *op. cit.*, p. 45.

[10] A marker was placed on this site by the San Jacinto Chapter of the Daughters of the Republic (1928). See also Lubbock, *op. cit.*, p. 67.

imagination and largeness of conception gave him faith to act for the future, while his critics complained of his idealism, and procrastinated. And the quality about Lamar which most disturbed his detractors was his proneness to translate these "dreams" into action.[11]

His first concern was for the protection of the frontier from both Mexicans and Indians. He believed that the poorest citizen, "whose sequestered cabin is reared on our remotest frontier, holds as sacred a claim upon the government for safety and security as does the man who lives in ease and wealth in the heart of our most populous city." [12] On account of his experiences with the Georgia Indians of Governor Troup's time, Lamar felt that the only restraint that the Indians would ever acknowledge was a competent military force in the field. After all efforts of a commission under Burnet and Rusk to treat with the savages had failed, and some of the chief men, in defiance of warnings, were caught, red-handed, plotting with the Mexicans, Lamar sent the small army voted him by his first Congress against the hostile tribes of the northeast. Some bands were peaceably removed from Texas and their improvements paid for; the Cherokees, under Chief Bowles, had to be expelled.[13]

This summary dealing with a menace that had threatened the very existence of the Republic had more far-

[11] Anson Jones, typical of the later anti-Lamar group, wrote: "His [Lamar's] mind is altogether of a dreamy, poetic order, a sort of political troubadour . . . Texas is too small for a man of such wild, visionary" dreams (*Memoranda*, p. 34).

[12] Brown, *op. cit.*, II, 152.

[13] *Lamar Papers*, No. 361 (I, 370); Barker, "Mirabeau Bonaparte Lamar," University of Texas *Record*, V, No. 2 (Aug., 1903), 154; William P. Johnson, *The Life of Gen. Albert Sidney Johnston*, pp. 93-118.

reaching results than the immediate protection of the frontier and the consequent increasing of immigration. It convinced Mexico that Texas was able to take care of herself and, together with the new navy, contributed much to recognition by England, France, and Belgium. European commercial treaties followed, a project upon which Lamar had been most intent.

Lamar's educational policy was characteristic of the man's vision. In his first message to Congress he had said, in what has become the most celebrated utterance of any Texas statesman:

Cultivated mind is the guardian genius of democracy, and while guided and controlled by virtue, is the noblest attribute of man. It is the only dictator that freemen acknowledge and the only security that freemen desire . . . The present is a propitious moment to lay the foundation of a great moral and intellectual edifice, which will in after ages be hailed as the chief ornament and blessing of Texas.

When a public school was a novelty and the Republic's treasury and credit were at their lowest, only a daring mind and a champion of enlightened liberty could have conceived the idea for insuring the education of the future Texas generations. His plan was feasible enough. It involved setting aside for each county an amount of land sufficient to insure adequate public free schools, and in addition fifty leagues of land for "a university of the first class," eventually to be established. At his urgent insistence Congress passed a bill embodying his suggestions, and on that day—January 26, 1839—the Texas Public School System was born. Congress failed, however, to pass a later bill providing funds for surveying the University lands, and

Lamar himself assumed the responsibility of having much of this tract run off.[14]

Lamar was fortunate in gathering about him a corps of efficient and trustworthy lieutenants. Not all the men in Texas in the late 1830's were honest, and in political circles there was much assumed greatness. The misfortune about many of the leading men of Texas, wrote a Washington friend to Lamar, is

that they are not smart enough to know that they are not smart. Houston City is a famous place—for phantom fame—and if there were more *Misters* and fewer titles, it would not be so ludicrous. A lady asked me if the gentlemen of Texas were not *generals generally*. I told her the *Major* part of them were quite *Captains* in their own way. I *Judge* she would think so if she was in at a party at Congress time in Houston.[15]

Always a keen judge of character, Lamar selected as his appointees men of as unbending honor as himself. James Webb became Attorney General; Albert Sidney Johnston, Secretary of War; Barnard E. Bee, Secretary of State; Memucan Hunt, Secretary of Navy; and James H. Starr, Secretary of Treasury. With such men at his back, Lamar ushered in an era of official honesty in the young Republic. Corruption on a vast scale was being practiced in connection with fraudulent land certificates. The Auditorial Court, which was overwhelmed with fabricated claims, was suspended by the President until Congress, in accordance with his recommendations, put an end to the system of bribery and forgery. At the same time that he was saving

[14] Brown, *op. cit.*, II, 149-51; Dienst, "Mirabeau B. Lamar, Patron of Education," *East Texas* Magazine, July, 1929, p. 9; West, "Mirabeau B. Lamar," *Houston Chronicle*, Jan. 27, 1929.

[15] Henry Thompson to Lamar, *Lamar Papers*, No. 1441 (III, 102).

the public domain, he was, because of his own home-loving nature, laying the foundations of the homestead exemption laws, a code which, with improvements, has become dear to the hearts of Texans.[16]

Another evidence of Lamar's building for the future was his moving the capital from Houston to a location then in the western wilderness—now Austin. During 1835 and 1836 the seat of government had, in rapid succession, been at San Felipe, Washington, Harrisburg, Galveston, Velasco, and Columbia. Lamar was inaugurated at Houston. But it was felt elsewhere that the capital should be more centrally located. Congress therefore appointed a commission to select a proper site.

Legend tells that Lamar, on an expedition to the west early in 1839, camped with Jacob Harrell at a ford over the Colorado, called Waterloo. The next morning Harrell's little son informed them that the prairie was dark with buffalo. Lamar chased the biggest bull in the herd up a ravine that is now Congress Avenue (Austin), and finally shot him with a holster pistol. The hunters assembled on what is now Capitol Hill, and as Lamar looked down the slopes covered with wild rye—it was April—to the purple-crowned river, he exclaimed, "This should be the seat of Empire." [17] If the story is true, perhaps Lamar's suggestion had influence with the commissioners, for they recommended this very site.

Their choice could not be justified except in terms of the future. It was the expression of that same confidence in the growth of the country that had inspired Lamar to

[16] *The Colorado Gazette and Advertiser,* Aug. 1, 1839; Barker, "Mirabeau Bonaparte Lamar," University of Texas *Record,* V, No. 2 (Aug., 1903), 156; Johnston, *op. cit.,* p. 94.

[17] Alex W. Terrell, "The City of Austin," *Quarterly* of the Texas State Historical Association, XIV (Oct., 1910), 115.

plan for educating unborn millions of Texas children. The commissioners, under Lamar's persuasion, had put aside all considerations of personal comfort, and disregarded actual distribution of population as well as the grave danger of Indians, to select a capital to meet the needs of a great republic far in the future. The nearest town was Bastrop, thirty-five miles east.

In May, 1839, one square mile, bounded by the Colorado River and by Shoal and Waller creeks, was laid off in lots, and Edwin Waller commissioned to erect the government buildings. By October these temporary quarters were ready. The archives in Houston were loaded on thirty wagons and hauled the two hundred miles westward. An escort of honor under General Edward Burleson met Lamar and his Cabinet a few miles out of Austin at "Squire Hornsby's," and accompanied them to Mrs. Angelina Eberly's hotel—the Bullock House.[18] Here as a feature of the public dinner Edwin Waller delivered the address of welcome, in which he recited some of the hardships incident to the building of the new capital—including the menace of Indians and the handling of his motley crew of two hundred laborers, fed on beef, cornbread, and water from the spring.[19]

Lamar found that the "accommodations" proudly referred to by Judge Waller in his speech included a Capitol, a residence for the chief executive, and various departmental buildings. The temporary Capitol, on the corner of Colorado and Eighth, facing Congress Avenue, was a

[18] The Bullock Hotel, its first story of hewed logs, its second of cottonwood plank, was on the southeast corner of Block 70, the northwest corner of the intersection of Congress and Sixth.

[19] P. E. Pearson, "Reminiscences of Judge Edwin Waller," *Quarterly* of the Texas State Historical Association, IV (July, 1900), 47-48.

sprawling, U-shaped, one-story building, constructed of Bastrop pine. The next Congress erected a stockade around it for protection against Indians. The President's "Mansion," a neat two-story frame building of native post oak and cedar, painted white, was on a hill one block east of Congress Avenue, now the site of St. Mary's Academy.[20] Lamar's business office was in a double log-house on the east side of Congress Avenue at its intersection with Eighth. The Treasury Building, another one-story, frame structure, shaped like a U, occupied the west side of Congress Avenue, mid-way between Sixth and Fifth; its yard—the building was fifteen paces from the street—was for years the favorite summer lounging place for official circles.

Thus did the young Republic, under Lamar, build for itself a capital on the very fringe of its frontier, and deliberately fix there the center of its future dominions. Government calmly hung out its "at home" sign literally within earshot of the Comanche's war whoop. The dramatic move pulled the Texas population rapidly westward and pushed forward a new frontier. It also gave to the Texas individuality and to Texas institutions a distinct Romance flavor, for the new capital was closer to San Antonio, predominantly Spanish, than to the Teutonic cities of the East.[21]

Even with heavy official duties Lamar found time for such pleasures as the frontier capital offered. He saw Mrs. Barker in *Romeo and Juliet* at Corri's theater in Houston,

[20] Lamar built also a cottage in Austin, near the present site of Grace Hall (Whitis and Twenty-Seventh).—*Lamar Papers*, No. 2376 (VI, 163).

[21] For the building of Austin see *ibid.*, Nos. 1294 (II, 587), 1363 (III, 40), 1390 (III, 57), 1430 (III, 91), 1468 (V, 313); Terrell, "The City of Austin," *Quarterly* of Texas State Historical Association, XIV (Oct., 1910), 113-28; Lubbock, *op. cit.*, p. 143; Johnston, *op. cit.*, pp. 113-15.

and heard her sing "Roy's Wife"; [22] he attended the San Jacinto Ball at Galveston in 1839; and was present at various semi-official functions. He gave a dinner honoring his Cabinet, another honoring the Senators, and a third honoring the Representatives, at a total cost to himself of five hundred dollars.[23] He rode in a twenty-three-hundred-dollar carriage, and drew the then munificent salary of ten thousand a year—more than half of which he gave to his friends.[24]

Lamar's prominence and the fact that he was unmarried made him a ready target for provincial gossip and frontier speculation. As early as 1837 one friend in New Orleans asked, "Can I congratulate you yet?" Lamar's Secretary of War, Memucan Hunt, warned from Mississippi, "One lady promised anything if I should aid her to preside as madam at the Executive Mansion in Texas"; and his rakish friend, S. A. Plummer, wrote from New Orleans, "There was a few days ago from Mississippi a very handsome and accomplished young lady. She is determined to remove to Texas. She is worth they say half a million—intends setting her cap for you. I think you rather old for her." [25] If the dangerous lady ever came to Texas, she left no footprints.

Lamar's old friends, the Roberts family, had moved to Galveston in 1837, and Olivia made frequent and rather indiscreet visits to the capital, the first of them prefaced by the following note to Lamar: "Do you remember giving

[22] *The Morning Star* (Houston), April 20, 1839. For the melodramatic story of Mrs. Barker in Texas, see Marquis James, *The Raven*, p. 301.

[23] *Lamar Papers*, Nos. 1440 (III, 99), 1133 (II, 495), 1163 (II, 511). Thomas R. Stiff, a vindictive gentleman who furnished these dinners, later sued Lamar for a balance due on the account.

[24] These figures are in "Star money"; in U. S. currency the carriage, purchased in New Orleans, cost $1400.—Letter from William Bryan to Edward Hall, Feb. 10, 1839, preserved in the Dienst Collection.

[25] *Lamar Papers*, Nos. 542 (V, 134), 561 (unpublished), 1366 (V, 299), 1207 (II, 534).

me permission to talk to you with the same freedom that I
would talk to my brother? . . . I have taken a fancy to
come to see you next week . . . one or two days." [26] The
frontier, always thirsty for gossip, seized eagerly upon a
situation so rich in possibilities. During the presidential
campaign, Lamar was warned of "a great deal of gossiping
about some little picadillos [sic] . . . which have a powerful influence among the better halves. . . . I have no
doubt," his informant went on to assure him, "that the
pretty little foot of a certain pretty little widow would not
only kick over the objections of the wise dames, but
also . . ." And William Bryan, the New Orleans Consul,
when shipping the carriage purchased for the Chief Executive, remarked that "General Lamar and the pretty widow"
would have an opportunity to commend his taste.[27] In
both cases Mrs. Olivia Roberts Mather was intended; but
those unacquainted with Olivia unfortunately put a false
interpretation on such allusions, and started trends of talk
wholly without authentic basis.[28]

Lamar wisely paid little attention to such under-currents
of gossip; and it probably did him no harm, besides occasionally arousing his irritability. In the face of it all, a
contemporary historian wrote: "Perhaps no man preserved
a reputation more unsullied both in public and private
life than General Lamar." [29]

[26] *Ibid.*, Nos. 1214 (II, 538), 1749 (V, 412).
[27] Letter from Edward Hall, March 1, 1838, *ibid.*, No. 683 (II, 39); letter from Bryan, Feb. 10, 1839 (Dienst Collection).
[28] *Lamar Papers*, No. 686 (V, 177); K. V. Pauls, *Mrs. Catharine Flood*
(no date), p. 22.
[29] Jacob De Cordova, *Texas: Her Resources and Her Public Men*, p. 187.
Gossip of the 1850's concerned Juan Lamar, who rumor said was an ille-
gitimate son. See the correspondence of Edward Hall, Joel Roberts, H. P.
Bee, and Lamar (1851–1858), preserved in the Dienst Collection; also the
Lamar Papers, Nos. 2306 (VI, 83), 2327 (VI, 92), 2478 (IV, 289), 2479
(IV, 289).

Much of this gossip subsided after Lamar's removal to Austin. Yet his two years in the frontier capital were not happy ones. Since the beginning of his administration his health had steadily failed,[30] until late in 1840 he wrote to Vice-President Burnet that illness had compelled him to retire from official duty "for the present." "In taking my leave," his letter continued, "I beg to assure you that the regrets . . . are greatly softened by the reflection that one who has at all times been so devoted to the country will be placed in my stead." [31] He started to New Orleans, but became so ill en route to Galveston that he stopped at the home of his friend, Dr. J. B. Hoxey, at Independence. He found conditions here much to his liking, and though soon strong enough to travel, preferred to remain. His recovery was rapid, and by March, 1841, he was back in Austin, enjoying better health than at any time since his inauguration.[32]

Upon his arrival he found the capital enthusiastic about a new project, being discussed everywhere—the expansion of Texas westward, even to Santa Fe and beyond. Acting President Burnet had told Congress, "Texas proper is bounded by the Rio Grande—Texas as defined by the sword may comprehend the Sierra del Madre. Let the sword do its work." [33] Congress talked freely of extending the "limits of Texas from the mouth of the Rio Grande to

[30] *Lamar Papers*, Nos. 1347 (V, 296), 1352 (V, 297), 1365 (III, 41); he was suffering from acute hemorrhoids.

[31] Letter of Dec. 13, 1840, printed by A. M. Hobby, *Life and Times of David G. Burnet*, p. 23.

[32] *Lamar Papers*, No. 1955 (III, 475).

[33] Burnet's message to Congress (Dec. 16, 1840), Texas *House Journal*, Fifth Congress, First Session, p. 292.

the Pacific Ocean, and along the coast to the Oregon territory." [34] Lamar favored the idea for the possibilities of increased revenue. Texas did not need more territory, but it did need money; for such projects as protecting the frontier, constructing a navy, and building the new capital had proved expensive. Even with the "Red-backs" of 1839 and the international commercial treaties, the Republic by 1841 was facing bankruptcy.

Lamar believed that trade with the Santa Fe region would fill the governmental coffers. This popular idea of the day he proceeded to crystallize into action by equipping an expedition to invite the people of that section to throw off Mexican rule and join hands with Texas. It was a heterogeneous crowd of traders, merchants, and private gentlemen that set out from Austin June 21, 1841, accompanied by a small military escort under Brigadier-General Hugh McLeod, and armed with a peace proclamation from Lamar, done into Spanish by the President's friend, José Antonio Navarro.[35] The failure of the expedition is an old story—its wanderings, hardships, betrayal, and final capture. Missourians in Santa Fe, jealous for the trade of their home state, were probably more to blame than the Mexicans. Texans promptly forgot their own former enthusiasm, and bitterly criticized the President. Had the expedition succeeded, it would have been undoubtedly the brightest star in Lamar's glory. As it turned out—an apparent failure—it was still worth ten million dollars to Texas in the

[34] *The Telegraph* (Houston), Feb. 2, 1842.

[35] McLeod had married Lamar's cousin, Rebecca Lamar, the sister of Gazaway Lamar. For the proclamation see *Lamar Papers*, No. 2033 (V, 474).

settlement with the United States at the time of annexation.[36]

Lamar's positive policies and his governmental housecleaning had, by the end of his administration, brought him many enemies, the chief of whom was Houston. Lamar and Houston were diametrically opposed in character even more than in policy. The one, a daring idealist, building institutions for the future; the other, a conservative pragmatist, mainly concerned with the present. The one, a statesman; the other, a consummate politician. The one, impatient, inclined to drive too directly toward his goal; the other, tactful, almost wily in his deliberateness. The two men were symbolic of different civilizations: Lamar, of the Old South, its culture and its traditions; Houston, of the new frontier of the Southwest in its most victorious mood. No wonder that the two came into sharp and lasting conflict, with a challenge by the first and a refusal of the challenge by the second! [37]

It was apparently becoming a habit with the Texans to retire their presidents under a shadow of disapproval, and Lamar went out of office almost as much abused as Burnet and Houston had been. None realized better than he, however, that his administration, though a financial failure, had laid the secure foundations of a great state in terms of homes, schools, and clean government. In his farewell address to Congress, he said, "I have discharged my duty

[36] George W. Kendall, editor of the New Orleans *Picayune*, who was with the expedition, wrote the best account of it, *Narrative of the Texan Santa Fe Expedition;* see also Brown, *op. cit.*, I, 189-98.

[37] Houston fought only one duel, and that with General William White. His challengers were many, including Albert Sidney Johnston, President Lamar, Commodore Edwin Moore, and President Burnet. (Alex. W. Terrell, "Recollections of General Sam Houston," *Southwestern Historical Quarterly*, XVI (Oct., 1912), 129.

to the country and to you. . . . I am more than willing to submit every act of my administration to the most rigid investigation. I seek no concealments and I shrink from no verdict." Feeling that he had dealt justly with both the present and the future Texas, he retired to private life, confident that oncoming generations would render the thanks that his own day somehow neglected to offer.

V

HOME ON THE BRAZOS

———•———

ALWAYS a careless correspondent, Lamar had allowed official business to crowd out many personal relationships during the last months of his term. The efficiency of such secretaries as H. J. Jewett and William Sandusky encouraged laxness in personal letter-writing. Rebecca Ann made frequent appeals to him to write: "You are so much occupied with your business that I dislike to trouble you to write to me," she apologized in her childishly stilted manner, "but nevertheless it would be highly gratifying to me to get a letter from you once in a while." [1] And again, "Oh, to receive a letter from you, what would I give!" [2] There is a note of pathos in an old friend's appeal from Galveston: "May I tax you so much as to send me a letter written by your own hand . . . And when you write, just write on to the end of the sheet. Such a thing would revive me as much as a shower of rain in a long dry season." [3]

[1] Unpublished letter, Rebecca Ann to her father, June 6, 1840.
[2] *Ibid.*, June 1, 1841.
[3] Willis Roberts to Lamar, April 12, 1841, *Lamar Papers*, No. 1995 (V, 467).

64

It was with a certain relief, then, both to himself and to his friends that Lamar retired to private life. He went at once to his farm near Richmond, Fort Bend County, which he had considered his home since 1838. At that time his friend Robert Handy had superintended the building of a low frame house near the Brazos. He had retired from office heavily in debt, but his brother Jefferson had left him by will a small amount, and he borrowed two thousand dollars more from his cousin Gazaway Lamar.[4] With these sums he set about making improvements on the Richmond plantation, as he liked to call it. The slaves Caroline and Black John, whom he had had with him in Austin, he put in charge of the house, and later added Dilsey[5] and Mammy Fanny. His field hands came from Georgia. Just as the master of the new plantation had established himself, he suffered the second great emotional upset of his life—the death of his daughter, Rebecca Ann.

During his administration she had made him a second visit, this time accompanied by her Aunt Mary Ann and her grandmother, Lamar's mother. They had scarcely arrived at Houston when the aged Mrs. Lamar was stricken with "congestive fever"—probably malaria—and died.[6] Rebecca Ann also fell ill, and spent the remainder of her visit at Galveston in the home of James Love.[7] From here she wrote to her father, "Have taken quinine every day regular since you left, and the Doctor told me to keep on

[4] *Lamar Papers,* Nos. 672 (II, 36) and 1756 (III, 360). The will of Jefferson Lamar is recorded in the Office of the Ordinary, Lumpkin, Georgia, Book A, pp. 21-24; Rebecca Ann also received a gift.

[5] Dilsey had the voice of a prima donna. Repeatedly promoters offered her a career in the North, but always she refused. She was later stolen (Letter, Lamar to Hall, Jan. 7, 1857, Dienst Collection).

[6] *The Morning Star* (Houston), July 27, 1839.

[7] *Lamar Papers,* No. 1400 (III, 61).

taking it three times a day . . . I shall miss Dr. Smith a great deal. I have become so accustomed to his society that he seems almost like one of the family." Rumors of yellow fever caused her hurried return to Georgia,[8] whence she wrote again: "I cannot help desiring to be in the second garden of Eden . . . Oh, if only I could see and converse with you!"[9] At her insistence Lamar spent the spring of 1843 with her in Georgia. It was probably her education, as well as the condition of her health, that prevented her return with him. He had scarcely reached Richmond after his visit when his brother Thomas wrote from Macon: "God grant you strength to sustain the dreadful blow. Rebecca Ann has been taken from us—she is no longer of earth."[10] That sentence, coming without warning, hit the very heart of Mirabeau Lamar. Rebecca Ann, sixteen, had been fast blossoming into a brown-haired, blue-eyed replica of his long lost Tabitha. Her death destroyed the last vestige of that happy little family in Columbus on the banks of the Chattahoochee, and again brought Lamar to the black pit of despair.

His brother Thomas realized the danger when he added to his letter, "Let me beseech you to meet this affliction with firmness—suffer it not to overwhelm you with gloom and despondency." But it did overwhelm him, and for months he remained in seclusion at Richmond, stunned by the blow. He was awakened from his stupor of grief by the love of his old friend, Edward Fontaine.

This militant Irish preacher, the grandson of Patrick

[8] Red, "Allen's Reminiscences," *Southwestern Historical Quarterly,* XVII (Jan., 1913), 293.

[9] Letters, Rebecca Ann to Lamar, Aug. 30, 1839 and April 13, 1841.

[10] Letter from Thomas Lamar, Aug. 2, 1843. Rebecca Ann died July 29. An obituary appeared in *The Georgia Telegraph* (Macon), Aug. 8, 1843.

Henry, had followed Lamar to Texas from Georgia. On account of his big heart and delightful humor, he had been a favorite with Lamar, and had served for a few months in 1841 as the President's private secretary. He escaped the ill-fated Santa Fe Expedition only through the insistence of his wife, but on the Somervell Expedition this lovable Don Quixote had suffered comical and "ignominious defeat on the spines of the giant prickly pear." In resigning his secretaryship—to go filibustering, ecclesiastically, in new fields—he had told Lamar, "Whatever my head, heart, and hands can do for you, shall always be at your service." [11]

The warm Irish heart did not forget its promise. "Knowing the deep anguish you must have suffered," he wrote to Lamar, "and your capacity for mental agony, I am filled with uneasiness." Under the guise of soothing the bitterness of his own feeings, he penned a consolatory poem. The verses, though mere doggerel, carried between the lines a wealth of sympathy. [12] Lamar replied with "On the Death of My Daughter," the writing of which marks his return to normal thinking and living. Though he found no remedy for his irreparable loss, yet the mere expressing of his grief, like a woman's weeping, broke through the shadows of his night.

The old restlessness was soon upon him, and early in 1844 he started East. He stopped at Mobile to renew acquaintance with a woman whom, when she had played

[11] *Lamar Papers*, Nos. 2007 (III, 512), 2111 (V, 491), 2114 (V, 493); Brown, *op. cit.*, II, 237. Fontaine was one of Lamar's best contemporary biographers, his account being published anonymously in Richardson's *Texas Almanac* for 1858 (Galveston, 1857), pp. 109-13. For the authorship, see *Lamar Papers*, No. 2591 (VI, 365).

[12] Both the letter and the accompanying verses are printed in the notes, p. 308; for Lamar's reply, see p. 236.

dolls with his sister Mary Ann, he had known as Octavia Walton. The grand-daughter of a signer of the Declaration of Independence of 1776 and the daughter of a governor, she was now married to a prominent surgeon, Henry S. LeVert, and was popularly known in Mobile as "Madame LeVert." Though Lamar had heard of her in recent years, he was scarcely prepared for the altogether charming person he found. "Only one such woman is born in the course of an empire," Irving said of her—and certainly Irving was a connoisseur of the female sex.[13]

She lived in a substantial but elegant mansion on Government and St. Emanuel streets. Here she held her "Mondays," the nearest approach to a *salon* which America had ever known. Among her intimate acquaintances were Henry Clay, Jefferson Davis, John C. Calhoun, Alexander Stephens, Edwin Booth, Henry W. Longfellow, and N. P. Willis. The list of her weekly callers looks like a reprint of Davidson's *Living Writers of the South*. Every visitor of distinction sought her acquaintance. In her drawing room Lamar met Richard Henry Wilde, who had been living in New Orleans since 1840, and whose "My Life Is Like the Summer Rose" had appeared in half the newspapers of Texas. Here also he met A. B. Meek, who lived in Mobile on the same street. Lamar and Meek at once became congenial, intimate friends. Sitting on the latter's front veranda they read together much of the manuscript for Meek's *Songs and Poems of the South,* which later appeared with a dedication to Lamar.[14] Meek praised highly

---

13 Elizabeth Ellet, *Queens of American Society* (New York, 1867), p. 392; *The Texas Sentinel,* Oct. 24, 1854; *Lamar Papers,* No. 726 (II, 157).

14 The dedication: "To Gen. Mirabeau B. Lamar, Ex-President of Texas, The Soldier, Statesman and Poet: These Songs, Which He Has So Kindly Approved, are Affectionately Dedicated."

Lamar's "On the Death of My Daughter," which was still in manuscript, and subsequently sent it to the editor of *The Southern Literary Messenger,* where it was published.[15] Certainly Lamar owed to Mrs. LeVert and to those to whom she introduced him at this time a marked revival of interest in things literary.[16]

In Georgia Lamar found that loving aunts had already erected an elaborate stone over the new grave in Rose Hill Cemetery in Macon, inscribed, "Sacred to the Memory of Rebecca Ann Lamar, Daughter of Mirabeau B. and Tabitha Lamar," with extracts from the obituary. He avoided all public appearances in Macon, refusing invitations to speak at dinners and patriotic gatherings. The new year, 1845, found him in New York, where he was hailed as "an unassuming but most romantic specimen of Southern chivalry," and was asked to receive callers at the City Hall.[17] He doubtless found time to visit his cousin, Gazaway Lamar, who had recently become President of the Bank of the Republic in New York. At Washington he was accorded the courtesy of a seat in the senate.[18] In the Capital City he found Mrs. Cazneau (known in the literary world as Cora Montgomery), wife of his old friend William L. Cazneau, to whom he had given office in 1839.[19] Lamar's presence inspired her to write "The Presidents of Texas," published with a full-page portrait of Lamar. Her sketch of him, the

---

15 *The Southern Literary Messenger,* XV (July, 1849), 398.

16 The scrap-books and correspondence of Mrs. LeVert are preserved at "Bellevue," her birthplace near Augusta, Ga. See also *Library of Southern Literature,* VII, 3221-26.

17 *The New York Herald,* Jan. 11, 1845; *The Republic* (Macon, Ga.), Jan. 15, 1845.

18 *The Georgia Telegraph* (Macon), Feb. 25, 1845.

19 *Lamar Papers,* Nos. 395 (I, 408), 1531 (V, 324).

most sympathetic ever penned, glows with warm feeling—
the gossips of the day insisted that it was more than friendship. She wrote,

He is scarcely of middle height, and of the full and rounded
proportions that we associate with a love of ease and self-
indulgence. This is true of him, but with an exciting cause,
he courts peril and is indifferent to privation. This benign,
meditative, repose-loving expression indicates strong domestic
virtues. . . . He is remarkably gentle and affectionate in his
manners, habitually self-controlled. . . . Each of his high
qualities, and he has many, walks hand in hand with some
collateral fault; but his faults spring so naturally from his
unpruned virtues that they are excused with a warmer love
than we give to the cold merits of more correct men.[20]

Mrs. Cazneau introduced Lamar to a coterie of literary
figures in Washington, New York, and Philadelphia. There
were Mrs. Ann Stephens, poetess and editor of the *Ladies'
Companion;* Mrs. Caroline Sawyer, writer of children's
verse; Mrs. Sarah J. Hale, editor of *Godey's Ladies' Book;*
Margaret Fuller, J. M. Storms, Horace Greeley, and Hamil-
ton Boone. Both Mrs. Stephens and Mrs. Sawyer wrote
tributary poems to Lamar, who repaid the compliments
when he published his volume.[21] To each Lamar deeded
a half section of land, perhaps as a gesture symbolic of the
bigness of Texas.[22] The letters of both women reveal a
warm personal friendship. Mrs. Stephens wrote to Lamar:

It seems a week since we left you, and yet here we are only

[20] *The United States Magazine and Democratic Review,* XVI (March,
1845), 282-91; the portrait appeared as the frontispiece in the June issue.
[21] *The Knickerbocker,* XXV (March, 1845), 242; *The Georgia Telegraph,*
April 1, 1845; *Lamar Papers,* No. 2181 (IV, 101).
[22] *Lamar Papers,* No. 2376 (VI, 163).

forty miles apart. . . . Instead of finding ourselves on the sofa with you cozily seated between us, here we are like three birds in a nest chirping for want of our other mate and laughing very loud when you are mentioned with the solemn resolution of deceiving each other into a belief that we have no disposition to cry. . . . You are great enough for your friends if only with them.[23]

And Mrs. Sawyer, always the gossip of the group, wrote to him:

I went on Sat. last to spend the day at Mrs. Greeley's in company with Mrs. Storms, and saw Margaret Fuller for the first time. I cannot say how I like her yet, because I could not get acquainted with her. Mrs. Storms proposes another visit in order to have an opportunity of turning Mrs. Stephens loose upon Miss Fuller. It would be amusing, and quite surprise her out of her dignity.[24]

Lamar enjoyed his association with this literary group. Always deeply interested in things cultural, he had served as president of the Philosophical Society of Texas, and had also been an honorary member of the Phi Gamma Society of Emory College.[25] During his decade in Texas he had been almost the only patron of the arts in that broad land. He was responsible for William Jones' chronicle of the Santa Fe Expedition, and he encouraged Mrs. Holley to publish her *Texas*. David Wood asked Lamar for contributions to his newly established *Richmond Telescope*, and again consulted him about the *National Intelligencer*. Frances Keeper asked his advice about establishing in

[23] *Ibid.*, No. 2182 (IV, 101).
[24] Letter to Lamar, March 5, 1845 (unpublished).
[25] *Lamar Papers*, Nos. 889 (V, 216), 2146 and 2148 (V, 497).

Texas "a literary magazine like Ann Stephens' *The Ladies' Companion,*" and Lewis Washington sent him a prospectus of his proposed literary periodical, *The Rambler's Sketch Book.* J. A. Veatch wrote to him: "My poeticals are progressing . . . my principal attention has been bestowed upon the piece which you spoke approvingly of . . . inclosed I send. . . ." [26] Such instances could be multiplied almost indefinitely, for the writers of the Republic of Texas turned instinctively to Lamar for advice and help. After busy years on the frontier he found his cultural life revived by this group of eastern authors. His renewed enthusiasm was to culminate, more than ten years later, in the publication of his own volume of poems.

Lamar had gone to Washington chiefly in the interest of annexation. During his administration he had been violently opposed to union with the United States, and he had been largely responsible for the withdrawal of the proposition of annexation by the Texas Congress in 1839. But his opinions rapidly underwent a complete change, for he thought he saw signs of England's engulfing Texas, with a consequent smothering of slavery. He became an earnest advocate of union, therefore, because he saw in this course not only a guarantee of slavery in Texas, but also a strengthening of that institution throughout the South.[27] As soon as the House of Representatives passed the Annexation Bill, Lamar wrote congratulations to Moses Beach, of the New York *Sun,* "on the resolution of your favorite

[26] E. W. Winkler, "The Bexar and Dawson Prisoners," *Quarterly* of the Texas State Historical Association, XIII (April, 1910), 292; Mattie Hatcher, *Mary Austin Holley* (Dallas, 1933), p. 81. *Lamar Papers,* Nos. 1243 (V, 280), 1334 (V, 291), 1270 (V, 284), 1807 (V, 427), 2388 (IV, 198).

[27] Mirabeau B. Lamar, *Letter on Annexation; Lamar Papers,* No. 2202 (IV, 112).

hope," assuring the editor that Texas would respond with filial warmth.[28]

Lamar spent most of the summer in Macon, Georgia, where lived Miss Cassandra Flint, a beautiful, sparkling brunette, as proud as she was popular. Her parents, Thomas and Matilda Flint, kept a boarding house at Poplar and Second streets. Lamar, it seems, had already won her when she heard that his kinsfolk had remarked that she would not make a suitable wife for the Ex-President of Texas. She at once returned his ring—a cluster of nine diamonds. Lamar refused to accept it, but instead wrote for her "My Gem of Delight." He asks her,

> What gift shall I bring thee to merit thy love—
> Some pearl from the ocean, or star from above?

And invites her,

> Then fly with me, Cassa—there's bliss in the flight,
> And glory shall circle my Gem of Delight.

But Cassa's hurt pride was greater than her love, and Lamar hurried—alone—to Texas, over which the Mexican War clouds were already gathering.[29]

Before buckling on his sword, Lamar spent a few weeks in Galveston, mainly because of a troupe of players there. He was always very fond of the drama, even in the primitive style in which it was served up on the Texas frontier in 1845. Harry Watkins, one of the actors, has left a de-

[28] *The Georgia Telegraph* (Macon), Feb. 11, 1845.
[29] Cassa soon afterward married Zachariah Whitehead, and later married David Little. Her daughter, Mamie Little Schoffield, became well known in the South as a singer; an organ in Christ Church, Macon, where she sang for years, was dedicated to her.

lightful picture of those nights in Galveston. Since Lamar, he says, was "no wealthier than the rest of the Lone Stars, he always came with the editor of the News, Captain Lewis. Of the company, I was Lamar's favorite," Watkins continues; "I shall never forget how on seeing me play on my benefit night *Richard III, Dick the Apprentice,* and harlequin in a pantomime, he paid me the compliment of saying that for a young man I possessed remarkable powers of endurance. . . ."

Lamar's acquaintance, it seems, was invaluable in a culinary way to the half-starved actor. For every evening after the performance the three of them—Watkins, Lewis, and Lamar—repaired to a shell-fish saloon, kept by a generous Spaniard, to dine on stew. Aside from the savory food, what feasts those must have been—with an actor, an ex-president, and an editor at three sides of the board! Lewis paid for them in advertising.

On one such occasion, the last night of 1845, Lewis suddenly started up from the table, exclaiming that he had promised his newsboys a New-Year's Address, and here it was twelve o'clock and not a line written! After a little coaxing, the three adjourned to the *News* office. Lamar wrote, Watkins carried copy, and Lewis did the setting up; and by four o'clock in the morning a rhymed "New-Year's Address to the Patrons" was ready for the carriers. When Watkins left Galveston, his parting tribute to the Ex-President was, "A more lovable man never lived"; Lamar's parting gift to the actor was a sword used at San Jacinto, presented with the remark that it would do for the mimic combats of the stage.[30]

[30] W. A. Croffut, "How They Did It," *Detroit Free Press,* April 2, 1885; reprinted in part in *The Galveston Daily News,* April 10, 1885. Unfortunately no issue of the *Galveston News* for Jan. 1, 1846 (which should contain the "Address") is known to exist.

Of the four American presidents participating in the Mexican War, Lamar was the only one from Texas.[31] He joined the army of General Taylor at Matamoras, with the title of Inspector-General, and fought at Monterey. At the head of the Second Regiment, he led the charge that brought victory. Colonel George Wood in his report of the battle mentioned "the gallant bearing and lofty courage" displayed by the Inspector.[32] His "To a Mexican Girl" (Matamoras) and "Carmelita" (Monterey) suggest the local color around him at the time.

Though he held the rank of lieutenant-colonel, he found himself virtually without a command, and therefore resigned, hoping to join General Scott at Vera Cruz. Complications and delay arose, caused, Lamar believed, by Senator Sam Houston's influence with a weak president in Washington. Impatient for action, Lamar organized a company of Texas Mounted Volunteers, and with this corps was stationed by Governor Henderson at Laredo.

The Laredo Guards protected the frontier from the Comanche Indians and bands of Mexican marauders. Many stories are told of these quick-moving cavalrymen, usually under the leadership of Lamar himself. Upon one occasion, when a soldier started up a bank to investigate a supposed ambush, Lamar halted him with, "Don't you know they will kill you up there"—and then Lamar himself went up. There is no better instance of Lamar's uncom-

[31] The other three: Jefferson Davis, Taylor, and Grant.

[32] The vest which Lamar wore at Monterey has been much melodramatized. It has been preserved, and though there is some red, the color is predominantly gold. Jefferson Davis, quoted by West ("Mirabeau B. Lamar," *Houston Chronicle*, Jan. 27, 1929) and Lubbock (*op. cit.*, p. 609), called it red. Certain recent biographers have dyed all Lamar's vests a "bright scarlet."

75

promising attitude toward dishonesty than his summary dismissal of his quartermaster.[33]

But Lamar was not satisfied with his border position. Both he and his men repeatedly petitioned to be allowed to advance into Mexico, but to no avail. He blamed Houston for his continued assignment to the minor frontier post, and wrote bitterly to David Burnet: "The post I occupy in this war is certainly a very petty and unsuitable one, but the President is determined to gratify his favorite, —your demented monster—in all his resentments . . . I can regard Texas as very little more than Big Drunk's big Ranch." [34] The end of the war came without any opportunity for Lamar of a major engagement after Monterey.

During his last year at Laredo he served one term as representative from Nueces and San Patricio counties, and then retired to his plantation in Richmond. Here he found awaiting him a gift from an actor-friend of former days—a copy of Sol Smith's *The Theatrical Apprenticeship and Anecdotical Recollections*. Sent immediately before the outbreak of the Mexican War, it arrived at Richmond after Lamar had gone to the front. Upon his return home the ex-President wrote to Smith:

If, in consequence of my long silence, you have been induced to drop me from your list of friends, I hope you will not deny me the privilege, under fair explanation, of reinstating myself in your good graces! Our acquaintance began at that halcyon period of life when the heart is most susceptible of strong and lasting impressions; and I can assure you, my old friend, that the attachment which then grew up between us,

[33] *Lamar Papers*, Nos. 2226 (IV, 136), 2247 (IV, 26); DeCordova, *op. cit.*, p. 186.

[34] *Ibid.*, Nos. 2323 (IV, 164), 2336 (IV, 172), 2324 (IV, 165); letter from Henderson to Lamar, Jan. 9, 1847, Dienst Collection.

making us two as one man, has not been weakened in me by the years. But on the contrary it has rather been improved by time, the great maturer, which converts the flowers of spring into the ripe fruits of autumn. My life, like your own, has been somewhat checkered by adventure; but I account it one of the greatest blessings of fortune that, amidst all her buffetings, she has not deprived me of the cheerful companion of my happier days—my old Sol Smith. A three-years' entombment of myself in Mexico and the frontier wilds has prevented my receiving your little book, which you kindly dedicated to me, and which now meets my sight for the first time. Its laughing tone and animated stories show that you have not lost the joyous spirit of your younger years—that you are still the man of infinite jest, in spite of all your ups and downs. And surely, my friend, if the ancients were right in saying that a brave man struggling with adversity was a sight worthy of the gods, I know of no claimant more worthy of their favors than yourself—than you who have contributed so much to lighten the burthens of others while bravely bearing your own. You have played many parts in your time—have played them all well, and most certainly none better than that of the true philosopher and friend. Then *here's a double health to thee,* old Sol. Long life and a happy one to him who knows how to enjoy prosperity with gratitude, and whose happy alchemy of mind can turn even misfortune into pleasantry.[35]

Perhaps Smith's book, an account of histrionic trials and travels in Georgia, reminded Lamar that it was time to busy himself with certain literary records that he had planned. At any rate, the most prolific period of his prose writing followed, with sketches of many Texas pioneers and Mexican celebrities.[36] He indulged much in travel,

---

[35] Smith, *Theatrical Journey-Work,* pp. 253-54.
[36] *Lamar Papers,* Nos. 2407 (VI, 171), 2414 (VI, 185), 2416 (VI, 196), and 2454 (IV, 261).

sometimes for the collecting of historical material, sometimes for the sake of seeing old friends. He liked to spend weeks at a time at the home of Judge James Webb, near Austin, where he had written "Gay Spring" to "the beautiful pink of Belle Mont, the fair little Florence Duval"— then six years old. He visited Washington again and made several desultory trips to Georgia, loitering usually at Mobile. The early weeks of 1851 found him at New Orleans, visiting in the home of Mrs. John A. Settle, the daughter of his life-long friend, Willis Roberts, and the sister of "the pretty widow"—Mrs. Olivia Roberts Mather. Mrs. Settle had in her home at this time also another guest— one suspects, by design—the beautiful Henrietta Maffitt, of Galveston.

Miss Maffitt's parents were John Newland Maffitt and Anne Carnic Maffitt, both originally of Ireland. By trade a tailor, Maffitt had come to America in 1819, and turned poet and preacher. His peculiarly emotional oratory soon brought him unusual popularity as an evangelist; he preached in churches so crowded that he had to be passed through a window, over the heads of the packed people to the pulpit. Gossip and scandal hounded him, however, until he died in 1850, literally, legend has it, of a broken heart. His wife in the early 1840's brought "the three graces," as her daughters were called, from Tennessee, where Henrietta had been born in 1827,[37] to Galveston. Here Eliza, Matilda, and Henrietta—the last two, twins— became famed for their beauty.[38]

[37] Ascertained from the funeral notice of Mrs. Caroline Matilda Johnson, Henrietta's twin. The date given by Frank Johnson (*History of Texas and Texans*, V, 2650) is incorrect, and other biographers give no date. Henrietta's head-stone (Richmond, Texas) carries no date of birth.

[38] Emma Maffitt, *The Life and Services of John Newland Maffitt*, [Jr.].

At the time Henrietta was visiting in New Orleans she was engaged to a gentleman in Galveston. Nevertheless she was persuaded by Mrs. Settle to delay her return, and Lamar readily agreed to prolong his visit. The two were thrown much in each other's company. Lamar had known Mrs. Maffitt and her daughters as early as 1846 [39] and had already addressed "Lovely Fanny Myer" to Henrietta. The popular Galveston beauty, encouraged by Mrs. Settle, was at first flattered and then fascinated by the attentions of so distinguished a gentleman as Lamar. Doubtless such poems as "In Deathless Beauty" (facsimile, p. 98) had much to do with winning the lady's heart. Together they heard Jenny Lind sing in New Orleans, an experience that Lamar never forgot. After a few weeks Miss Maffitt consented to a hasty marriage, and the two immediately left on a wedding tour of the South. [40]

Lamar delighted in showing his bride his favorite scenes in Georgia. They visited the old State House in Milledgeville, where Lamar wrote to her the tribute beginning,

> Oh, is it not a pity . . .
> That I am now, of fifty-three,
> Upon the shady side?

—an exact statement of fact. He might have added that his black hair was tinged with gray, but that the quick gesture and the latent sparkle in the blue eyes bespoke a man little past his zenith. There was a trip to the legended Chatta-

---

[39] *Lamar Papers,* No. 2216 (IV, 130); see also Lamar's "Home on the Brazos," stanza X.

[40] A brief account of the courtship was left in manuscript by the daughter, Loretto Lamar. The marriage took place between the first and the twentieth of February, 1851 (Letter, Lamar to Johnson, Feb. 26, 1851. Dienst Collection).

hoochee bluffs above Columbus, and almost a week at Fairfield, the old home of Lamar's boyhood, where Henrietta doubtless properly admired Mirabeau's painting, "The Nightmare," done by him more than a quarter of a century before. She found there also the violin on which he had played as a boy.[41] They spent most of 1851, however, in Macon; and here, in the city where Rebecca Ann lay buried, a second daughter was born early in 1852, named Loretto Evalina after two of Lamar's sisters.[42] The summer of 1852 they visited in the home of Harmong Lamar, at Glenville, Alabama. Here Lamar found time, under the spell of Henrietta's enthusiasm, to begin the preparation of a few of his poems for the press—a project which he was not to complete until five years later.

Back in Texas with his new family, Lamar, always in love with things domestic, began plans for their permanent home. The Richmond plantation seemed inadequate because it was small and its houses unsatisfactory. Lamar insisted that Henrietta be near Galveston, then the cultural center of Texas; he insisted also that his land have on it an abundance of timber. Lack of funds rendered the search embarrassing. On one scouting expedition for a proper location, he wrote back to his wife: "I love you more than language can express . . . and feel that your presence is all that I want. . . . Since we parted I have been going night and day in search of a home, and shall still persevere until I gain one. . . . Kiss the little one." His

[41] Lucian L. Knight, *Reminiscences of Famous Georgians,* p. 170; Lucian L. Knight, *Georgia and Georgians,* III, 1341.

[42] Sol Smith remarks (*Theatrical Journey-Work,* p. 94) that at the time of Lamar's marriage (1851) the ex-President had promised to name the first child after him, but when "it unfortunately turned out to be a girl, the idea of naming her Solomon was given up at once." See also the unpublished letter, Lamar to Hall, June 1, 1852, Dienst Collection.

next letter closes with, "I think I will never leave home again without you." [43]

In his absence Henrietta, very impatient at the delay, was completely converted to a plan proposed by Mrs. Jane Long, at whose house they had been boarding. Mrs. Long was to furnish additional acreage adjoining the Lamar place at Richmond and also money for renovating the buildings, and the two families were to share the enlarged plantation. Lamar, won over by his wife's enthusiasm, finally consented to the plan. The scheme was not completely put into operation before it proved unsatisfactory. Both financial and domestic troubles arose, the nature of which can be guessed from Lamar's later promise to Henrietta: "I never will again for everything on this earth subject you to such difficulties as must inevitably arise from having two families of equal authority in the same house. Our experience on that point suffices for the balance of my life." [44]

After the breaking up of the partnership, Lamar acquired more land on the Richmond plantation, and more debt, but still the houses were not in repair. The financial situation became most embarrassing. "My money matters are desperate," he wrote to a friend in 1854. "For many months I have had a use for five or six dollars which I am not able to raise, except by the slow process of selling a little butter which my wife saves from a few cows." [45] He refused to sell any of his bounty land, even to pay his debts, considering it a donation from the government, a part of his Texas head-right. In 1855 he made a hurried

[43] Unpublished letters, May 6, 1853; May —, 1853; June 11, 1853.
[44] Unpublished letter, Jan. 16, 1855.
[45] Letter, Lamar to Edward Hall, Aug. 29, 1854, printed in *East Texas Magazine*, July, 1929.

trip to Mobile in an effort to solve his financial difficulties. From New Orleans he wrote to his wife that he had been elected President of the Southern Commercial Convention, and added a message which he apparently considered of far greater importance—"Tell our pretty angel that I will bring her a rocking chair." [46] At Mobile he found his old friend, Willis Roberts, who had returned to Alabama. "Madame LeVert" had gone to Europe, but A. B. Meek still lived on Government Street, and Lamar again "enjoyed sitting on his front veranda." Before leaving Mobile he wrote to Henrietta: "Judge Meek has just read me his 'Red Eagle,' a poem of great merit abounding in gorgeous imagery. I think it cannot fail to take unless it should be assailed on the ground of its being Southern." [47] He carried back to Richmond a poem by Meek, "Impromptu to Mrs. Henrietta Lamar," a tribute from her "husband's friend." [48]

Lamar had decided to remedy his money-troubles, at least temporarily, by another loan from his cousin Gazaway. With this sum he opened up new farms adjoining his former plantation, and made of the house a comfortable and congenial home for his family.[49] Few men have had stronger domestic instincts than Lamar, and he found himself surrounded at Richmond by what was dearest to him. "Sweet little dashing Loretto"—as her god-mother aunt called her—had inherited the personal beauty and vivacity of her mother and the affectionate disposition of her father, and with her Negro mammy, Fanny, became a most

[46] Unpublished letter, Jan. 19, 1855.
[47] Unpublished letter, Jan. 19, 1855.
[48] See notes, p. 305.
[49] *Lamar Papers*, No. 2491 (IV, 17).

important part of the establishment.[50] Mrs. Lamar, with her love for everything growing, brought shrubs and flowers from the whole countryside into her yard, and visitors never forgot the bowls of pink roses and blue plumbago on her parlor table. To Lamar in poetic mood, she was always "the Lily of the Dell"—the "boasted flower of old Ft. Bend." Her sister, Mrs. Eliza Budd, an excellent musician, and Carrie Budd, were welcome additions to the congenial household.[51] Those who were guests—some of them for long periods of time because they had nowhere else to go—have paid tribute to the hospitable and harmonious home on the Brazos.[52]

But the heavy debt hung over the plantation like a cloud. The farms were barely self-supporting, and yet Cousin Gazaway Lamar was becoming impatient for his money. During the summer of 1857 a happy solution for the problem appeared for a moment when Lamar was appointed Minister to the Argentine Republic. The salary proved too small, however, to allow reasonable payments on his debts and to support his family. In distress he appealed to "dear Gaz" to accept land for the debt. "I ask this favor," he wrote, "because it will relieve me from a mountain of miseries, restore my peace of mind—and secure a little repose for me between this and the grave." [53] But Gazaway Lamar insisted that he have money—not land—and Mirabeau did not accept the appointment. Al-

[50] Unpublished letter, Mrs. Loretto Chappell (Lamar's sister) to Mrs. Henrietta Lamar, March 25, 1853; Elizabeth Brooks, *Prominent Women of Texas,* p. 23.

[51] During his wedding tour with Henrietta, Lamar had sent thirty dollars a month to Eliza at Galveston. (Unpublished letter, Lamar to Hall, June 1, 1852, Dienst Collection.)

[52] *Lamar Papers,* No. 2565 (VI, 356); see note to "Nora," p. 266.

[53] *Lamar Papers,* Nos. 2520 (IV, 40) and 2523 (VI, 343).

most immediately President Buchanan offered him another diplomatic post, this time as Minister to Nicaragua, with also the position of Minister to Costa Rica super-added, at a total salary of ten thousand dollars a year. Gazaway was appeased with a promise of a thousand a year until the debt was paid. His conscience must have told him he had been an insistent collector, for he wrote to Mirabeau: "I expect you to go off angry with me because I need my money." [54]

His wife accompanied Lamar to Washington for their credentials, for she intended going with her husband to Central America. At the Capital City she received many flattering attentions, among them an entertainment at the White House by the President's niece. After a violent attack of bronchitis, she gave up her proposed trip to Nicaragua, and early in December returned to Richmond to manage the plantation for the next two years. Probably the real reason for the sudden change in her plans was Cousin Gazaway's objection to "the expenses of those who had better stay at home." [55]

Before going to Washington, Lamar had decided to publish, at his own expense, his "scribblings," as he always called his verses. His old friends, James Webb of Austin and A. B. Meek of Mobile—not to mention Mrs. Cazneau and Mrs. Stephens—had for years been urging this obligation upon him, but Lamar was very diffident. Chiefly to please his wife, he overcame his reluctance, and selected from his album those poems which seemed most closely associated with friends and occasions. The slim printed

---

[54] *Ibid.*, Nos. 2545 (IV, 58), 2563 (IV, 68), 2605 (VI, 367).

[55] *Ibid.*, Nos. 2545 (IV, 58), 2601 (VI, 366); unpublished letter, Lamar to Hall, Dec. 3, 1857, Dienst Collection; Brooks, *op. cit.*, p. 23.

volume appeared in September, 1857, appropriately titled *Verse Memorials.*

Early in the new year (he had spent Christmas in Washington), Lamar completed preparations for his departure to his diplomatic post. The night before leaving New York he wrote to Henrietta at Richmond:

It is now one o'clock at night, and I have just finished packing my trunks, preparatory to my leaving tomorrow in the new steamer (I forget its name) which will depart at twelve. . . . I found the "Verse Memorials" all sold here; I have only two copies left. The publishers have just failed, and I was lucky enough to drop in in time to get from them $200 worth of books, which closes the account between me and them. The books are tolerably well selected, and I think will afford you pleasant reading. . . . I shall take them with me to Nicaragua, where I hope they will be soon followed by yourself, a lovelier book to me than all the libraries in the world. I long to read the poetry of your bright face and hear the music of your voice. . . .

He sailed the next day on the "Moses Taylor," and completed his journey on the "Susquehanna." [56]

Upon reaching Managua, Lamar found a difficult situation made even more delicate by the almost rabid interest of his countrymen. Nicaragua and Costa Rica were quarreling as to the ownership of the banks of the San Juan River, and certain meddling European powers had injected international complications. Lamar found difficulty in assuming a proper diplomatic veneer, and was perhaps too direct and frank in his methods.[57]

[56] Unpublished letter, Lamar to his wife, Jan. 4, 1858; see also *Lamar Papers,* No. 2570 (IV, 73).

[57] *The Richmond Reporter,* Oct. 23, 1857; *The Texas Sentinel,* Oct. 3 and 31, 1857; *Lamar Papers,* Nos. 2403-6 (IV, 206-7) and 2573 (IV, 74).

True to his domestic instincts, he was soon negotiating with the Nicaraguan government for a plot of ground on which to build a home.[58] But he abandoned the project when he became convinced that the climate prohibited his wife's joining him. He established a temporary home in Managua, however, and employed as his secretary José Debrin, a Spanish boy, and as his housekeeper, José's wife. The young couple seemed peculiarly attached to Lamar, and insisted on calling him god-father. After Lamar's departure for Costa Rica, José wrote to him:

Mrs. Debrin has been touched at your kind remembrance of her, and wishes me to tell you that she is ready to take care of you as soon as you come back to this country. . . . There are not yet any signs of any future god-grand-daughter for you. I am, it seems, a good-for-nothing fellow. . . .

And in another letter:

I will do whatever you order very, *very* willingly. Try to be gay—and happy in Leon. Mrs. Debrin is ready to talk with you in Spanish.[59]

Though he felt acutely the absence of his family, he wrote to Henrietta that he could force himself to stay if only he could provide for her.[60] Various attacks, branded by his friends in Washington as abolition propaganda, had already been launched against him.[61] He was disappointed in the Zeledon Treaty, negotiated with Nicaragua in the

[58] *Lamar Papers,* No. 2612 (VI, 368).
[59] *Ibid.,* No. 2688 (VI, 389) and 2644 (VI, 379).
[60] Unpublished letter, Oct. 5, 1858.
[61] "Our Minister in Nicaragua," *New York Times,* Feb. 9, 1859; "Minister Lamar," *The States* (Washington), Feb. 8, 1859; *Lamar Papers,* No. 2731 (IV, 203).

spring of 1859, and after his health failed the following summer, he resigned his position.

The twenty months in Central America produced only two poems, "The Belle of Nindiri" and "The Daughter of Mendoza," both rich in native color and music, and both addressed to Spanish belles. Lamar loved beauty wherever he found it, whether in a woman or in a sunset.[62]

He reached Washington in September, and was back at Richmond by the tenth of October. He refused public dinners tendered him at Houston, Galveston, and Richmond, and preferred to remain quietly with his family on the plantation. The seventeen thousand dollars received for his diplomatic services had greatly relieved the financial stress, and he prepared to enjoy "the little repose between this and the grave," of which he had written to Cousin Gazaway. He had brought a monkey and a parrot to Loretto, both of which became later very loyal to their little mistress.[63] All was happy activity on the plantation, for preparations were under way for the merriest Christmas that the Lamars had ever enjoyed. Friends and relatives invited for the holiday season had already begun to arrive when Lamar was suddenly stricken with a heart attack on December 18, 1859. At ten o'clock the next morning he died.[64] The holly wreath was tied with black crêpe.

[62] The letters accompanying these poems (see p. 303) seem to the present editor to preclude any suggestion of gossip hinted at in certain sources (Dienst, "Mirabeau B. Lamar," *East Texas* Magazine, July, 1929).

[63] During Lamar's absence Mrs. Eliza Budd, Henrietta's sister, had married Dr. Alexander, whom Loretto cordially disliked. Family tradition says that more than once the Doctor had to be rescued from the clutches of "that child's vicious bird."

[64] Accounts of Lamar's death and funeral: *Galveston Weekly News*, Dec. 27, 1859; *Northern Standard* (Clarksville, Texas), Jan. 14, 1860; *Columbus* (Ga.) *Daily Times*, Dec. 30, 1859; *Georgia Telegraph* (Macon), Jan. 17, 1860.

VI

POET LAUREATE OF THE
SOUTHWEST

———•—•———

THE POEMS of Lamar for the present volume have been gleaned from many fields. The unpublished sources include Rebecca Ann Lamar's album of her father's verses, Lamar's manuscript album, William Sandusky's manuscript of the poems, Lamar's papers, and various scrapbooks, albums, and letters of his kinspeople and friends. The published sources include the newspapers of Georgia, Alabama, and Texas, and the volume which Lamar published in 1857, *Verse Memorials*.

Of the manuscripts, probably the most important is Rebecca Ann Lamar's album, which her father prepared for her in 1843. It is a gold-stamped, red leather quarto of more than a hundred pages into which Lamar carefully copied at least forty-seven of his poems.[1] Though not arranged chronologically, all these date between 1816 and 1843.

Lamar's own album—a quarto bound in gold boards, with his name stamped on the front—contains twenty-

[1] Nine stubs indicate the removal of other poems.

88

three poems, all in his handwriting. They do not appear in chronological order—an indication that Lamar used the book, not for original composition, but as a means of preserving his poems. It was written about 1851, as the verses in it date from 1823 to 1851, with numerous omissions, however, of poems belonging to this period.

The Sandusky Manuscript is a copy of twelve of Lamar's poems in the handwriting of William Sandusky, Lamar's private secretary during 1840–1841. Soon after his resignation from that post Sandusky wrote to Lamar (October 18, 1841):

I am not going to trouble you with one of those long letters you hate so much to read, but just going to ask you the favor of a copy of "The Parting Kiss". . . . I admire it so much that I wish to keep it among the collections of Poetry you gave me, which I am copying very neatly in an Album for a Keepsake.[2]

Lamar did not comply with Sandusky's request because "The Parting Kiss" had become the subject of Texas gossip most unpleasant to him, but two years later he sent twelve poems, which Sandusky beautifully penned in an album.[3]

The newspaper to print more of Lamar's poems than any other was *The Columbus* (Georgia) *Enquirer,* founded by him in 1828, owned by him until 1830, and again edited by him in 1834. Unfortunately the first four volumes of the paper have been lost, only a few scattering issues surviving. In the first two of these volumes (1828–1830) Lamar almost certainly published poems of his courtship

[2] *Lamar Papers,* No. 2112 (V, 491). "The Parting Kiss" is a short story by Lamar, published in *The Telegraph* (Houston), Feb. 17, 1838, and *The Columbus* (Ga.) *Enquirer,* November 10, 1841.

[3] Other manuscript sources are indicated in the notes.

and four years of marriage to Tabitha, the happiest period of his life. After her death in 1830 he destroyed all poems written to her, as he frankly confesses in "To My Daughter." The loss of these early issues, then, leaves a great chronological gap in Lamar's verse from 1825 to 1831. The numbers of the *Enquirer* for 1834 are richly sprinkled with his poems, some single issues containing as many as four. During his first visit to Texas in 1835, he contributed five poems to *The Texas Republican* in Brazoria. Afterwards he published very sparingly in the Texas press, for his political enemies were beginning to point to his poems as evidence of an idealism which rendered their author unfit for practical affairs.[4] His poems did appear, however, at rare intervals in such widely separated papers as *The Southern Intelligencer* (Austin), *The Red-Lander* (San Augustine), *The Northern Standard* (Clarksville), and *The Matamoras Flag.* During the same period *The Macon* (Georgia) *Telegraph* and *The Charleston* (South Carolina) *Courier* published his verses, probably only when Lamar's friends contributed them.

Lamar first seriously thought of collecting his poems in 1846 when Judge James Webb jestingly threatened to send them to press for him.[5] After his second marriage (1851) his wife became enthusiastic about a volume, and together they spent considerable time during the summer of 1852 at Glenville, Alabama, preparing his verses for publication. There is a legend that his wealthy kinsman, Harmong Lamar, at whose home he and his bride were summering

---

[4] Typical is Anson Jones' statement (*Memoranda,* p. 34) that Lamar "has fine belles-lettres talents, and is an elegant writer. But his mind is altogether of a dreamy, poetic order, a sort of political troubadour. . . . Texas is too small for a man of such wild, visionary. . . ."

[5] *Lamar Papers,* No. 2215 (IV, 128).

at Glenville, offered to finance the project. But Lamar lacked both the industry and the confidence in his poetry to push the matter to a conclusion; he was afraid, he said, of exposing himself to ridicule.[6] Upon his return to Richmond he laid aside the manuscript for five years. Renewed friendship with A. B. Meek then furnished the needed courage, and Lamar's nephew, Lucius Mirabeau Lamar, supplied the funds in exchange for Texas lands. The wide-margined volume, under the title of *Verse Memorials*, was published in September, 1857, by W. P. Fetridge and Company of New York, with a dedication to Mrs. William L. Cazneau ("Cora Montgomery"). As the title suggests, Lamar included only those of his poems vividly reminiscent of some particular occasion or person. He insisted that in presenting the volume to the public he was actuated mainly by the desire to manifest to his friends that he still held them "in grateful remembrance." [7] The first printing had scarcely been sold when the publishers went into bankruptcy.

Lamar's poems are, in great part, occasional in nature, "spontaneous effusions," written more often for albums than for publication. One feels that some of these lines of compliment were created to do service for a moment, as were the occasional lyrics of Edmund Waller or Robert Herrick. This narrowness of range may be largely the result of Lamar's conception of poetry. He considered his verse-writing always as a diversion, a recreation to be indulged in during moments of relaxation. His poems,

[6] Letter from Lamar to his wife, Jan. 19, 1855, Mobile.

[7] Preface to *Verse Memorials*. A recent biographer's statement—"The elderly office-seeker employed his idle time in preparing a volume of verse for publication in the hope that its sale would provide a small nest-egg for his little daughter" (Gambrell, *op. cit.*, p. 302)—finds little justification in Lamar's letters of 1855–1857.

"dropped like wild flowers along the rugged path of public duty," were, he said, only fragments of thoughts and feelings rescued from the turmoil of a life that permitted little leisure for literary recreation.

His native South, too, with its ill-founded prejudices against professional art, still further restricted the scope of his poems. Tradition dictated that he assume towards his verse the attitude of the Southern cavalier. Any excursion into the realm of *belles lettres* must be, his environment insisted, not a part of the stern journey of living, but rather the occasional picnicking along the way when one momentarily forgets the hard road. And so it was that Lamar throughout the hurrying changes of a busy life—whether he was the Beau Brummell of Georgia small-town society, the vigorous young editor and politician, the grieving husband, the pioneer hero of Texas liberty, or the far-visioned statesman of a new republic—was always inclined to pour his verse into the mould of tradition, and it came out too often the poetry of compliment or of reminiscence. It is so frequently couched in the album-like conventions of his time and section that its relation to the dramatic life of its author is usually a matter for inference and interpretation.

Lamar was born in the same year that Wordsworth's *Lyrical Ballads* appeared, and he died in the year that saw Darwin's *The Origin of Species*. If any man has a right to produce sentimentally romantic verse, surely he of those years when the world was making its best bow to "soft feelings in sweet words" may claim that privilege. But the literary South had been born during the English eighteenth century, and still retained the clear impress of its origins. Accordingly, Lamar's early verse is strongly reminiscent of Pope, both in form (couplet) and manner. "Anacreontic" and "The Gift" make no attempt to rise above cleverness, and the "New-Year's Address"—particularly the section descriptive of the country dance—contents itself with the homely and bare realities of the Georgia cracker. "The Source of Strife," a fable of religious feuds, suggests Dryden, and "The Ruling Passion" plays with one of Pope's dearest ideas.

But in the early 1820's the literary influence of the eighteenth century was breaking up even in the slow-changing South, and English romanticism was permeating the land. The long vogue of Pope was yielding to the popularity of Thomas Moore. The new romanticism, powerless to change the thinking of the South, succeeded only in adding another dash of sentiment to the Cavalier wine. Lamar, sadly lacking in humor, fell a ready victim to the tawdry fashion, and began generously mingling his wit and sentiment, as in "Love" and "Fair Captivity." At a time when the Southern plantation had become picturesquely heavy with its own richness—a field that a realist would have found most fertile—Lamar preferred to continue to fuse the occasional spirit of the eighteenth century with the sentimentalism of the nineteenth. In form, too, the same mingling is apparent, for in his early verse he vacillated between the couplet and the stanza. By 1823 ("Perpetual Love") he turned definitely to the stanzaic form, which he never deserted.

After 1820 the English echoes in Lamar's verse are distinctly from the romantic poets. One comes across a phrase from Gray or a rhythm from Burns.[8] Lamar borrowed most frequently, however, from Thomas Moore: his blend

[8] Compare Lamar's "The Rose, the Moon, and Nightingale" with Gray's "Elegy"; Lamar's "My Gem of Delight" with Burns' "Flow Gently, Sweet Afton."

of sentiment and music closely resembles Moore's; and, like Moore, he employs the rose, precious gems, and the moon and stars as symbols of woman's beauty; like Moore, Lamar allows youthful love to mellow into friendship, and beauty into virtue.[9]

It is significant that Lamar's advent into Texas wrought little change in his verse. To us of the present, the Republic of Texas—with its land-hunger, its revival meetings, its rough-and-tumble elections, its Indians, and its battles—may seem the ideal field for the romantic writer; but we feel so only because that environment has passed into shadowy tradition. To Lamar, who soon became a part of the frontier, these conditions were a very real part of everyday life. He therefore neglected them in his literary efforts exactly as he had avoided in his Georgia verse the Negro and the plantation. A region collects its cowboy ballads and tells its tall tales of the frontier only when its civilization is nearing sophistication. Surrounded by scenes that now seem more vividly colored with romance than any fiction, Lamar still looked back with eyes of affection to the days of the cavaliers, and remained the courtly poet of compliment even on the Texas frontier. One regrets that it was so.

Yet, must all America of all ages send forth a barbaric yawp or wear chaps? True to all the totems of the deep South, Lamar was employing in his new environment the

9 Compare Lamar's "Grieve Not, Sweet Flower" with Moore's "Oh, Take Thou this Young Rose"; Lamar's "On the Banks of the Chattahoochee" with Moore's "Guess, Guess"; Lamar's "Home on the Brazos" (the lot of women) with Moore's "The Day of Love" and "Rose of the Desert"; Lamar's "In Life's Unclouded, Gayer Hour" with Moore's "Our First Young Love"; Lamar's "Anna Cowles" with Moore's "Yes, Yes, When the Bloom." Lamar's "Nourmahal" borrows the name of Moore's Sultana in *Lalla Rookh*. Moore's second visit to the United States (1804) greatly enhanced his popularity in the South.

literary code in which he had been reared. Though often clothed too conventionally to harmonize with frontier surroundings, these poems express sincerely Lamar's own emotions—now his love for the six-year-old, cotton-haired little daughter of his friend, now his admiration for a beautiful Mexican woman, now his grief for his long-dead Tabitha, now his haunting fear that his dormant soul could never again vibrate to the music of life. The dress he chose for his verses may be old and sometimes cut by rather doubtful models, but the feeling so clothed—perennial and ever-springing in the human heart—can never grow old.

His lines are too often lacking in creative energy, and are sometimes blurred for the want of the bright, hard images dear to the hearts of certain more recent poets; but the music of his verse during his last twenty years compensates for the lack of pictures. During the last decade of his work he achieved a verse melody that no other Texas poet has yet been able to surpass. His chief musical devices are a short and varied refrain, and a cadence, the happiest effects of which are particularly apparent in such poems as "My Gem of Delight," "Gay Spring," and "The Daughter of Mendoza." The last, one readily guesses, was intended to be sung to the accompaniment of castanets.

In the final analysis Lamar appears to have been, culturally speaking, torn between conflicting forces. He was reared in an America that had its eyes definitely fixed on England for literary models. At the very moment that he was penning his best poems, *Harper's Magazine* was deferentially paying Dickens and George Eliot small fortunes for the American rights to their novels. Practiced in the poetry of compliment as interpreted by the traditions and conventions of the South, Lamar found himself suddenly transplanted to the fringe of the frontier in Texas. Here the conservative culture of the Old South which he had brought with him met a new environment, wholly foreign to it. In his own living he made the adjustment, he became a pioneer. That, perhaps, is the reason he never even dreamed of mixing the Texas scene and his cultural backgrounds. And we have the paradox of a man so much a part of the frontier that he took his afternoon nap, stretched at full length on the bare boards of his front porch, his crushed hat his only pillow—who yet wrote songs so courtly in manner that they must have appeared, even to him, incongruous in their Texas surroundings. A dash of Southern Puritan—strong enough to ensure that his very virtues should sometimes offend—added yet stranger flavor to this mixture of cavalier and pioneer.

Caught between these conflicting forces, the half-patrician Texas frontiersman turned to the conventional themes and forms for his verse, and Texas' most daring and far-visioned statesman became, in matters cultural, conservative. At the moment that the fusion of Southern tradition and Western environment was giving birth to a characteristic Texas culture, Lamar's poetry too often felt only the Southern influence. He seemed unable to associate the crude humor of the West, which became the chief poetic expression of the environment, with art. His poems, then, emphasize the traditional element of the Old South—only half of the early Texas culture. They are also, at their best, a melodic revelation of the emotions and inner nature of Lamar—an aspect of the man entirely absent from the pages of history.

PART II

Lamar's Poems
and
The Circumstances of Their
Composition

To.

Miss Henrietta Maffitt.

O, lady, if the stars so bright,
    Were diamond worlds bequeath'd to me,
I would resign them all this night,
    To frame one welcome lay to thee;
For thou art dearer to my heart,
    Than all the gems of earth and sky;
And he who sings thee as thou art
    May boast a song that cannot die.

But how shall I the task essay?—
    Can I rejoin the tuneful throng,
Since Beauty has withdrawn its ray—
    The only light that kindles song?
No, no—my harp in darkness bound,
    Can never more my soul beguile;
Its spirit fled when woman frown'd,
    Nor hopes for her returning smile.

Then blame me not—my skill is gone—
    I have no worthy song to give;
But thou shalt be my favorite one,
    To love and worship whilst I live;
What e'er betides—where'er I roam,
    Thine Angel image I will bear
Upon my heart, as on a stone,
    In deathless beauty sculptur'd there.

NO GIRL CAN WIN MY STUBBORN
BREAST

*"No Girl Can Win My Stubborn Breast" was addressed to
Laura Dent (daughter of W. B. Dent), Nancy Mason (daughter
of John C. Mason), Sarah Gordon (daughter of Charles P.
Gordon), Martha Fannin (cousin of James Fannin, of Texas
fame), and Mary Eliza Moore (daughter of J. J. Moore), all of
Eatonton, Georgia. Fairfield, Lamar's home, was nine miles
distant. The poem appears in Rebecca Ann Lamar's album
(the text here printed) and in* Verse Memorials.

1816   *82819* 1857

I

No girl can win my stubborn breast,
Unless with every beauty blest
That e'er in lover's fancy glowed,
Or Nature lavishly bestowed
                On Laura.

II

She must possess an active mind,
By books of taste improved, refined;
An abstract wit of easy flow,
That wounds no friend and makes no foe,
                Like Nancy's.

III

Her heart, where warm affection glows,
And social goodness overflows,
Must know no guile—have no deceit—
But with the truth and candor beat
                Of Sarah's.

IV

To win the love of one like this,
I'd never pray for brighter bliss;
For life would glide as free from woe
As those dear days, spent long ago,
        With Martha.

V

But where shall I the fair one find,
In whom these charms are all combined?
Oh, such an one I know there be;
To point her out, I'd turn to thee—
        My Mary.

TO CHLOE

The young Lamar was evidently practicing his love verses when he wrote "Chloe." It is an ode from Horace (I, 23) done into the English eighteenth-century music. It appears only in Rebecca Ann Lamar's album.

1816   1937

My timid Chloe, wherefore shun
The Bard thy beauties have undone?
Thou shouldst not to thy mother cling
Like some frighted fawn in Spring,
When lovers would thy ear employ,
And speak of hope and future joy.
Alarm'd the vernal breeze to hear
Or hidden reptiles rattling near,
The fawn may wish its mother nigh,
And with her o'er the mountains fly;

But no such cause can make you flee,
For Spring no terrors brings to thee;
Nor do I seek thee for a feast,
With feelings of a savage beast;
Then stop, my Chloe, wherefore fly?
Full fifteen Springs have past thee by;
'Tis time to quit thy mother's side.
Come, come and be my bonny bride.

ANACREONTIC

Sarah Gordon, to whom Lamar addressed "Anacreontic," was the first sweetheart of whom he left any record. She was the daughter of Charles P. Gordon, a lawyer of Eatonton, Georgia (see p. 8). In its attempt at cleverness, it suggests the eighteenth-century manner. The poem appears in the album of Lamar's daughter, Rebecca Ann (see p. 88), and was published in Verse Memorials.

1816   1857

You've pressed me oftentimes, sweet lass,
To sip with you the social glass,
Which I as often have denied,
And coldly put the wine aside:—
But now produce the spacious bowl,
I'll quaff the juice with generous soul,
Till every ill be merged in mirth,
By toasting Beauty, Wit, and Worth.
One glass I'll fill—to her whose mind
With wit and taste is most refined;
One glass I'll fill—to her whose soul
Is freest from all low control;

One glass I'll fill—to her I prize
My warmest friend beneath the skies;
One glass I'll fill—but "Hold!" you cry,
"Such numbers bring the bloodshot eye;
To drink to each of these a bumper,
Sure Bacchus's self could not get drunker."

Ah! lovely girl, for your sweet sake,
I only mean ONE glass to take:—
That single glass, when drunk to you,
Is drunk to all these virtues too;
For thou art Nature's nonpareil,
Who dost in everything excel—
The brightest and the best of earth,
Sweet queen of Beauty, Wit, and Worth!

THE ENVIOUS ROSE

When Lamar was a boy of eighteen, living at Fairfield, he addressed "The Envious Rose" to Sarah Gordon of Eatonton. The present text appears in both his and his daughter's albums. In Verse Memorials *the conventional* Mary's *is changed to* Anna's *and the poem inscribed to Anna Miles, a distant cousin in Charleston, Coles County, Illinois.*

1816   1857

The Rose I saw on Mary's breast
   I deemed the happiest of its race.
In such a world of beauty blest,
   How could it ask a brighter place?

Yet all its hues departed soon,
    Like fading clouds at closing day,—
It could not brook superior bloom,
    And sank in envy's pale decay.

FAIR CAPTIVITY

*Letitia Ewell of Richmond, Virginia, was Sarah Gordon's
bosom friend. She was probably visiting in the Gordon home
in Eatonton, Georgia, when Lamar presented her with the
cavalier compliment, "Fair Captivity." It was published almost half a century later in* Verse Memorials.

1817   1857

I

Tell me, book-worm, studious sage,
Who nightly pore o'er Learning's page,
Wouldst thou the realms of Thought explore,
And add new wealth to Wisdom's lore?—
Then fly, for ever fly the sheen
Of Richmond's bright and beauteous queen;
For on her glories shouldst thou gaze,
Adieu, adieu to Learning's maze;
Her face will be thy only book—
Thine only study her fair look.

II

Say, warrior clad in armor bright,
Shield of thine own and country's right,
Wouldst thou fair Freedom still maintain,
And scorn to wear the conqueror's chain?—

103

Then fly in time—for ever fly
The lightning of that regal eye;
For triple mail nor polished lance
Can aught avail against its glance;
And all who dare one flash to brave,
Must fall her captive and her slave.

SPRING

*The "Blue-eyed Queen" was Sarah Gordon (Eatonton), the
name changed here to the conventional* Mary. *The verses
mark the end of Lamar's first serious love affair. They appear
only in Rebecca Ann Lamar's album.*

1818   1937

O, Spring may be a welcome guest,
To many a dark December breast,
But vain her thousand charms combine,
To chase the gloom that dwells in mine.
When first I woo'd my bright-hair'd maid,
And prosperous love our bosoms sway'd,
The Blue-eyed Queen, with joy I hail'd,
And sadden'd when her beauties fail'd.
I plucked with joy the flow'rs of May,
But Mary sweeter were than they;
I heard with joy the warbling throng,
But Mary poured a softer song;
I watched with joy the streamlet glide,
It ran to keep by Mary's side;
But ah! sweet Spring, no more I feel
Thy influence o'er my bosom steal,

104

And all in vain with lavish hand,
Thou spreadst thy blessings o'er the land;
Still sad amidst the joys I rove,
And mourn the loss of her I love.

THE COQUETTE

*Lamar, twenty-one years old when he wrote "The Coquette,"
was not intensely serious. If the cruel-hearted lady was more
than a mere poetic convention, she was probably Sarah Gordon of Eatonton (see p. 8).*

The poem was published in The Cahawba *(Alabama) Press
for August 12, 1820 (the text here printed). It appears also in
the album of Lamar's daughter, in the Sandusky Manuscript,
and in* Verse Memorials *(with the first four lines omitted).*

1818   1820

Oh mine has been the rose's fate,
    The favorite of a day,
To bask awhile, in beauty's smile,
    Then idly thrown away.
But what shall be the fair one's doom,
    Who seeks a vain renown,
By luring victims with her smile,
    To murder with her frown?—
Oh, she shall feel what she inflicts,
    A passion unrepaid;
Be wooed by many—wed by none—
    Still flattered and betrayed;
And when her triumphs are no more—
    When all her charms depart—
Her guilty victories will coil
    Like adders round the heart.

THE GIFT

Sparta, Hancock County, Georgia, is less than thirty miles from Fairfield, the Lamar homestead near Eatonton, and was therefore easily within the range of Lamar's early social activities. Here lived Miss Eliza Springer, whom Lamar often visited during the latter part of 1818, and to whom he wrote "The Gift" a short time before leaving Georgia for Cahawba, Alabama (see p. 10).

1819   1857

Whene'er a lover's doomed to part
With her who has transfixed his heart,
A custom—founded long ago—
Bids him some little gift bestow—
Which gift the fair is bound to take,
If only for politeness's sake.
Now, as the time is drawing nigh
When you, sweet girl, will say, "Good-by,"
And in the lurch your lover leave,
With sad, desponding heart to grieve,
He fain would make some gift to you,
As a pledge of love for ever true.
What shall it be—a diamond ring?
Ah! that, you know's a costly thing,
And my scant coffers may not bear
To purchase gems so rich and rare.
I will not give the full-blown rose,
For that with transient beauty glows,
And you might say, just like that flower,
My love would wither in an hour.
Suppose I labor, morn and eve,
In Fancy's loom a lay to weave—

Ah! wouldst thou not deride each line,
Because it could not equal thine?
No ring—no rose—no rhyme—no pelf—
What shall I give? I'll give myself!
Wilt thou accept?—the gift is poor,
But, 'pon my word, I've nothing more.

THE SOURCE OF STRIFE

*Lamar had little patience with religious or denominational
controversy, the evil condemned in "The Source of Strife." He
published the poem in* The Cahawba (Alabama) Press *for
July 17, 1819, soon after his arrival in Alabama (see p. 12).*

1819   1819

Once on a time in sunshine weather
A farmer's poultry basked together.
A pigeon chanced to strike their eyes,
Whose neck displayed a thousand dyes.
"Oh!" said a cock, without design,
"That bird's blue neck is very fine."
A neighboring cock who marked its hue,
But from a different point of view,
Replied, with no small mark of spleen,
"Blockhead! His neck's not blue but green."
A third exclaimed, "Confound you both,
His neck is red, I'll take my oath."
To give the chanticleers their due,
What each averred was very true—
But none had sense enough to see
His neighbor spoke as true as he.
The champions in an instant rose,

From angry words advanced to blows,
Maintained a combat long and sore,
And fell, alas, to fight no more!
Observe in these, my cocks and pigeon,
The feuds of men about religion:
From one fixed point our eyes we strain,
And see her color very plain;
Then persecute and rend our brother,
Because he viewed her from another,
And struck with fainter lights or fuller,
Beheld her with a different color.
    The moral—Hence let all feuds cease,
And each enjoy his rights in peace.

LOVE

While Lamar was editor of The Cahawba *(Alabama)* Press,
*he published "Love," without title and without signature, in
the issue for July 13, 1821. A revised version—perhaps not
Lamar's—appeared anonymously in* The Columbus *(Georgia)*
Enquirer *for June 9, 1836, under the title "Mary's Bee." It
appears in the album of Lamar's daughter, Rebecca Ann,
under the title "Love." Lucinda is likely a mere literary convention, referring to no particular individual.*

1821
                                       1821

Oh, envy not the happy state
Of those who seem with joy elate—
For all things are not what they seem,
And bliss is but a morning dream;
And much of what we crave below,
If ours, might work us endless wo.

I envied, once, a happy fly,
That glanced along Lucinda's eye,
And lit upon her velvet lip.
Oh, then said I—"Could I but sip
The nectared sweets with that poor fly,
What prince on earth so blest as I?"—
And as I spake, impelled by Fate,
I seized upon the tempting bait,
And stole a warm, unbidden kiss.
But ruin lurked amid the bliss;
For through my soul and through my frame
There shot a fierce and quenchless flame—
A fire that never is at rest,
Unsleeping Ætna of the breast,
Consuming all my joys on earth.
O Love, thou murderer of Mirth!

THE RULING PASSION

*During his early years of verse writing Lamar was much under
the influence of Pope. In "The Ruling Passion" he is playing
with one of the favorite ideas of the English poet. The poem
was published in* The Cahawba (Alabama) Press *(May 11,
1821) while Lamar was co-editor, and reprinted in* Verse Memorials *(1857) and in Dixon's* The Poets and Poetry of Texas
(Austin, 1885).

1821   1821

Alas! in all the human race,
We may some ruling passion trace—
Some monarch-feeling of the breast,
That reigns supreme o'er all the rest.
With some, it is the love of fame—

A restless and disturbing flame,
Which still incites to deeds sublime,
Whether of virtue or of crime.
With others, 'tis the love of gold—
Sad malady of rooted hold,
Which closer round the bosom twines,
As virtue dies and life declines.
With many, 'tis the love of pleasure—
A madness without mete or measure,
Which never faileth, soon or late,
To plunge its votaries in the fate
Of thoughtless flies in comfits caught—
Dying 'mid sweets too rashly sought.
But woman, always good and bright,
Great Nature's pride and earth's delight,
What is this monarch of thy soul—
This tyrant of supreme control,
That tramples with despotic force
All other feelings in its course?—
Thou needst not speak—thou needst not tell,
For all who know thee know it well:—
We read it in that downcast eye,
We learn it from that stifled sigh,
We see it in the glowing blush
That gives thy cheek its rosy flush;
And though compelled, by shame and pride,
Deep in thy heart its sway to hide,
Still do we know it as a fire
Which only can with life expire—
Sole inspiration of thy worth,
And source of all that's good on earth.
O Love! all-conquering and divine,
We know where thou hast built thy shrine.

GRIEVE NOT, SWEET FLOWER

During 1819 Lamar lived in the home of Dr. Willis Roberts at Cahawba, Ala. The next year, after Dr. Roberts had moved with his family to Mobile, Lamar was frequently his welcome guest. On one such visit Mirabeau wrote "Grieve Not, Sweet Flower" to Olivia, the eldest daughter. She was the "Young Lady of Mobile" to whom the lines were inscribed in Verse Memorials. *See "In Life's Unclouded, Gayer Hour," also written to her.*

The poem was printed in The Texas Sentinel *(Austin), September 12, 1857, and the* Charleston *(South Carolina)* Daily Courier, *November 27, 1857.*

1821   1857

Grieve not, sweet flower, to leave these shades,
 Grieve not to say farewell;
Ye soon shall find a happier home,
 Where heavenly beauties dwell.
Transplanted on my fair one's breast,
 To shed your fragrance there,
Each breath of life will far outweigh
 Whole centuries elsewhere.

'Twas thus I whisper'd to the Rose,
 As from the dewy dell
I plucked it for my favorite fair—
 The lass I love so well.
Nor will a gentle one like her
 Reject the gift I bring,
Because she is herself a flower,
 Out-blooming all the Spring.

111

Then take, fair maiden, take the Rose—
    It blooms alone for thee;
And while it basks beneath thy smile,
    More blest than I can be,
Oh, may it whisper what I feel,
    Yet tremble to avow,
A passion deep and long indulged,
    But never named till now.

NEW-YEAR'S ADDRESS
To the Patrons of *The Cahawba Press*

Lamar was co-publisher and editor of **The Cahawba Press** *for almost two years (see p. 12). The "Address" was written for the New-Year's issue of 1822, probably after Lamar had severed his connection with the paper. On the back of the copy sent to his brother, Lamar scribbled the note: "I pen'd this address in with a running quill . . . you will find many typographical errors, and as many more of the head."*

Lamar attended, around Eatonton and Cahawba from 1815 to 1822, many country dances like the one he describes in sections VI and VII, though none of the names mentioned there can now be identified.

1821   *1822*

I

Yearly doth the Laureate sing
In honor of his country's King,
And poets annually raise
To Patrons tributary lays.
With Printers too it is in vogue
To write to friends a New Year's ode,

And in compliance with the fashion
I'll make some rhymes if I can match 'em,
And conjure up a short Address
To the fair patrons of the Press.
Through learning's maze I never stray'd
Nor woo'd the Muse in sylvan shade,
Yet I'm resolv'd no more to doze;
Hail doggrel verse and farewell prose.
Where my own wit and fancy fail
Old Horace's will still prevail;
To take from him a hint or two,
'Tis only what my betters do.
Half that poets write they steal
But some have talents to conceal,
Nor do I think them much to blame;
Do as they may their fate's the same,
For genius is a wing to sail
With flying colours to a jail.
But there are knaves besides the poet:
Lawyers and Doctors daily show it,
One robs your purse, the other kills,
Death rids you of their fees and pills.
The Fair themselves are rogues, I know,
For sad experience taught me so;
They'll steal one's heart and after all
Will laugh and say the theft is small.
And must I then some book explore,
And write what others wrote before?
I'd rather own my genius small,
For borrow'd wit's no wit at all.
Muses, descend! inspire my theme,
Around your poet shed a gleam;
O, with thy aid a dunce may rise,

And spite of genius skim the skies.
Tony—catch me old Pegassus—
I'll seek the top of Mount Parnassus,
In order that my eye may range,
And notice what is new and strange.
Why may I not this steed bestride
And well as others, take a ride?
He is, I know, hard on the rein
And may perhaps dash out my brain,
Yet I will every danger face
And even risk a Gilpin race.
But as I am a rider young
I may be in a mudhole flung;
And if I should I beg the reader
To overlook the sad procedure
And leave me not as Obadiah
Left Doctor Slop stuck in the mire,
But patiently the laugh restrain
And wait 'til I can mount again.—
Behold me mounted on my steed.
Now up the hill like lightning speed,
O'er crags and stumps and bogs I go,
The lessening plain grows dim below;
Old Ariosto's Griffin horse
Never winged so swift a course.
Now swifter still—still swifter flies,
He seems almost to cut the skies—
And now I've gained Parnassus height,
O, what a dear enchanting sight!
I'll turn my flying horse to graze
Whilst with enraptured view I gaze
Upon the sons to genius dear
That animate this Heavenly sphere.

Old Spenser here is to be seen
Attended by a *Fairy Queen;*
In yonder distant cool retreat
Young Thomson takes his happy seat,
His Musidora in the stream
Is bathing near, but not unseen;
For youthful Damon, blissful lover,
Doth all her latent charms discover.
Old Virgil shakes his Dryden's hand,
And Pope and Homer join the band,
And hundred others here I find
In dearest harmony combined.
Bold Milton stands in awful state
O'er all pre-eminently great;
But sweet immortal Shakespeare, you
With gladsome heart I turn to view,
Dear favorite of my early days!
Still, still I love to read thy lays
For thou art Nature's darling child
That warbles thy native wood notes wild.
And when thy genius ranges round
The world's for it too small a bound.
Thou each passion canst control
That actuates the human soul,
Bid grief and joy alternate rise,
Depress to Hell—exalt to skies.
What stoic can restrain the laugh,
At the fat coward, Jack Falstaff?
But when old Shylock treads the stage
Each breast indignant swells with rage;
To see despotic Richard draw
His sword against his country's law,
And ride supremely on the heath,

115

Horribly bent on blood and death,
What heart is there to valor dear
Feels not the freezing pant of fear?
To hear Queen Kate for justice plead,
To view sweet Desdemona dead,
Unhappy Juliet lying low
Beside her hasty Romeo,
To hear Ophelia o'er the surge
Singing—alas, her funeral dirge—
And bold mad Hamlet swear and rave
In mournful wildness o'er her grave,
Is there a heart that will not bleed
At scenes like these?—'tis hard indeed!
What man is there with torpid breast
Loves not his native land the best,
Who would refuse his sword to draw
For her defence and Freedom's law,
But with a trembling, coward soul
Would bow to Despot's cursed control?
If such there be, let such go read
When Marcus made a great Julius bleed,
And should his heart be callous still
And feel not patriotic thrill,
May he in life imprisoned dwell,
Doomed upon earth for future Hell.

II

Here too among the tuneful band
Great Coleridge takes an equal stand;
No fabled Nine to him belong
For God alone inspires his song.
His genius soars from pole to pole

Boundless as the rays of Sol.
Like Homer's self he strikes the lyre,
Now full of strength, now beaming fire.
Through all his strains, in gentle stream
Religion pours its lucid beam.
Great bard, thy works will ever shine,
Will triumph o'er the lapse of time
When Jeffrey's slanderous race is run,
His works forgot and he unsung.
Bold Byron sits in monkish mood;
His genius strong as Niger's flood,
A soul of wrath and vengeance warm,
He speaks like Demon of the storm;
No tender thrill his bosom knows,
The child of misery—heir of woes;
Lays to Love he never caroled.
His themes are Corsair and Childe Harold,
Demons dark, and dread, and drear,
That yell of murder in the ear.
I love not Bards of rugged mind,
Whose heroes are of sooty kind;
They do my inmost soul affright,
And make me dream of hell at night.
Give me the bard of fancy gay
That sings like birds in blue-ey'd May,
Warbling within some flow'ry dale,
A simple song or moving tale
As Milton says, *in winding 'bout*
Of linked sweetness long drawn out.
I love the bard whose tender soul
Feels youthful Cupid's soft control,
O'er whose lays in dear delight,
Love gayly waves his purple light,

117

Whose Muse forever on the wing,
Collects the treasures of the spring,
And in profusion renders us
The sweets of flowery tenderness;
Whose sportive, gay, and laughing style
Will make the dull misanthrope smile,
Gorgeous as the rainbow's hue,
Sparkling as the morning dew,
Flowing ever in silver light,
Like limpid stream of crystal bright.
Such is the bard who can impart
Enrapturing transports to my heart,
And such the strains that Tommy Moore,
The young Anacreon's learnt to pour.
Dear melodious bard sing on
Forever sweet as Syren's song,
That makes old ocean's waves rejoice,
And dance the enchanting voice.
Continue still those songs to raise,
That *Little* tuned in youthful days;
Haunt again the eastern bower,
And sip the sweets of every flow'r,
Then from your old scholastic nook,
Pray give us one more *Lalla Rookh*.

III

Obsequious to the rolling day
Another year has passed away,
Forever passed, forever flown
Like Hobson's ghost, not to return.—
Dear reader, did you ever see
A little book of A B C,

For children made, by Mr. Murry?
Then if you're not in too great hurry,
I beg of thee to stop and look
To the tenth chapter of that book,
And pictured there, I think you'll find
A creature of curious kind,
With grizzly beard and piebald head
And flying pinions half way spread,
Whilst in his hand of mighty strength
He swings a scythe of dreadful length.
Know then, this creature's name is *Time,*
Who flies the world from clime to clime
And in his course of falcon flight
Sweeps boldly every living wight,
Nor kindly spares one earthly thing,
From Egypt's worm to Eastern king.
He cuts down pyramids and flowers,
School boy's traps, and lofty towers,
It was his hand that did destroy
Old Berch's mills—and walls of Troy,
Laid Thebes with all her gates in dust
And likewise Dame Quickly's sign post.
Where is now imperial Rome?
Her palaces and piles are gone,
Her liberty pole is tumbled o'er,
And Pompey's statue is no more.
Time has swept the whole away
Nor left a trace where once they lay.
Where are all those heroes bold
Of whom we are in history told,
And all the mighty legions, they
Together drew for battle's fray,
Xerxes' army and Hannibal's,
Thirsting for blood like cannibals?

No more do they with valor glow,
For time, alas! has laid them low.
Such is the fate that waits us all,
Each in his *narrow cell* must fall,
And there lie still, till that bright morn
When Gabriel winds his large French horn;
The hand that scrawls these verses o'er
In some few years shall scrawl no more,
And he whose eyes the lines may trace
With critic sneer, or smiling face,
Shall likewise fall, as sure as U
Doth follow after letter Q.
It matters not how fair a face,
Nor what may be your mental grace;
Beauty and wit can never save
One victim from the hungry grave;
For if they could old Albion's isle
Would still be lit with Wortley's smile,
And sweetest Shakespeare had not died,
But still have sung on Avon's tide.
Yet there is that which never dies;
The soul the pow'r of Time defies,
For it in endless youth will bloom
Beyond the confines of the tomb,
When Time, grown craz'd, himself shall smite,
And with his scythe, cut his wind pipe.

IV

I hate the fool who always chatters
On politics and public matters,
Who cannot speak, but what he mentions
States, Constitutions, and Conventions;

You must your printer's boy excuse
For in this way he has no news.
'Tis true that he might something say
Of Jackson and Don Calava,
And scrawl a few sarcastic things
On Queens defunct, and drunken Kings,
And from this height direct a glance
At the affairs of Spain and France;
And South America, then viewing,
Tell you what they there are doing,
How some for Liberty are struggling,
Some absconding, and some smuggling;
But all these things are growing old,
They have a hundred times been told,
And if you search, all public capers
You'll find recorded in our papers.
Solomon says there's nothing new,
And 'pon my word I think so too,
For nincompoops to legislate,
And asses grow in pow'r and state;
For candidates to 'lectioneer
And friends prove base and insincere;
For banks to fail, and cashiers steal,
And officers to serve with zeal,
Their private more than public weal;
For the young men at midnight gloom,
To roam the streets, when shines no moon,
To smoke segars—with drunken head,
To reel at one o'clock to bed;
For girls of gay fifteen to wear
In public an affected air,
And learn at home before the glass
Each pretty trick and sweet grimace;

121

All this is nothing new we know,
It has been thus for years ago.
The world's not altered in its course,
Or if it has 'tis for the worse.
Still do the rich as heretofore
Monopolize the public pow'r.
Still bows the merchant like an ape
To sell a pin or bunch of tape,
The meager jejune Doctor still
Gets license of M.D. to kill,
And still the tavern keepers do
Charge as they did five years ago.
Of all the world this class I hate
For one good reason, which I'll state:
'Tis simply this, they're too much like
A little bird we call the snipe;
They favor in their feature strong
For both have bills tremendous long.
And after all it doth appear
There's nothing new but a New Year.

V

I am too fast—on second view,
I find that I have something new.
Another dandy came to town
Last Christmas day, in high *bon ton.*
A sprightly youth, quite neat and tight,
As rockets tall and head as light;
With broadcloth coat and breeches too
And little jacket bound in blue;
His ruffles deck'd with breast pin bright
That glitters like the source of light;

But by my books I've oft been told
That all which glitters is not gold.
His beaver's cocked in foppery's pride,
On corner of his skull one side,
For fear it should his ringlets spoil
Dressed sweetly in Macassor oil.
With his right hand he swings his chain,
And in his left a long sword cane,
From which he'd draw the polish'd steel,
And bravely—run off by the heel.
And who is he, this flaming star?
A coxcomb licensed to the bar,
Frolicking round in folly's whirls,
Scorned by men, admired by girls.
With brass heel boots he struts in court,
Under his arm a large report,
His long green bag with papers full,
More in the satchel than his skull.
He has a speech well memorized,
Which he to any case applies.
So when he spouts 'tis with the ease
Of him who thundered to the seas;
United comes on the evidence,
Which cools his fire of eloquence:
There ends his speech—in vain he tries
On rhetoric's wings again to rise;
He flutters, flounds, and fain would soar,
His pinions cropt, he sails no more;
He rose like eagle o'er the fowl,
But tumbled headlong like an owl.
O cease, dull sir, to prate your law,
Go hew the wood and water draw,

Lay Blackstone's Commentaries down
And take up Aesop and Tom Thumb.

VI

Now pause we here a while to tell
What at a country dance befell,
In Christmas times, at father Grumpus'
Where they cut a dreadful rumpus.
He lives three miles from Doctor Sneak,
On what is called the Rackoon Creek,
In cabin built of swamp oak strong,
Twenty feet wide and thirty long,
The chinks well daub'd with straw and clay
That ne'er admits the solar ray;
A cyprus roof and puncheon floor,
A four square window and a door,
Screaking on new hickory hinges,
At which your very bosom scringes.
A bed, a barrel, and a broom
Grac'd south-east corner of the room.
Another held a cross'd leg'd table,
A tripod, bench, and rocking cradle;
In the third lay pots and griddles,
The fourth cleared out for him that fiddles,
Whilst round the walls in gay festoons
Swung petticoats and pantaloons.
Such is the spacious drawing-hall
In which was held our lively ball.
'Bout three o'clock in afternoon
An hour unusually soon,
All the neighboring beaux collected;
Some from distance were expected.

There were Belch and Tony Grumbo,
Corporal Crane and Captain Sligo,
Doctor Dunce and Justice Bibo,
All dandies of the higher class
That shared the smiles of every lass.
The latter one is as fair as
Adonis or the Trojan Paris.
I will for those who never saw
This lovely youth, his picture draw,
For of the beauties great and small
He tops the climax of them all.
Then figure to yourself a beau,
Just six feet long from top to toe
With crooked back and frozen thin sides
And brains as soft as pumpkins' insides,
A little meager baboon face
As tadpole sleek, and thin as plaice;
His eyes you hardly can discover
So far his brows projecting over;
Between them hangs a bottle nose
Which with the flaming jorum glows;
Were he at midnight to look at us
We'd take his snout for *ignis fat'us*.[1]
His spider legs are long and slim
And crooked as a black-jack limb;
They interlock above his heels
And work like cogs in trundle wheels,
So when he moves he hobbles on
Like horses foundered on new corn.
Among the dashing belles, there were
Miss Kitty Perce as good as fair,
Dorothy Snap and Peggy Wild,

---

[1] *Ignis fat'us,* Will-o-the-Wisp.

Two lovely girls as ever smiled,
Tabitha Brass and Widow Jabber,
Patty Bland and Molly Badger,
Betty Bounce and romping Nelly,
And many more than I could tell ye.

VII

But now they light the pine torch tapers.
Yonder come the music makers;
They soon arrive in marching band
And in their corner take their stand.
The head one of the grand procession
Has gourd fiddle in possession,
On which in jollity and fun, he
Plays old *Possum up the gum tree*.
Another on a long necked banger,
To the delight of every stranger,
Thrums *old Virginia never tire*
Eat parch corn and lie by the fire.
The last not least among the band
Holds stirrup iron in his hand,
Which he rattles with a spindle,
Making a delightful jingle.
Each moves his head in dodging motion,
And plays a tune, to his own notion,
Producing music on the plan
Maintain'd in Pope's *Essay on Man,*
That *discord is* (they prove good)
Sweet *harmony not understood*.
For the dance they now prepare;
Each beau leads out his gentle fair.
Dr. Dunce in dexterous flounce

126

Took the head with Betty Bounce,
And Corporal Crane and Patty Bland
Quick occupied the second stand,
Whilst Tony Grumbo, active chap,
Hopped up next with Dorothy Snap
And left poor Bibo in the lurch,
To take the foot with Kitty Perce.
And now they all begin to reel,
High bounding on the sturgeon heel,
The beaux exerting every spring
To dance breza and pigeon wing.
The girls as light as air balloons,
Fandagoes cut, and rigadoons.
No sooner than one reel is run,
As soon another is begun.
Thus on they danced with main and might
Till twelve o'clock at least at night,
And would have danced, how long, God knows,
Had not a sad disturbance rose.
Belch and Sligo were two rivals,
Cock'd and primed to fight on trifles,
Both endeavoring to surpass,
In marked attention to Miss Brass.
The captain wed the widest row,
Which made poor Belch with dudgeon glow,
The latter went with smiling grin,
And ask'd Miss Tab to dance with him,
Whom Sligo afterwards engaged.
Now this the beau so much enraged,
That off he turned in dreadful wrath,
And dragged his happy rival forth
To seek upon his tawny hide
A just revenge for wounded pride.

Now back his mutton fist he drew,
And in the captain's face it flew.
At which the crimson current flows
In dreadful fluxion from the nose.
But soon our Sligo's fist let fly
A mighty punch in Belch's eye.
Then grasping hold a stave of oak
He drove the grinders down his throat.
At this they clinch, like tigers fighting,
Kicking, scratching, gouging, biting,
Over pots and pans they stumble,
Now they have it rough and tumble.
The girls affrighted left the room.
Their torches lit, and sallied home.
I too in the dreadful flurry
Took French leave in the greatest hurry.

VIII

Ah, badly doth the world requite
The carrier's labor and his wit.
His fate indeed is so severe
He never smiles but once a year,
He cracks a joke on New-Year's day
For which he gets dam'd little pay.
If it should rain, or hail or snow,
He like a ticking watch must go;
Must take his old hebdomadal round
And risk his neck on slip'ry ground.
For one to trudge through mud and mortar
Now the town, bale-full of water,
Is not so pleasant all must know,
Yet this the carrier has to do:

But his sad case I won't expose
Nor move your pity with his woes,
For long recitals of his grief
I fear would not produce relief.
Do *you* at present something pay
And *he* in duty bound will pray
This year may be a year of joy
To Patrons and the Printer's boy.
So from Parnassus' lofty height,
Swift as the darting beams of light
I with my coursers do descend,
And now upon my friends attend
In hope that they will not refuse
To recompense my weary muse.

FROM THE CHURCH STEEPLE

In 1822 Lamar returned to Fairfield, near Eatonton, after three years in Cahawba, Alabama, where his ventures in the business world had failed. Upon his visit to the Union Church at Eatonton (which had been completed during his absence) he wrote these lines in a whimsical mood of self-satire. They appear only in Rebecca Ann Lamar's album.

1822   1937

In early life, when hope ran high,
And tow'ring fancy wing'd the sky,
I thought I should, ere life was o'er,
Above the vulgar level soar,
And make the great folks of the nation,
Look up to me, in my high station.

Behold, I've gained my heart's desire!—
Whilst standing on this lofty spire,
I can from the bold height look down
Upon the greatest lords in town,
And they, as only common people,
Look up to me—while on this steeple.

PERPETUAL LOVE

"Perpetual Love" belongs to Lamar's first year in Milledge-
ville, when he was Governor Troup's secretary. He wore a
sword and was socially very popular.
    Lucy may be Lucy Bell, the daughter of the hotel-keeper
with whom Lamar had boarded the year before in Cahawba
(see p. 12). Laura may refer to Laura Thompson of Macon,
to whom Lamar addressed a later poem. "Perpetual Love"
appears as "Song" in the Sandusky Manuscript, in Lamar's
manuscript album, and in Rebecca Ann Lamar's album.

1823   *1857*

I

Perpetual love plays round my heart
    For some fair form—I don't know who;
I would not with the passion part,
    Although its object mocks my view.

II

To meet a girl with sparkling eye—
    She is that phantom of my breast;
But if a brighter pass me by,
    I'm sure to love the brighter best.

III

I thought, dear LUCY, long ago,
    For none but thee my soul could sigh;
But LAURA spread superior glow—
    Love waved his wings and bade good-by.

IV

Oh, do not say that I'm to blame—
    'Tis Nature's fault that made me so;
Heaven knows my love's a constant flame,
    But who I love—I do not know.

THE MAIDEN'S REMONSTRANCE

Lamar wrote "The Maiden's Remonstrance" soon after leaving Cahawba for Milledgeville, where he found the social atmosphere of the new capital very pleasant. The poem depicts probably a wholly fictitious situation. It was published in The Columbus Enquirer *(November 29, 1834) under the title "The Remonstrance." The same text, with present title, appears in Rebecca Ann Lamar's album. It was extensively revised (see notes, p. 305) for* Verse Memorials *(present text).*

1823   1834

I

The hand you have so often pressed,
    You vow you'll ne'er forsake it,
And yet you have no wish expressed
    In wedlock's right to take it;—

The heart you have so warmly wooed,
    You vow you'll ever shield it,
And yet you have a course pursued
    That must to sorrow yield it.

II

You say you love the opening rose—
    Ah! dost thou know its fleetness?
Then why not pluck it while it blows,
    Before it lose its sweetness?
You say you love me as your life—
    Ah! wouldst thou not deceive me?
Then why not take me for your wife,
    Ere beauty's light shall leave me?

III

Cease, Oh cease the flatterer's part,
    An upright mind disdains it;
Your guile may win a maiden's heart,
    But truth alone retains it.
If thou hast wooed, but not to wed,
    If falsely thou hast spoken,
Oh, leave me to the tears I shed—
    My heart, my heart is broken!

TELL ME NOT THAT WOMAN LOVES

"Tell Me Not That Woman Loves" was dedicated to Miss Laura Thompson, the daughter of a physician in Macon. It is preserved in Rebecca Ann Lamar's album ("Song") and in Verse Memorials.

1823   1857

I

Nay, tell me not that woman loves,
   Because her bosom heaves the sigh;
And, tell me not that pity moves,
   Because she hath a tearful eye;
How easy 'tis to seem to feel,
How easy for the tear to steal!
Oh, Affectation's practised part
Makes Nature seem less true than Art.

II

Each tale of unrequited love,
   My feeling Laura weeps to read;
No flower that withers in the grove
   But makes her gentle bosom bleed;
Yet while she mourns the faded rose,
And gives her tears to fictious woes,
She still derides my real distress,
And still withholds her power to bless.

WRITTEN IN A LADY'S ALBUM

These lines, the first addressed to Sarah Rossetter (Milledge-ville), mark the beginning of a friendship which was later to take on a more serious aspect, at least for Lamar. The verses, which he called a parody, owe something to Gray's "Elegy." They appear only in Rebecca Ann Lamar's album.

1823   1937

Friend of the Muse, this Album read,
    'Twill please thy polish'd mind;
It may not claim the highest meed,
    Yet still 'tis much refin'd.
        Just like its owner's mirth,
            It makes dull care depart;
        And like her sterling worth,
            It sinks into the heart.

No vicious Muse the song inspires,
    Unmeet for beauty's ear;
'Tis friendship's pure and sacred fires
    That light the records here.
        Some flowers of humble bloom
            To every bow'r belong;
        Yet many a rich festoon
            Here genius strews along.

TO A VILLAGE COQUETTE

*The "fair renegade," Lamar said, lived at Monticello, the only
information about her that has survived the years. The poem
was probably Lamar's graceful manner of discontinuing a
friendship that was proving inconvenient to him at Milledgeville, for Monticello was thirty miles to the northwest, in Jasper County, and Sarah Rossetter had already dawned upon his
horizon at the State Capital.*

The poem was published anonymously in The Columbus
Enquirer *for August 2, 1828, and also in* Verse Memorials *(the
present text).*

1824   1828

I

Fair renegade of faith and love,
  Apostate to thy vow,
The ruin of my earthly hopes
  Is written on thy brow!
'Tis vain to smile—I trust no more
  The light that leads astray;
The triumphs of thy arts are o'er—
  Thou canst no more betray.

II

Among the gems that decked thy youth,
  To me a heavenly host,
It was the lovely star of truth
  That charmed my spirit most;
But when that star, that rose so fair,
  Went down in Beauty's sky,
It left no other planet there
  For me to wander by.

III

Yet, lady fair, despite my wrong,
  I will not now upbraid;
If thou hast peace, my parting song
  Shall not that peace invade.
I will not seek thy hopes to mar,
  Thou art no more my ruling star,
  Yet still I wish thee well.

IV

The ring you gave, I may not wear—
  'Tis meet that I restore
The gem that deepens my despair,
  And makes me mourn the more;
But back I may not give to thee
  The memory of the past;
For that must dwell a thorn with me
  While life itself shall last.

V

The bleeding soldier, feeling yet
  The arrow near his heart,
May quite forgive—but not forget—
  The hand that sped the dart.
So do I blend, amid my woes,
  Forgiveness with regret;
But she who murdered my repose—
  Oh, how can I forget!

VI

While yet in Jasper's valleys green
  Is left a lingering tree,

136

To mind me of how blest I've been,
  But never more may be—
So long shall I thy change lament,
  And weep that one so fair
Should doom the heart that loved her most
  To darkness and despair.

THEY SAY THOU ART AN ANGEL BRIGHT

*Addressed to Martha Clark, daughter of B. W. Clark of Eaton-
ton, the poem was written when Lamar was secretary to Governor Troup at Milledgeville. The theme belongs to the cavalier tradition of the ante-bellum South.*

1824   1857

I

They say thou art an angel bright,
  A seraph from on high;—
Alas! I may not censure those
  Who breathe the pleasing lie;
For lo! thou art so beautiful,
  So fraught with every grace,
They well might make the sweet mistake
  While gazing on thy face.

II

And yet, despite thy heavenly charms,
  No angel thou in truth;
For how can she an angel be,
  Who murders without ruth?

137

And does thou ask me for the proof?
   Behold it in my woes—
Hast thou not stabbed me with thine eye,
   And murdered my repose?

III

Then do not deem thyself, fair maid,
   A creature from the skies,
Because the light of those blessed spheres
   Is sparkling in thine eyes;
But if thou wouldst the being be
   Thou seemest unto the sight,
Then soothe the pangs thy charms have wrought,
   And be an angel quite.

SONNET TO SOLITUDE

*The "sonnet" is an acrostic to Sarah Rossetter, in whose album
Lamar wrote the lines on May 19, 1825, at Milledgeville. At
the time, he was secretary to George Troup, and the "mad
Governor of Georgia" was engaged in a winning struggle with
the Federal authorities over the Indian lands along the Chattahoochee—a fact that explains "these jarring times" and Lamar's half affected longing for quiet. The poem appears in the
album of Rebecca Ann Lamar, and in* Verse Memorials.

1825   1857

Say, why will man with fellow-man contend,
And kindle passions that in ruin end?
Reason and Nature prompt to social life,
And fly the cursed concomitants of strife.
Hail! gentle Solitude, unknown to crimes,

Retreat of Virtue in these jarring times—
Oh, let me in thy peaceful shades abide,
Secure from all the wars of power and pride;
Some nook be mine, in which to clear a field,
Erect a cottage, and to quiet yield.
There could I dwell, contented and confined,
To God devoted and to death resigned;
Enough of turbulence—I mourn its woes—
Religious Solitude, I court thy calm repose.

TO SARAH

Lamar addressed the lines to Sarah Rossetter of Milledgeville, during his secretaryship with Governor Troup. They are preserved only in Rebecca Ann Lamar's album, into which her father copied them in 1843.

1825   1937

Full many ills my heart hath borne.
  Its joys have been but few;
Yet still some shining days I've known,
  Those days were spent with you,
                                   Sarah.

I've lassies seen with beauty blest,
  With wit and goodness too,
But O, the loveliest ne'er possessed
  The pow'r to please like you,
                                   Sarah.

For some small fault would seem to lurk
  In all I ever knew;
But Nature, smit with her own work,
  Forgot a fault for you,
                  Sarah.

Then let the nobler minstrel sing
  The praise to others due;
Whene'er my humble harp I string,
  Its chords shall sound for you,
                  Sarah.

ODE TO FISHING CREEK

Fishing Creek is a tiny stream, only ten miles in length, that empties into the Oconee River at Milledgeville. Lamar wrote the "Ode" in the album of Sarah Rossetter, to whom he was earnestly paying court in 1825. It is an acrostic to Susannah T. Rossetter, Sarah's younger sister. In 1843 Lamar copied it into the album of his daughter, Rebecca Ann, and fourteen years later published it in his Verse Memorials.

1825   1857

Sweet stream, although thou glid'st along
Unknown to fame and classic song,
Still on thy banks I oft abide,
As glad as the swains on Levan's tide;
Not that thy banks are gayly green,
Nor that thy waves are silver sheen;
All other streams might boast thy bowers,
Have equal flocks, and fields, and flowers,

Their cadenced waves as sweetly shine,

Reflecting light as pure as thine—
Oh, still no stream so dear to me;
Some fond remembrance dwells with thee—
Some pleasing thought of fleeted days,
Enjoyed upon thy banks and braes:—
Thou mind'st me of my much-loved maid,
The times we've loitered in thy shade,
Each cheerful word, each pleasing smile,
Replete with joy and free from guile.

LOVE'S NO SOURCE OF GLADNESS

The "Song," as Lamar entitled these lines, seems to suggest that Sarah Rossetter's gallant lover did not find his lady particularly tractable in Milledgeville in 1825. The verses appear in Rebecca Ann's album.

1825   1937

O, love's no source of gladness,
    Say rather 'tis of woe;
It is a kind of madness,
    Have I not found it so?

Its hopeless victims languish,
    Their youth—their beauty dies;
A prey to all its anguish,
    My life's a life of sighs.

Is there no joy beguiling,
    To cheer the sinking mind?

II

I'll mention one—the low, abandoned knave,
  Who publishes a paper called "Diurnal": [1]
A ready rascal and a shameless slave,
  He labors daily in his task infernal,
To vent on truth his heeleboric breath—
A human Upas, spreading moral death.

III

Oh Mr. Grantland,[2] never like that elf
  Withhold the meed to worth and talents due;
And from the right be never swerved by pelf,
  But still your old accustomed course pursue,
To scourge the graceless scoundrels of the times—
Be sure—nay, very sure—you print my rhymes.

IV

I do not write for popular applause;
  I can not lie, the multitude to please;
Nor heed I aught your plodding schoolman's laws;
  I take whatever course may suit my ease,
At random steering by the rudder rhyme—
Bound to no port, and careless of the clime.

V

And ask ye, reader, wherefore I aspire,
  In spite of genius, to a rambling song,

[1] *The Journal* (Milledgeville), edited by Robert Lucas, was politically, after 1819, an organ of the Clarke faction, bitterly opposed to Crawford and Troup.
[2] Seaton Grantland, editor of *The Southern Recorder* (Milledgeville), was an enthusiastic supporter of Crawford and Troup—Lamar's party.

Regardless of the critic's vengeful ire?—
  Perhaps ye think it is unwise—nay, wrong—
To con the verse that can not purchase fame;
A skilless effort is the heir of shame.

VI

I write obsequious to my fair one's will,
  And seek no recompense beyond her smiles;
If she can tolerate my want of skill,
  I little heed who censures or reviles;
At her command I'll rhyme till reason reels,
Though every critic cur comes yelping at my heels.

VII

I know that Nature never did infuse
  In my lethargic clay poetic fires;
Nor did I ever wish to woo the Muse.
  Sad is the lot of him whom she inspires—
Especially if poor. He ne'er shall claim
The smiles of beauty or the meeds of fame.

VIII

I had a friend [3]—the best I ever had—
  The sweetest minstrel of his day and time;
He was, indeed, a very gifted lad,
  And oft the village echoed with his rhyme.
But he in life was spurned—in death, forgotten;
And why?—because he'd neither cash nor cotton.

[3] Stanzas VIII to XIV refer to Henry Denison, whose poems were collected and edited by B. F. Tefft.

IX

No more rememb'red is the child of song—
   The warm, devoted, and aspiring youth,
Whose spirit was a river rolling strong,
   Melodious in love, and powerful in truth;
His worth, his genius, and his tuneful strains,
Were all sepulchred with his cold remains.

X

By menial hands the humble bier was borne,
   And he was placed at rest, with few to weep;
But Nature seems her fav'rite bard to mourn—
   For in the valley, where his ashes sleep,
She plants perennial flowers of every hue,
And bathes them nightly with her tears of dew.

XI

No marble rises by the willow-tree,
   No verse invokes the tribute of a tear;
Unlettered dullness scorns his memory,
   And kindred genius ceases to revere;
These lowly lines,—which may not hope to live—
Are all I have, and these I fondly give.

XII

In token of my love.—I have no art
   To paint his virtues, or describe my wo;
But surely he must have a marble heart,
   Insensible to every generous glow,
Who can not weep—who has no tears to shed—
When memory wakes to view some friend long dead.

146

XIII

Poor HAL has winged his way to realms above
  Where none can enter but the pure in heart;
That I may meet him in that land of love,
  Oh, let me from his maxims ne'er depart.
How pleasant will it be to recognize
Each other, as we tread along the skies!

XIV

I've thought the sweetest flower that scents the grove
  Was oft the first to lose its vernal bloom;
I've thought the child of poesy and love
  Was oft the earliest victim to the tomb.
Is there no power the sinking rose to save?
Can no one snatch bright genius from the grave?

XV

O Doctor Pangloss! [4] what avails thy skill,
  If thou canst not delay the parting breath?
Hast thou no compound rare—no potent pill—
  With which to combat and to baffle Death?
Methinks, indeed, a brain like thine, prolific,
Should never be at fault for a specific.

XVI

Long hast thou been thy teeming genius training,
  To perpetrate a book with wisdom rife—
Perchance of deep philosophy—explaining
  The grand phenomena of human life.
When wilt thou print?—then none shall physic need;
Thy book will physic every one who'll read.

[4] Probably Dr. Horace Shaw; see p. 8.

XVII

Go on, dear doctor,—in thy closet work—
  I laugh sometimes, but still admit thy worth;
No gall nor envy in my heart can lurk;
  And sure thou canst forgive a little mirth,
E'en at thy own expense. In former times
Didst thou not pen some quite unsparing rhymes?

XVIII

Oft have I read thy high-resounding verse
  With profit and delight;—but since thy Muse
Doth not disdain to play at cut and tierce,
  Thou must not murmur if my own should choose,
In sportive mood, to have at thee, old friend,
And for thine Oliver a Rowland send.

XIX

Then on, I say—the critics may deride
  Thy words of learned length and thundering sound;
And they may say thou hast pedantic pride,
  And call thy noodle an *obscure profound;*
But never let them work thee to vexation—
To murder honest fame is their vocation.

XX

As for myself, I scorn the rabid throng;
  I don't their wit nor hateful malice dread;
Deaf to their rage, I still pursue my song,
  Though dull it be as Johnny's anvil-head.
'Tis Sally Riley that demands the lay;
'Tis fame to please her—pleasure to obey.

XXI

Oh, Sally Riley is a lovely lass,
  In whom the light of every virtue dwells—

A bright divinity that doth surpass
  All earthly forms in weaving magic spells;
The fetters which her young, aurora face
Entwines around the heart, no other can displace.

XXII

I well remember when I met her first,
  And all the rapture of the heavenly sight;
She broke upon me like a sudden burst
  Of glory from the realms of love and light;
And never did a Chaldee watch his star
With more devotion than I worshipped her.

XXIII

She had that day been through the city shopping,
  And called at Mr. Shaw's to buy a sash;
And I—as if by accident—did pop in
  The moment she was counting down the cash;
And from the very time that I first met her,
I vowed I'd marry her—if I could get her.

XXIV

Two other girls were with her—soon the three,
  Together linking with their 'kimbo arms,
Departed from the store in merry glee,
  With such high lustre streaming from their charms,
As gave a double brilliance to the day,
And swept all shadows lying in their way.

XXV

The one [5] was of a tall, attractive shape,
  But seldom equalled, and surpassed by none;
She wore a deep vermilion Canton crepe,
  That glistened as its foldings caught the sun;

[5] Laura Dent of Eatonton, Georgia.

Her ostrich-feathers nodded to the skies,
And lambent lightnings arrowed from her eyes.

XXVI

The other [6] was of stature rather low,
  And was in cambric very neatly drest;
Disdaining gewgaw and fantastic show,
  She deemed that simple beauty was the best—
And never sought a dandy dunce to win,
With shining tinsel or a practiced grin.

XXVII

No—she was Nature's unaffected child,
  Exempt from all the blandishments of art;
Her modest mien, and manners ever mild,
  Bespoke the gentle nature of her heart.
And he who weds that girl need never roam
For bliss—she'll make a paradise of home.

XXVIII

But Sally [7] was the gem for me—far, far
  Outshining every pure and sparkling thing;
Hers was the beauty of a new-born star,
  The morning's glory, and the bloom of spring.
No mortal might behold her eyes and live,
Did not her sweetness soothe the wounds they give.

XXIX

The moonbeams dancing on the waters bright,
  The singing of the birds at dewy dawn,
The sweet-brier's odor, and the lily's white,
  The waving osier, and the gliding swan,

[6] Nancy Mason, also of Eatonton.
[7] For identification, see introductory note, p. 143.

Are all delightful things—in which we trace
Her smiles and melody, her purity and grace.

XXX

I will not try to paint the rainbow's hues,
 Nor sketch the splendor of supernal day.
What bard may render justice to the rose,
 Or concentrate its fragrance in his lay?
And yet these tasks were easier far, I ween,
Than weave in song my fair one's heavenly sheen.

XXXI

She is, indeed, the jewel of her race,
 And, like the diamond, shines without a peer;
The fairest belle that worships her own face,
 Is but the dark antithesis of her;
And he who would her dazzling lights portray,
Must dip his pencil in celestial ray.

XXXII

One girl hath a good heart—another, sense;
 A third, distinguished for her beauty bright;—
But where is she, of such rare excellence,
 In whom these qualities do all unite?
Such fair perfection, Envy must allow,
Was dear Maria's [8] once—is Sally's now.

XXXIII

Ay—not to beauty's fascinating power
 Is Sally Riley's loveliness confined;

[8] Mary Eliza Moore of Eatonton; see p. 9.

Beauty is rightly called a fading flower—
  Its glories soon are scattered in the wind.
Heaven did to her two richer gems impart—
A mind reflective, and a feeling heart.

XXXIV

Who that has ever heard her counsels wise,
  Can doubt the soul of goodness whence they came?
When laughs her heart, and sport lights up her eyes,
  What stoic breast, so spiritless and tame,
As not to revel in the wit that flows?—
I always wish the strain might never close.

XXXV

O ye proud belles in whom no merit glows,
  Whose value quadrates with your fathers' pence,
Be it your task to win the brainless beaux—
  'Tis Sally's praise to please all men of sense;
The world may woo you—woo you for your pelf;
The world loves Sally—loves her for herself.

XXXVI

To genius, truth, and modesty unknown,
  Go, flutter like the moth, in rich brocade;
For, nursed in folly, and in pride full-blown,
  Your low ambition lies in vain parade.
To bankrupt gentlemen ye are a prize,
But never need ye hope to win the wise.

XXXVII

Go, wed some doctor with cadaverous jaw,
  Whose idle drugs are moulding on the shelf;

Go, wed some lawyer, who can't practise law,
　But's doomed to have it practised on himself;
Or, take the merchant, who must shortly fail—
Be locked in wedlock, or be locked in jail.

XXXVIII

Oh, these will tell you that you're fresh and fair,
　Though horrible as Milton's Death and Sin;
And that you're witty too they'll freely swear,
　Though all Boeotia's darkness reigns within.
'Tis gold extorts their praise—not wit nor beauty—
And well they know that flattery gains the booty.

XXXIX

Far nobler conquests Sally makes than these;
　Her frowns repel the mercenary slave;
But ah! she has the power and will to please
　The virtuous, generous, and the brave.
Then come, ye witless belles, in her behold
What ye have not—some worth that is not gold.

XL

She is—but stay!—some other time I'll sing
　Her praise, in bolder verse, if I am able;
But now I hear the bell for dinner ring,
　And this is Mary's week to grace the table.
Excuse me—I must go—indeed, I think
That bards, as other folks, should eat and drink.

Lamar continued with Canto II twenty years later.
See p. 225.

153

NOURMAHAL
Written In A Ballroom

Lamar wrote "Nourmahal" in a ballroom at Milledgeville, "on being rallied," he said, "by a young lady for not joining in the amusements of the evening." It reflects strongly his reading of Thomas Moore, especially "Lalla Rookh."
First published in The Columbus Enquirer *(December 13, 1834), it was reprinted, with many variants, in* Verse Memorials *(the present text). It appears also in Rebecca Ann Lamar's album.*

1825   •   1834

I

While beauty is shedding its magical light,
   And music and merriment mingle their power,
To chase from each bosom its sorrowful night—
   Oh, may not a lover, in such a sweet hour,
The charms of his far-distant beauty forget,
   And whisper of love to the belles that are by?
No, no—I would rather my spirit should set
   In darkness for ever, than leap to the eye
Of any—the brightest—that beam in this ball—
   The light of my bosom is fair Nourmahal.

II

O Mary, if beauty and sweetness could chase
   My long-cherished love, and a new one supply,
It might be the smile of thy luminous face—
   It might be the glance of thy soul-stirring eye.
Like a Peri from heaven you float in the dance,
   As light as a zephyr from orient bowers;

154

I now and then give you a transient glance,
    Just such as I'd throw upon winter wild-flowers;
For never, oh never thy splendor can thrall
    The bosom that's bound to my fair Nourmahal.

III

Oh, Nourma was copied from angels above,
    And all of their goodness enlivens her breast;
I never can sigh for another one's love,
    So long as with hers I am happily blest.
Oh, wonder not then that I join not in the mirth,
    Since I find not my star of idolatry here;
The purest of pleasures that brighten this earth,
    And all of the bliss of a far better sphere,
I'd freely relinquish as valueless all,
    Unless I could share them with fair Nourmahal.

OCTAVIA

Octavia Walton, grand-daughter of a signer of the Declaration of Independence and daughter of a governor, found herself socially prominent from birth. She removed from Georgia with her father to Florida in 1821, and was visiting in Milledgeville at the age of fifteen when Lamar addressed his verses to her. It is significant that twenty years later, after she had become the sophisticated "Madame LeVert" of Mobile, whose drawing-room was the social center of the South, Lamar did not alter the lines (see p. 68).

In Rebecca Ann Lamar's album the conventional Amanda *is substituted for* Octavia.

1825   1857

I

When first to town Octavia came,
All eyes were pleased, all hearts were flame;
Aside the students' books were laid,
And every bard a rhyme essayed.
Our native girls no longer prized,
Their wit forgot, their worth despised—
All, all gave place to that bright Star,
Who touched so well the Light Guitar.

II

Oh, let them to that fair one bow,
And chaplets weave to grace her brow—
My native maids I still admire,
To them alone I tune my lyre;
Nor in my heart shall they give place
To higher birth or richer race—
Not e'en to thee, thou shining Star,
Who touch'st so well the Light Guitar.

156

LEST I BECOME A PERJURED BARD
To Sophia

Always restless, Lamar found time for travel even while he was Governor Troup's private secretary. He was a guest in the home of his old friends, the Roberts family, in Mobile, when Sophia, the second daughter, reminded him of his promise to write her a poem. He complied with these verses.

Lines 9 and 10 refer to his recent break with Sarah Rosset-ter, who had ridiculed his "Sally Riley." The poem appears in Rebecca Ann Lamar's album ("To Sophia"), and in Verse Memorials.

1825   1857

I own I promised, t'other day,
To frame for thee a cheerful lay;
But, lady fair, I can't comply—
Oh, do forgive the little lie!
Some other boon demand—you know
My heart, my life, my all may go;
But when you bid me build the rhyme,
You only urge me on to crime;
For once I penned a sprightly lay,
To please the fair—but missed the way;
And since that time, I've often *swore,*
For those I *love,* I'd rhyme no more;
Then, lady, urge me not too hard,
Lest I become a perjured bard.

THE SONG-VISION

Written during the happiest year of Lamar's life, when he and Tabitha and Rebecca Ann were living in the cottage in Columbus, "The Song-Vision" follows the Romantic tradition of the period rather than pictures a real situation. The heroine's name, Fanny, reappears years later in Lamar's short story, "The Parting Kiss" (1837) and in his "Fanny Myer" (1848).

The poem was published in The Columbus Enquirer *for June 21, 1828, when that paper was less than a month old.*

1828   1828

Oh, warble not that fearful air!
    For sweet and sprightly though it be,
It wakes in me a deep despair
    By its unhallow'd gaiety.

It was the last my Fanny sung,
    The last enchanting playful strain
That breathed from that melodious tongue,
    Which none shall ever hear again.

From memory's fount what pleasures past
    At that one vocal summons flow;
Bliss which I vainly thought would last—
    Bliss which but deepens present woe!

Where art thou, Fanny? can the tomb
    Have chill'd that heart so fond and warm—
Have turn'd to dust that cheek of bloom—
    Those eyes of light—that angel form?

Ah no! the grave resigns its prey:
  See, see! my Fanny's sitting there;
While on the harp her fingers play
  A prelude to my favourite air.

There is the smile which ever bless'd
  The gaze of mine enamour'd eye—
The lips that I so oft have press'd
  In tribute for that melody.

She moves them now to sing: hark! hark!
  But ah! no voice delights mine ears:
And now she fades in shadows dark;
  Or am I blinded by my tears?

Stay yet awhile, my Fanny, stay!
  Nor from these outstretched arms depart;
'Tis gone!—the vision's snatch'd away!
  I feel it by my breaking heart.

Lady, forgive this burst of pain
  That seeks a sad and short relief,
In coming from a 'wilder'd brain—
  A solace for impassioned grief.

But sing no more that fearful air!
  For sweet and sprightly though it be,
It wakes in me a deep despair
  By its unhallow'd gaiety.

THOU IDOL OF MY SOUL

Lamar wrote "Thou Idol of My Soul" at the grave of his wife, Tabitha, who died in 1830 (see p. 26). Twenty-seven years afterward he called the elegies to her "memorials, not only of departed worth, but also of a period of sorrow and suffering whose dark shadows are in sacred contrast with the calm sunshine" of his last years. The verses somehow associate themselves with the inscription on Tabitha's memorial tablet: "Erected by Mirabeau Lamar in memory of his wife whose death has left him no other happiness than the remembrance of her virtues."

Lamar copied the lines in the album of his daughter, Rebecca Ann, but never published them except in Verse Memorials.

1830   1857

I

Thou idol of my soul, adieu!
 With one so loved, 'tis hard to part;
Thine angel-form still haunts my view,
 And lives within the constant heart
  That soon must break for thee.

II

When spring return, each modest flower
 That wears thy grace, shall blossom here;
And oft I'll come, at twilight hour,
 To bathe their beauties with the tear
  Of memory shed for thee.

III

But none shall ever mark that tear,
    For none can rock my soul to sleep;
Do thou, blest shade, but hover near,
    When in my lonely walks I weep
        My life away for thee.

IV

That life no hope survives to cheer,
    Except the one that thou art blest,
And that the day is drawing near
    When mine shall with thine ashes rest,
        My spirit wing to thee.

V

Oh, yes—though doomed so sad to part,
    We'll meet in heaven's eternal day;
For thou my saving angel art,
    To light my footsteps in the way
        That leads to God and thee.

VI

E'en now I feel thy peaceful sway;
    I hear thy voice, I see thy smile.
Oh, do not pass like dreams away;
    Tarry, my love, a little while—
        I come, I come to thee!

AT EVENING ON THE BANKS OF THE CHATTAHOOCHEE

The cottage of Tabitha and Lamar was so near the Chatta-hoochee River that the spring floods of 1829 inundated the floors. Their favorite evening stroll was the quarter mile of river bank only three blocks from their home, for which Lamar predicted a future as a promenade (see p. 26). Two years after his wife's death Lamar wrote "At Evening on the Banks of the Chattahoochee," as he sat here at the spot made dear by its association with her.

The poem, one of Lamar's favorites, appeared in The Colum-bus Enquirer *of November 7, 1834 without title; in* The Texas Republican *(Brazoria) of October 24, 1835, under "Stanzas," signed "Z"; in Lamar's manuscript album, in Rebecca Ann Lamar's album, and in the Sandusky Manuscript, with the title here used; in* Verse Memorials *(the text here printed) with the title "Monody"; in* The Library of Southern Literature *(At-lanta, 1907), VII, 3000.*

1832   1834

I

Oft when the sun along the west
    His farewell splendor throws,
Imparting to the wounded breast
    The spirit of repose—
My mind reverts to former themes,
    To joys of other days
When love illumined all my dreams,
    And hope inspired my lays.

II

I would not for the world bereave
    Fond Memory of those times,

When seated here at summer eve,
   I poured my early rhymes
To one whose smiles and tears proclaimed
   The triumph of my art,
And plainly told, the minstrel reigned
   The monarch of her heart.

III

Enriched with every mental grace,
   And every moral worth,
She was the gem of her bright race,
   A paragon on earth;
So luminous with love and lore,
   So little dimmed by shade,
Her beauty threw a light before
   Her footsteps as she strayed.

IV

But all the loveliness that played
   Around her once, hath fled;
She sleepeth in the valley's shade,
   A dweller with the dead;
And I am here with ruined mind,
   Left lingering on the strand,
To pour my music to the wind,
   My tears upon the sand.

V

I grieve to think she hears no more
   The songs she loved so well—
That all the strains I now may pour
   Of evenings in the dell,

Must fall as silently to her,
  As evening's mild decline—
Unheeded as the dewy tear
  That Nature weeps with mine.

VI

Oh, if thou canst thy slumbers break,
  My dear departed one,
Now at thy minstrel's call awake,
  And bless his evening song—
The last, perchance, his failing art
  May o'er these waters send—
The last before his breaking heart
  Shall songs and sorrows end.

VII

I fain would let thee know, blest shade,
  Though years have sadly flown,
My love with time has not decayed—
  My heart is still thine own;
And till the sun of life shall set,
  All thine it must remain,
As warmly as when first we met,
  Until we meet again.

VIII

If I have sought the festal hall,
  My sorrows to beguile,
Or struck my harp at lady's call,
  In praise of beauty's smile—

Oh, still thou didst my thoughts control
    Amid the smiling throng;
Thou wert the idol of my soul,
    The spirit of my song.

IX

Take, take my rhyme, O ladies gay,
    For you it freely pours;
The minstrel's heart is far away—
    It never can be yours.
The music of my song may be
    To living beauty shed,
But all the love that warms the strain—
    I mean it for the dead.

FAIR, WITTY, AND WEALTHY

"Fair, Witty, and Wealthy," whimsically satirical, reflects La-mar's scorn for him who would marry for material gain. At the time he wrote the poem, his family had fears—unfounded, as later events proved—that he might marry Mary Ann Jeter, a penniless widow of Columbus. These verses, published anonymously in The Columbus Enquirer *(March 10, 1832), were his ironic reply to their objections. The text here printed is that of Rebecca Ann Lamar's album (1843).*

1832   *1832*

O'erwhelm'd with debt and daily dunn'd,
    My fancy flown, my feeling dead,
My mind is like a ruined harp
    Whose chords are broke, its music fled.

Then ask me not for flow'ry lays;
    The gift of song is not with me.
I sigh for cash, and not for bays,
    And woo no muse but Betsy Lee.

Prometheus-like could I but steal
    From her bright mind a kindling ray,
The readers of this page would feel
    The magic of a deathless lay.
Her face so fair, her cash so sheen,
    The subject of my song should be;
I would be wedded to my theme—
    What theme so rich as Betsy Lee?

MUSINGS

Lamar's recovery from the shock of Tabitha's death was slow and seems to have been marked in his verse by a tendency toward moralizing. "Musings," like "The Painter's Mimic Powers," was written during this period at Fairfield, the old homestead south of Eatonton. In Rebecca Ann Lamar's album ("Random Stanzas") it appears without inscription, but in Verse Memorials *(1857) it is inscribed to Lamar's sister, Mrs. Louisa M'Gehee of Summerfield, Alabama, probably because she had recently lost a son.*

1833　　　　　　　　　　　　　　　　　　　1857

I

This morn the sun rose bright and clear,
    And seemed in gladness shining;
Deep in the west 'twill soon appear,
    With all its beams declining.

Thus sanguine men the world begin,
  With prospects bright before them;
As life speeds on, the light grows dim,
  And darkness soon comes o'er them.

II

Oh, who in manhood ever found
  The joy his youth expected?
And who o'er dark affliction's wound,
  Has never wept dejected?
Oft are we soonest called to sigh
  O'er things we hold the dearest;
And oft when bliss seems smiling by,
  The spoiler's hand is nearest.

III

The fairest hopes of virtue born,
  But leave the heart to languish;
We seize the flower and feel the thorn—
  All earth is doomed to anguish.
If transient joys are sometimes caught
  From fortune, fame, or beauty,
Dark Vengeance comes in after-thought,
  And points at murdered Duty.

IV

With me, the flowers of hope are dead,
  My path no more adorning;
As transient was the light they shed,
  As dewdrops in the morning.

167

Bereft of all that might elate,
  Of all that once was shining,
Oh, let me meet the ills of fate,
  And bow without repining.

V

And was it for this lowly lot
  The lamp of life was lighted—
To sigh for joys and find them not,
  And then go down benighted—
Down to the dust without a tear,
  Unheeded, unregarded,
And e'en by Him who placed us here
  Unpitied and discarded?—

VI

No, no—beyond the Morning Star
  A brighter world is beaming;
We hail the day-spring from afar—
  The dawning light is streaming!
There will the weary find repose,
  The peace that earth has blighted;
Eternal bliss will crown their woes,
  And all their wrongs be righted.

VII

Then thither let us wend our way,
  Our lives no longer wasting
On seeming joys that fade like day,
  Or turn to gall in tasting.

We all may win that land of love,
Whate'er on earth betide us,
If we but watch the Star above,
That God hath lit to guide us.

ARM FOR THE SOUTHERN LAND

*In 1833 Lamar was one of the moving spirits in the birth of
the new State Rights Party at Milledgeville, Georgia (see p.
27). In the same year he wrote "Arm For the Southern Land"
when the relative power of the State and of the Federal Government was becoming a burning question.* The Columbus
Enquirer *(Aug. 19, 1833) published the poem in its present
three-stanza arrangement, when Lamar was a candidate for
Congress on the State Rights ticket. After he came to Texas,
he revised the poem to fit the Texas situation, and published
it as "Song," signed "Z," in* The Texas Republican *(Brazoria)
for October 10, 1835, a form appearing also in the Sandusky
Manuscript and in Graham's* Early Texas Verse *(Austin, 1936).
For the Texas version, see notes, p. 306. For* Verse Memorials *Lamar chose the original Georgia version (the text here
printed), inscribed there to his nephew Lucius M. Lamar.
This same form, with title "Nullification Song," appears in
Rebecca Ann Lamar's album. It was appropriately reprinted
at the beginning of the Civil War in the* Macon (Georgia)
Daily Telegraph *(April 17, 1861).*

1833   1833

I

Arm for the Southern land,
All fear of death disdaining;
Low lay the tyrant hand
Our sacred rights profaning!

Each hero draws
In Freedom's cause,
And meets the foe with bravery;
The servile race,
And tory base,
May safety seek in slavery.
Chains for the dastard knave—
Recreant limbs should wear them;
But blessings on the brave
Whose valor will not bear them!

II

Stand by your injured State,
And let no feuds divide you;
On tyrants pour your hate,
And common vengeance guide you.
Our foes should feel
Proud freemen's steel;
Where'er they die,
There let them lie,
To dust in scorn descending.
Thus may each traitor fall,
Who dare as foe invade us;
Eternal fame to all
Who shall in battle aid us!

III

Proud land! shall she invoke
Another's hand to right her?—
No!—her own avenging stroke
Shall backward roll the smiter.
Ye tyrant band,

With ropes of sand,
Go bind the rushing river;
More weak and vain
Is slavery's chain,
While God is freedom's giver.
Then welcome to the day
We meet the proud oppressor,
For God will be our stay—
Our right hand and redressor.

THE PAINTER'S MIMIC POWERS

The poem was intended as an inscription for a painting, a floral design in oils, done by Lamar's sister, Evalina, and hung in the dining room at Fairfield. It was here at the old homestead that Lamar wrote these verses soon after Evalina's death (1833). The poem appears in Rebecca Ann Lamar's album. The last line, though suggesting the theme of "The Psalm of Life," preceded Longfellow's poem by five years.

1833   1857

I

Behold the painter's mimic powers!
The pictured seem like living flowers;
The rose—it wears such natural red,
We think it freshly from the bed.

II

But take a more observant view—
Its freshness is not drunk from dew,
No sweetness from its beauty flows;
'Tis but the semblance of a rose!

III

While thus the painter's happy skill
Deceives the eye, yet pleases still,
We may this homely lesson glean—
Things are not always what they seem.

SUNSET SKIES

*In Verse Memorials Lamar inscribed "Sunset Skies" to Mrs.
Loretto Chappell, his youngest and favorite sister. Her unusual affection for his first daughter, Rebecca Ann, who died
at Mrs. Chappell's home in 1843, made Loretto doubly dear
to Lamar, and he named his second daughter (b. 1852) after
her.*

*The poem was published, without inscription, under the
title "Sunset" in* The Columbus Enquirer *for March 1, 1834.
It appears also in Rebecca Ann Lamar's album.*

1834   1834

I

The sunset skies—the sunset skies!
  Their splendor, Lord, is thine;
Those golden hues—those Tyrian dyes—
  And all yon glow divine,
Are shadows of a regal gem—
Dim flashings of God's diadem.

II

O radiant West—O radiant West!
  Thou seem'st, to Fancy's eye,

A lovely land, a home of rest—
   Bright realm 'twixt earth and sky,
Where kindred spirits sing and soar,
And meet again to part no more.

III

Perchance to heaven so near they dwell,
   They hear the seraphim;
Perchance their own glad voices swell,
   Responsive to their hymn;
Oh, when shall I, in that blest land,
Unite me with that choral band?

IV

While gazing on the splendid scene,
   I sometimes think I see
My long-lost friends, with smile serene,
   Waving their hands for me—
As if they fain, from earthly woes,
Would call me to their own repose.

V

Ye clouds, so beautiful and bright,
   Floating in rich array,
Oh, bear me on your pinions light
   From this dull world away—
I heed not whither—anywhere,
If truth abide, and friends are there.

THE SEASONS

"The Seasons" was published in The Columbus Enquirer *for November 7, 1834, without inscription. It was reprinted in* Verse Memorials *(the text here used), where it was inscribed to Susan Wiggins, the daughter of Lamar's brother Lucius. It appears, without any important variants, also in Rebecca Ann Lamar's album, in the Sandusky Manuscript, and in Lamar's manuscript album. It was reprinted in* The Library of Southern Literature *(Atlanta, 1907) VII, 2995.*

1834   1834

I

The *Spirit of Spring*, from the regions of light,
Brought music, and odor, and all that was bright;
But vain were the blessings—they shed no delight
On the heart that lay locked in a Lapland night.

II

The *Spirit of Summer* then came with a glow,
And warmth on the beauties of Spring did bestow;
But all of the sunshine ne'er melted the snow
That fell on the heart in the Winter of wo.

III

The *Spirit of Autumn* now chills with its wing
The blushes of Summer and the beauties of Spring;
But light is the mischief its breezes may fling,
Compared to the ruin that sorrow can bring.

IV

The *Spirit of Winter* will come very soon,
On the wings of a cloud that shall darken the noon,
More welcome to me than perennial bloom,
For the frown of the storm is the type of my gloom.

THE BEAU'S FAREWELL

*Instead of a farewell, the poem is really a salute, for it marks
Lamar's resuming of social life after the death of Tabitha, his
wife, four years before. It was published in* The Columbus Enquirer *(November 15, 1834) under the title, "Song of an Antiquated Beau." In Lamar's manuscript album the title is the
same, but in Rebecca Ann's album and in the Sandusky Manuscript it is "The Antiquated Beau's Farewell." The title and
the text here printed are those of* Verse Memorials.

1834   1834

I

When I was young—when I was young,
   And spun my harmless rhymes,
I dashed the shining dames among,
   The Brummell of the times;
But now, alas! I'm growing old,
   My locks are turning gray,
And by the fair I'm kindly told
   'Tis time to march away.

II

At Fate 'tis folly to repine—
   Our fortunes to deplore;
For beaux, like kingdoms, must decline,
   To reign and rule no more;
Yet who the tears of sad regret
   Has firmness to restrain,
That sees his star of glory set,
   Never to rise again?

175

III

Adieu, adieu, ye flowery lays—
And, ladies fair, good-night;
I sing no more in beauty's praise,
Nor bow before its light.
'Tis meet that I, who've had my day,
To younger beaux should yield:—
Ye vet'rans grown unfit for fray,
Why linger in the field?

THE HARP I DARE NOT WAKE

*During the restless, melancholy years immediately following
Tabitha's death, Lamar was a frequent visitor in the home
of Samuel W. Goode, Montgomery, Alabama. When Emily
Goode, one of the four daughters, asked him to write in her
album Lamar refused, but later sent her these verses, under
the title, "Apology for not Writing in a Lady's Album." Two
years afterward he did write in her album (see p. 35).*

The poem, really an elegy to Tabitha, was published in The
Columbus Enquirer *of November 15, 1834 (see note, p. 307,
for variant form). It appears also in Lamar's manuscript
album, in Rebecca Ann Lamar's album, and in* Verse Memorials *(the title and text here printed).*

1834   1834

I

No, no—the harp I dare not wake,
So long neglected lain;
My heart, my heart would surely break,
To hear its voice again.

176

The tones that once so sweetly threw
  Oblivion o'er my cares,
Would only bring to memory's view,
  The woes of vanished years.

II

To Love's celestial, higher home,
  My life's enchanting light
Hath on the wings of morning flown,
  And left my soul in night;
Yet sometimes from that lovely sphere,
  All beautiful and blest,
A gentle seraph comes to cheer
  The minstrel's lonely breast.

III

Oh, while that seraph dwelt on earth,
  It was her smiles alone
That gave my lyre its wonted mirth,
  And sweetened every tone;
From her my inspiration came,
  With her it passed away,
And how can I resume the strain,
  Unkindled by her ray?

IV

Then marvel not that I withhold
  The boon that Beauty claims;
My heart, my heart is dark and cold—
  Extinct are all its flames;

177

And well I know, when love is gone,
　And grief alone remains,
More dreary is the poet's song,
　Than winter o'er the plains.

LOVE AND MARRIAGE
A Song of Similes

*"Love and Marriage" was to Lamar's maturity what "No Girl
Can Win My Stubborn Breast" had been to his youth. Pub-*
lished in The Columbus Enquirer *for November 15, 1834, it
appears also in Rebecca Ann Lamar's album, in the Sandusky
Manuscript, and in Lamar's manuscript album (the text here
printed).*
　In Verse Memorials *Lamar dedicated the poem to "Fanny
Fern"—Mrs. Sarah Willis Parton, the sister of N. P. Willis—an
indication that he knew not only her identity (which was not
disclosed to the public until after the Civil War), but also the
story of the hardships following her marriage.*

1834   1834

I

Say, have you seen Aurora rise,
　The face of Nature bright'ning,
And then beheld the evening skies
　Deformed with stormy lightning?—
Oh, Love is like that morning ray,
It speaks a warm and cloudless day;
　But Marriage is the evening storm
　That breaks the promises of morn.

II

Say, have you seen an early flower
  Its thousand charms displaying,
And then beheld at twilight hour
  Its beauties all decaying?—
Oh, Love is like that morning rose,
We think its beauties will not close;
  But Marriage is the twilight dew
  That blights its freshness and its hue.

III

Say, have you seen wet-weather streams
  O'er shining rocks careering,
And then beheld, at Sol's bright beams,
  The waters disappearing?—
Oh, Love is like that hasty rill,
Its courage is bright, but downward still;
  And Marriage is the noonday beam
  That dries the fountain of the stream.

IV

Say, have you seen at summer eve
  A calm upon the ocean,
And then beheld the tempest heave
  The waves in wild commotion?—
Oh, Love is like that halcyon sea,
We think the voyage will stormless be;
  But Marriage is the tempest dark
  That wakes the waves and wrecks the bark.

BEAUTY

Close to "Love and Marriage" both in spirit and in time, "Beauty" was published anonymously in The Columbus Enquirer *for November 22, 1834. The next year when Lamar was entering Texas (see p. 34) it appeared, signed "Z," in* The Texas Republican *(Brazoria) for July 4, 1835, along with other poems by Lamar so signed.*[1] *It was printed in the* Dallas News, *October 11, 1935, and in the* Fort Worth Press, *March 3, 1936.*

1834   1834

Round Love's Elysian bow'rs
   The softest prospects rise,
There bloom the sweetest flow'rs,
   There shine the purest skies.

And joy and rapture gild awhile,
The cloudless haven of beauty's smile.

Round love's deserted bow'rs
   Tremendous rocks arise,
Cold mildews blight the flow'rs,
   Tornadoes rend the skies.

And pleasure's waning moon goes down,
Amid the night of beauty's frown.

Then Youth, thou fond believer,
   The wily syren shun,
Who trusts the fair deceiver
   Will surely be undone.

When beauty triumphs—ah, beware!
Her smile is hope, her frown despair.

[1] For further identification of the author see Philip Graham, "An Unsigned Poem by Lamar," *Studies in English* (University of Texas), No. 13 (July 8, 1933), p. 113.

TO A LADY

Similar in theme and occasion to "The Harp I Dare Not Wake," "To A Lady" was addressed to Mrs. Mary Ann Jeter (Columbus, Georgia), formerly the wife of Oliver Jeter. Lamar wrote the poem in Mrs. Jeter's album, and published it, signed "The Academician," in The Columbus Enquirer *of November 22, 1834. At the time William L. Jeter, Oliver's brother, was part-owner of the paper.*

The verses are preserved in Rebecca Ann Lamar's album and the Sandusky Manuscript (with two additional stanzas, later given to "Grieve Not For Me"). The Enquirer four-stanza form appears in Lamar's manuscript album, with the title here printed, and also in Verse Memorials *(present text), with the first line as title.*

1834   1834

I

Oh, let my harp, like Judah's lyre,
　　To silence be consigned;
Each sound extorted from the wire,
　　Brings madness to the mind.
It wakes a train of painful thought,
　　Beyond my strength to bear—
Reviving scenes with misery fraught,
　　In days of my despair.

II

I may not breathe her name adored,
　　My life's lost paragon,
For whom my early strains were poured,
　　Herself the soul of song.

181

In all my notes she bore a part—
    She sang them o'er and o'er—
Delighted with my minstrel art,
    But with the minstrel more.

III

And shall that harp—that fav'rite harp,
    She lives no more to hear—
Be touched to win another's heart,
    To please another's ear?
No, no—to break its tranquil sleep,
    Would break my life's repose;
Its voice would only make me weep
    Afresh o'er former woes.

IV

Then ask me not my hand to fling
    Across the wires again;
To thee, they could no rapture bring—
    To me, consuming pain.
Soon may they wake in yonder sphere,
    The heavenly choir among,
Responsive to the voice of her,
    For whom they first were strung.

SONG OF A MAGDALENE

Columbus grew from a trading post on the Indian Reserve in 1828 to one of the most prosperous, most commercial-minded cities in Georgia in 1834. This mushroom growth resulted in social conditions that would have shocked some of the older Georgia cities. In an age strangely self-righteous, Lamar was pleading in these verses for victims of these conditions. He published the lines anonymously in The Columbus Enquirer *for December 20, 1834. They appear also in Rebecca Ann Lamar's album (the present text).*

1834   *1834*

I

When heedless man shall wander wide
   From virtue's sacred fane,
He finds in time, a Lethean tide,
   That sweeps away his shame;
But go thou, woman, where thou wilt,
   There flows no potent stream
To drown the memory of thy guilt,
   Thou erring Magdalene.

II

For other crimes and other woes,
   There may compassion be;
The world's cold charities are closed
   To sinful ones like me;
Where'er I go—where'er I roam,
   No eyes with pity beam;
"Go, go away, thou guilty one,
   Thou art a Magdalene."

III

With shame upon my burning brow,
   A scorpion in my breast,
O, whither shall I wander now,
   For succor or for rest?—
The wolf finds safety in his cave,
   The fox in thickets green;
There is no refuge but the grave,
   For me, a Magdalene.

IV

Poor outcast of the human race,
   To vice and misery born,
Unpitied victim of disgrace,
   Condemn'd to deathless scorn,
No wonder that the world can find,
   No mildness in my mien;
The madness of despair is mine,
   A wretched Magdalene.

V

Behold the doom'd, the destin'd bark,
   With all her canvas spread,
Sent helmless o'er the waters dark,
   To wreck and ruin sped.
Such is my fate—awhile to glide
   O'er life's polluted stream,
Then flounder in the Stygian tide,
   Ill-fated Magdalene.

VI

And wilt thou, Lord, like man, forsake
  A sufferer here below,
Whose guilty wanderings have been great,
  But greater still her woe?
O, must my eyes forever pour,
  Grief's unavailing stream?
Can no repentant tears restore
  A mourning Magdalene?

VII

Yes, Lord, thou didst thy promise keep
  When weeping Mary came;
Like her I kneel—like her I weep—
  Confess my guilt and shame,
And humbly hope thy boundless love
  Around my path may beam,
And light to thy blest home above
  Another Magdalene.

THERE IS A MAID I DEARLY LOVE

The maid was Lamar's cousin, Mary Ann, daughter of his maternal uncle, Zachariah Lamar of Milledgeville (see p. 5). The poem, written at Fairfield in a mood of playful affection rather than of serious love, was presented to Mary Ann at the time of her marriage to Howell Cobb.

It is preserved in Lamar's manuscript album and in Verse Memorials.

1834   1857

I

There is a maid I dearly love,
    A fascinating girl,
As modest as the lily white,
    And beautiful as pearl.
I long have been her worshipper,
    And evermore must be;
Yet colder far than Zembla's snows
    That maiden is to me.

II

From early youth to womanhood
    I've seen her charm expand,
And fondly hoped, some happy day,
    To win her heart and hand;
But oh, the bud that was so sweet,
    And long my secret pride,
Has only blushed into the rose,
    To be another's bride.

III

She soon will wear a garland bright,
    A wreath upon her brow,

And will before the altar stand,
  To breathe the bridal vow.
I know she will not think of me,
  Nor heed the grief she makes;
Yet warmer than the heart she weds,
  Will be the heart she breaks.

IV

O Cousin Anna, wouldst thou know
  Who may this maiden be?—
Then to thy mirror turn, sweet girl,
  And there her beauties see;
For thou art she, that cruel one,
  The source of my distress—
Yet all too beautiful for me
  To ever love thee less.

THE MARRIAGE DAY

*"The Marriage Day" was addressed in the spirit of banter to
Martha Kennedy of Eatonton, Georgia, and presented to her
a few weeks before her marriage to Dr. J. Mather of New Orleans. It was published in* The Columbus Enquirer, *April 17,
1835. It is preserved also in Rebecca Ann Lamar's album.*

1834   *1835*

I

Come, Martha, view the streamlet sheen,
That glides so gayly down yon green;
As pass its waters swiftly by,
So doth the youthful season fly:—

187

Then haste, my fair—no more delay—
And fix in youth the MARRIAGE DAY.

II

That current's source may never fail—
Long will its waters seek the vale;
But, lovely one, thou must not deem
Thy youth can last like that bright stream;
'Twere best, before it fleets away,
To haste, to haste the MARRIAGE DAY.

III

Behold the field with roses spread—
Pass some brief time, and all are dead.
So will thy beauties shed, fair maid,
A transient gleam, and sink decayed;
And when they're gone—ah! none will say,
"Come, Martha, haste the MARRIAGE DAY."

IV

Full soon will Spring, with genial powers,
Rebeautify the field with flowers;
But ah! the bloom of youth once o'er,
No Spring its glories can restore:—
Then, ere they fade like flowers away,
O haste, O haste the MARRIAGE DAY.

WOMAN

"Woman" was the last poem Lamar wrote before setting out for Texas—his note of thanks, as it were, to the fair sex. The first stanza, as printed in The Columbus Enquirer *(April 17, 1835), seems to anticipate his departure, for it begins (notes, p. 308),*

> *O, I have left a sunny clime.*

The poem appears in Lamar's manuscript album (the text and title here printed), in Rebecca Ann Lamar's album ("Song"), and in the Sandusky Manuscript ("Song"). For a revision of the last stanza, see the notes, p. 308.

In Verse Memorials *(1857) the poem is quite appropriately inscribed, with stanzas IV and V omitted, to Mrs. Sarah J. Hale, the celebrated editor of* Godey's Ladies' Book, *who was then "guiding the taste of thousands of women away from indelicacy," she believed, "and carrying on decorous conversations with her readers on the privileges and duties of women." Lamar met "the lady of* Godey's" *during his visit to the East in 1845 (see p. 70).*

1835   1835

I

Oh, twine no laurel-wreath for me,
  Nor Mammon's stores impart;
I ask no fame but woman's smiles,
  No treasure but her heart.
The flash of glory fades like day,
  And riches have their flight;
But love—the star of woman's life—
  Knows no declining light.

II

Go travel in the reindeer's track
  Beneath the polar skies,
Or with the camel tread the sands
  O'er which the siroc sighs;
Still woman's love and loveliness
  Will temper every clime,
And leave for man's ungrateful heart
  No reason to repine.

III

What though along the realms of ice
  No vernal beauties blow;
What though along the burning waste
  No cooling waters flow;
Amidst the snows—amidst the sands
  Her smiles will still impart
A spring-like feeling in the mind,
  A fountain in the heart.

IV

When dread contagion spreads abroad
  And man for safety flies,
She lingers by the sufferer's side
  And every want supplies;
When friendship mourns no more the dead
  And mirth succeeds despair,
Go seek at eve the burial place—
  You'll find her weeping there.

190

V

Does fortune fail and friends fall off?
  Do foes come trooping on?
I find a refuge in her love,
  A solace in her song.
The ills of fate, I heed them not,
  The darkest frown I scorn,
If woman's rainbow smiles be left
  To light me in the storm.

VI

Oh woman, beautiful and kind,
  A blessing everywhere,
I want the skill to sing thy praise
  My homage to declare;
In poverty, my comforter,
  In wealth my diadem;
Through weal and woe my shining light,
  My star of Bethlehem.

GIVE TO THE POET HIS WELL-EARNED PRAISE

Written on the Prospect of Battle

Written between July and October of 1835, during Lamar's first visit to Texas (see p. 34), "Give to the Poet His Well-Earned Praise" is the first poem which Lamar composed on Texas soil. It was published in The Texas Republican *(Brazoria) for October 10, 1835, six months before San Jacinto, Lamar's first battle. The sub-title first appears in* Verse Memorials *(1857), when the poem was inscribed to General E. B. Nichols, prominent in Houston and Galveston since 1838, when he came to Texas to engage in banking and shipping. The poem is preserved also in Rebecca Ann Lamar's album, and has been reprinted in Dixon's* The Poets and Poetry of Texas *(Austin, 1885), and in Graham's* Early Texas Verse *(Austin, 1936).*

1835   1835

I

Give to the poet his well-earned praise,
    And the songs of his love, preserve them;
Encircle his brows with fadeless bays,
    The children of genius deserve them;
But never to me such praises breathe,
    To the minstrel-feeling a stranger—
I only sigh for the laurel-wreath
    That a patriot wins in DANGER.

II

Speed, speed the day when to war I hie!
    The fame of the field is inviting;

Before my sword shall the foemen fly,
  Or fall in the flash of its lightning.
Away with song, and away with charms!
  Insulted Freedom's proud avenger,
I bear no love but the love of arms,
  And the bride that I woo is DANGER.

III

When shall I meet the audacious foe,
  Face to face where the flags are flying?
I long to thin them, "two at a blow,"
  And ride o'er the dead and the dying!
My sorrel steed shall his fetlocks stain
  In the brain of the hostile stranger;
With an iron heel he spurns the plain,
  And he breathes full and free in DANGER.

IV

When victory brings the warrior rest,
  Rich the rewards of martial duty—
The thanks of a land with freedom blest,
  And the smiles of its high-born beauty.
Does victory fail?—enough for me,
  That I fall not to fame a stranger;
His name shall roll with eternity
  Who finds the foremost grave in DANGER.

SAN JACINTO

The night before the battle of San Jacinto, Benjamin Rice Brigham rushed into the tent of his friends, in search of a substitute for guard duty. "Boys," he said, "I've stood guard two nights, and am detailed for the third. I want to be in the battle tomorrow. Will somebody take my place tonight?" A comrade (F. J. Cooke) volunteered, and Brigham went to sleep. In the battle next day (April 21) he was among the first to fall, and died a few hours later.

Lamar was deeply moved at sight of his body, and after retiring to his tent he wrote "San Jacinto." The poem appears in Mrs. Edward Fontaine's album (the present text). An unrevised or a corrupted version was printed in the Educational Free Press *(Austin) for March, 1902 (I, 1, p. 7).*

1836   1902, 1937

Beautiful in death
   The soldier's corse appears,
Embalmed by fond affection's breath
   And bathed in his country's tears.

Lo, the battle forms
   Its terrible array,
Like clashing clouds in mountain storms
   That thunder on their way.

The rushing armies meet,
   And while they pour their breath,
The strong earth trembles at their feet,
   And day grows dim with death.

Now launch upon the foe
  The lightnings of your rage!
Strike the assailing tyrants low,
  The monsters of the age!

They yield! They break! They fly!
  The victory is won!
Pursue! They faint, they fall, they die!
  O stay! The work is done.

Mourn the death of those
  Who for their country die,
Sink on her bosom for repose,
  And triumph where they lie.

Laurels for those who bled,
  The living hero's due.
But holier wreaths will crown the dead—
  A grateful nation's love!

TO MARY ANN

After his visit to Georgia in 1837 Lamar wrote "To Mary Ann"
immediately upon reaching Velasco, Texas. Mary Ann was
Mrs. Jeter of Columbus, Georgia. Before her marriage to Ol-
iver Jeter (1829) Lamar had known her as Mary Ann Gartrell.
He had addressed "To A Lady" (p. 181) to her after her hus-
band's death.

In 1837 she was expectantly awaiting Lamar's return to
Georgia, but his feeling for her remained a sympathetic, af-
fectionate friendship. The one surviving letter from her to
Lamar was written almost simultaneously with his verses to
her (see p. 45).

The poem is preserved in Lamar's manuscript album and
Rebecca Ann Lamar's album. It was published in **Verse Me-**
morials.

1837   *1857*

I

O Mary, when we parted last,
   Beneath our fav'rite tree,
You bade me watch the evening star,
   And strike my harp to thee.
That harp is not what once it was—
   Confusion o'er it reigns;
The chords have caught my own despair,
   And breathe bewildered strains;
There is no gladness in their voice,
   They shed no welcome balm—
They only deepen my lament
   For thee, my MARY ANN.

196

II

Then be my lyre in silence laid,
    Till brighter days shall bloom;
And should no future morning break,
    Its spirit to relume—
Oh, should it waft no more, my love,
    Its wonted strains to thee—
Thou must not deem thyself forgot,
    Or less beloved by me;
But let its tones in happier days,
    When first our love began,
Still be my soul's interpreter
    To thee, my MARY ANN.

III

Long have I been, my lovely one,
    A worshipper of thee—
Long hast thou been a pure and bright
    Divinity to me;
And though denied by Fortune now
    To bow before thy shrine,
My heart beats on, all warmly still—
    Its every pulse is thine;
Nor can I cease, while yet remains
    Of life a lingering span,
To pour my daily orisons
    For thee, my MARY ANN.

IV

Why should I change?—I know the flowers
    Are bright in Texan dells,

197

And brighter still the sparkling eyes
   Of Texas sprightly belles;
Yet in this land of light and love,
   All beautiful—divine—
There is no flower or living thing
   Whose charms can equal thine;
O'er all that's pure, and sweet, and bright,
   Thy beauty bears the palm—
Thou art the rose of all thy race,
   My blue-eyed MARY ANN.

V

That matchless rose—that matchless rose!
   Though blooming far away,
Can I allow its loveliness
   In memory to decay?
No, loved one, no—by day and night
   My thoughts are tuned on thee,
And every recollection wrings
   A silent tear from me:—
For mine's a love that's full of grief,
   A life-consuming pang,
That will not let me cease to weep
   For thee, my MARY ANN.

VI

My home is in the battle-field—
   My resting place the grave;
Where trampled Freedom shrieks for aid,
   There must my banner wave.
The hope of thy approving voice
   Will still my soul inflame—

Will pour fresh valor in the heart
　And light me on to fame;
But oh, the wreath the soldier wins
　In danger's stormy van,
Is not so welcome as one smile
　From thee, my MARY ANN.

VII

Adieu, adieu, thou cherished one,
　Beloved of early years,
Whose beauty threw a rainbow light
　O'er all my cloud of cares.
When fortune failed, and friends fell off,
　And foes came trooping on,
I found a refuge in thy smiles,
　A solace in thy song.
Then be thy life prolonged and blest,
　Thy death serene and calm;
We'll meet again—if not on earth—
　In heaven, my MARY ANN.

SERENADE

*"Bonnie Jane" was probably Mrs. Jane Long, the widow of
James Long, the Texas filibuster. Lamar had known her since
his first trip to Texas in 1835 (p. 34).*

*The present text is that of Rebecca Ann Lamar's album
(1843). In* Verse Memorials *(1857), long after the break between Mrs. Long and the Lamar family (p. 81), Ann was substituted for* Jane, *and the poem inscribed to Miss Anna Truesdell, whom Lamar had met in Brooklyn in 1845.*

1838   1857

The moon, the cold, chaste moon, my love,
　　Is riding in the sky;
And like a bridal veil, my love,
　　The clouds are floating by.
Oh, brighter than that planet, love,
　　Thy face appears to me;
But when shall I behold its light,
　　Through bridal drapery?

We owe our gratitude, my love,
　　To Sol's enlivening ray;
And yet I prize the moonlight, love,
　　Above the glare of day.
O bonnie Jane, thou art to me
　　Whate'er in both is best—
Thou art the moonbeam to mine eye,
　　The sunbeam to my breast.

IN LIFE'S UNCLOUDED, GAYER HOUR

The "Lady in Houston" to whom Lamar dedicated "In Life's Unclouded, Gayer Hour" in Verse Memorials *(1857) was Mrs. Olivia Roberts Mather. The Roberts family had been among his close friends at Eatonton, Cahawba, and Mobile; and in 1838 followed him to Texas (see "Grieve Not, Sweet Flower," p. 111). During his administration as President, Olivia, living with her father at Galveston, was a frequent visitor at Houston. These lines explain his seeming lack of feeling for her, the grief referred to in the last stanza being the death of his wife, Tabitha, in 1830.*

The poem appears in Lamar's manuscript album and in Rebecca Ann's album, with the title "Stanzas"; in Verse Memorials *(1857); in* The Library of Southern Literature, *VII, 2994; in Dixon's* The Poets and Poetry of Texas *(Austin, 1885); and in Greer's* Voices of the Southwest *(New York, 1923).*

1839   1857

I

In life's unclouded, gayer hour,
   I bowed to beauty's sway;
I felt the eye's despotic power,
   And trembled in its ray;
But beauty now no more enthralls—
   Its magic spell hath flown;
Upon my heart it coldly falls,
   Like moonlight on a stone.

II

The chords of feeling soon were broke,
   Where love delighted played;
Affliction dealt too rude a stroke,
   And all in ruin laid;

Yet, lady fair, there was a time
   I might have worshipped thee;
Thy beauty would have been the shrine
   Of my idolatry.

III

That time is past, and I am left
   A sad sojourner here—
Of hope, of joy, of all bereft,
   That makes existence dear.
Despair hath o'er my bosom cast
   The gloom of starless night—
A darkness which through life must last,
   Unpierced by beauty's light.

FROZEN NOTES

*"Frozen Notes" is one of three poems, much alike, which
Lamar originally titled "Apology for Not Writing in a Lady's
Album." The lady, this time, was Olivia Roberts Mather, liv-
ing at Galveston with her father, Willis Roberts, whom Lamar
had appointed Collector of Customs (see "In Life's Unclouded,
Gayer Hour," also addressed to her). The "bright seraph" of
Stanza V was his wife, Tabitha, who had died nine years before.*
   *The poem appears in the Sandusky Manuscript, in Rebecca
Ann Lamar's album, and in* Verse Memorials, *where it is in-
scribed "To a Lady in Galveston."*

1839   *1857*

I

And must I touch the chords again,
   At Beauty's high behest?
And must I pour a formal strain,
   Unechoed from the breast?—

No, lady, no—I will not wrong
   Exalted charms like thine;
I will not pour a lifeless song
   At Beauty's sacred shrine.

II

Oh, how couldst thou, of soul and sense,
   Thy deep-felt scorn conceal,
For him who sings in lady's ear
   The songs he does not feel?—
Whose songs at best would only shine
   Like phosphor of the tomb,
Shedding a light that gives no heat,
   Yet shows surrounding gloom!

III

And if his cold, unkindling lay
   Excite thy just disdain,
Oh, how much more thy pride would spurn
   The high, impassioned strain,
If thou shouldst know that all the light
   Around the numbers thrown
Was struck from recollected love,
   And beauty not thine own!

IV

Yet such were mine—my frozen notes
   Would fall like flakes of snow;
Or, if the memory of the past
   Should wake a genial glow,

Still unconscious of the light
　　Of beauty sparkling near,
My soul and song would rise to one
　　Who gems another sphere.

V

I know I shall, on some blest strand,
　　Where souls of goodness throng—
Some Jordan of the Spirit-Land,
　　Whose waters roll in song—
My own bright seraph meet once more,
　　Renew her fav'rite lay,
And all my soul's devotion pour
　　Through Love's eternal day.

VI

Yet now with me, all minstrel fire
　　Is quenched in sorrow's tears;
And though the lyre I still retain,
　　Its spirit dwells with hers;
And vain it were to touch the chords—
　　The notes would sound in vain!
For where would be her smiles, to fling
　　Enchantment o'er the strain?

VII

Then, lady, ask me not to sing—
　　A bard of low degree,
Whose songs, if warm, would not be thine,
　　If cold, unworthy thee.

Some happier one, of higher art,
　Should strike to thee the strings,
Whose inspiration is his theme—
　The beauty that he sings.

VIII

Or dost thou love the minstrelsy
　With which Creation teems—
The lute-like winds—the vocal grove—
　The sweetly-sounding streams?
These, these, my fair, should raise to thee
　Their music rich and wild,
For Nature's voice is best attuned
　To Nature's fav'rite child.

THE STAR AND CUP

Lamar said with reference to the poem: "The second of March —the anniversary of the Declaration of the Independence of Texas—was on one occasion celebrated in a grove in Washington County, and the rigid exclusion of wine made a special feature of the rural banquet. The cup which circulated on that day under our Single Star *was filled with the pure crystal of the spring." The celebration occurred in 1840, during Rebecca Ann's second visit to her father. Lamar's sister, Mrs. Mary Ann Moreland, was also present—a fact that may explain the dedication of the poem to her in the* Verse Memorials *(1857).*

The first Texan gesture against intoxicating drinks was made in 1839, when even Sam Houston made a temperance speech at the capital—and then slipped out a side door to escape signing the pledge! (Quarterly of the Texas State Historical Association, XVII (Jan., 1913), 289). In Lamar's manuscript album the title is "Song," and in the first line "lonely star" takes the place of "bright Lone Star." It was reprinted in D. F. Eagleton's Writers and Writings of Texas *(New York, 1913).*

1840   1857

I

I love the bright Lone Star, that gems
　　The banner of the brave;
I love the light that guideth men
　　To freedom or the grave;
But oh, there is a fairer Star,
　　Of pure and holy ray,
That lights to glory's higher crown,
　　And freedom's brighter day:—

206

It is the Star before whose beams
  All earth should bow the knee—
The Star that rose o'er Bethlehem,
  And set on Calvary.

II

Let others round the festive board
  The madd'ning wine-cup drain;
Let others court its guilty joys,
  And reap repentant pain.
But oh, there is a brighter Cup,
  And be its raptures mine,
Whose fragrance is the breath of life—
  Whose spirit is divine:—
It is the Cup that Jesus filled—
  He kissed its sacred brim,
And left the world to do the same,
  In memory of him.

GRIEVE NOT FOR ME

In 1840 Lamar found it necessary, on account of his failing health, to retire temporarily from the Presidency to the home of J. B. Hoxey (Independence, Texas). While his recovery was still uncertain he wrote "Grieve Not For Me," which appears in Rebecca Ann's album with the sub-title, "Written During Illness."

Stanzas V and VI were added to the 1841 version of "To A Lady" (p. 181), but in 1857 were finally given to "Grieve Not For Me." In Verse Memorials *Lamar inscribed the poem to his sister, Amelia Randle. It appears also in his manuscript album, and was reprinted in Dixon's* The Poets and Poetry of Texas *(Austin, 1885).*

1841   1857

I

There is a sorrow in my heart
　　The world may never know—
A pang that never will depart,
　　Till Death shall lay me low;
Yet light and cheerful still I seem—
　　No signs of sorrow see;
I wear to all a cheerful mien,
　　That none may GRIEVE FOR ME.

II

My suff'rings soon, I know, must end,
　　For life is on its ebb;
The autumn leaves that first descend
　　Will find me with the dead:—

208

I wish my fall may be like theirs,
  From lamentations free;
I ask no unavailing tears,
  No friends to GRIEVE FOR ME.

III

Grieve for themselves, that they are left
  A thorny world to tread,
But not for him who goes to rest
  Among the quiet dead;
For there no dreams disturb the mind,
  Though dark the mansion be;
And if in faith I sink resigned,
  Why need they GRIEVE FOR ME?

IV

Oh, if they knew my soul's unrest,
  The agonies I bear—
If they could view my inmost breast,
  And see the vulture there—
They would not chain me to my woes,
  But freely let me flee,
Nor break their own pure heart's repose
  By GRIEVING AFTER ME.

V

Around my bed no brothers bow,
  No sisters vigils keep;
No mother bathes my aching brow,
  Or fans me while I sleep.

Alas! I would not have them near—
   Sad would their presence be;
I could not bear their plaints to hear,
   Or see them GRIEVE FOR ME.

VI

But there are those I dearly love,
   Whose pilgrimage is o'er,
Called to the shining realms above,
   Where sorrow is no more.
I humbly hope, O God, to find
   A home with them and thee;
And strengthen thou each suff'ring mind
   That vainly GRIEVES FOR ME.

SOLDIER OF THE CROSS
To the Pioneer Preachers of Texas

When Lamar's failing health forced him in December, 1840, to retire temporarily from the Presidency, he remained at the home of Dr. J. B. Hoxey at Independence, Washington County, Texas, until he fully recovered, in March, 1841 (see p. 60). During this period of rest Mrs. Hoxey suggested to him, he said (Verse Memorials, p. 45), the theme of this tribute to the pioneer preachers. The poet may have had particularly in mind the staunch Irish preacher, Edward Fontaine, who was his close friend and secretary during 1841, and who also lived near Independence.

The poem appears in The Columbus Enquirer *(October 19, 1842) under the title, "The Missionary's Hymn," without inscription; in* Verse Memorials *(1857) with the title and inscription here printed; in Rebecca Ann Lamar's album; and in Lamar's manuscript album under the title "Missionary Hymn" (the text here printed). No important variants occur.*

1841   ·   1842

I

Nay—tell me not of dangers dire
   That lie in duty's path:
A Warrior of the Cross can feel
   No fear of human wrath.
Where'er the Prince of Darkness holds
   His earthly reign abhorred,
Sword of the Spirit! thee I draw,
   And battle for the Lord.

II

I go, I go to break the chains
　　That bind the erring mind,
And give the freedom that I feel,
　　To all of human kind;
But oh, I wear no burnished steel,
　　And seek no gory field;
My weapon is the Word of God,
　　His promise is my shield.

III

And thus equipp'd, why need I fear,
　　Though hosts around me rise?—
There is a power in gospel truth
　　No heathen can despise;
And he who boldly fights with that,
　　Will through more perils wade
Than the vain warrior, trusting to
　　His bright Damascus blade.

IV

No blasts by land or sea can shake
　　The purpose of my soul;
The tempest of a thousand winds
　　May sweep from pole to pole,
Yet still serene, and fixed in faith,
　　All fear of death I scorn:
I know it is my Father's work—
　　He's with me in the storm.

V

Then let me go where duty calls,
  Where gratitude demands,
Bearing the Banner of the Lord
  To dark and distant lands;
And if the high and holy cause
  Require my early fall,
A recreant he who would not die
  For Him who died for all.

ONE THING LACKEST THOU YET

Lamar wrote these verses of cavalier compliment in the album of Genevieve Meur of New Orleans, in response to an earlier request (Lamar Papers, No. *1322* [III, *13*]), *as he was on his way to Georgia for his first visit after the expiration of his term of office. They are preserved, without title or inscription, also in Lamar's manuscript album.*

1842   1937

In form and face, and gentle grace,
  No lady with thee vies,
And all thy thoughts are diamond sparks,
  That dazzle like thine eyes.
One virtue only dost thou need,
  Thy nature to exalt—
Take pity on thy lowly bard
  And be without a fault.

TO MY DAUGHTER

*Rebecca Ann was almost sixteen when her father visited her
in 1843. Brought up by her "dear Aunts" with the duty con-
stantly before her of improving her "writing and composing,"
she was much interested in her father's verses, and asked him
to write her a poem. In response he prepared an album in
which he wrote "To My Daughter," along with forty-five earlier pieces (see p. 88). It appears also in Lamar's manuscript
album and in* Verse Memorials.

*Resembling closely Canto II of "Sally Riley," "To My
Daughter" is Lamar's last elegy to Tabitha. Perhaps it explains
(Stanza IV) why no songs belonging to Lamar's courtship of
her have survived.*

1843   1857

I

Oh, do not ask me now for rhyme,
 For I am lonely-hearted;
And lost are all the dear delights
 The Muses once imparted.
I sigh no more for Hybla's dews,
 Nor Helicon's bright water;
I only crave a sable wave
 Of Lethe's stream, my Daughter.

II

And wouldst thou share thy father's woes,
 Partake his bitter weeping?
Then seek with him yon valley's shade,
 Where beauty's wreck is sleeping;

For in that dark and lonely place—
    Death's solemn, silent quarter—
Was laid the pride of all her sex,
    The mother of my Daughter.

III

She was all bright and beautiful,
    A floating star before me,
Whose lustre was my guiding light,
    For ever shining o'er me;
So much of heaven in all her ways,
    How often have I thought her
Some angel sent us from the skies,
    To bless this earth, my Daughter!

IV

It was from her alone I drew
    My minstrel inspiration;
But when she died and left me here—
    My soul in desolation—
I broke the shell she loved so well,
    Destroyed the songs I wrought her;
Nor can my voice again rejoice
    In cheerful strains, my Daughter.

V

Then name some other boon, my child;—
    Thou know'st I can deny thee
No gift thine innocence demands,
    While thou art smiling by me:

But should I dare re-string the harp
By Chattahoochee's water,
The bitter tears of other years
Would flow afresh, my Daughter.

APOLOGY FOR VERSE

Lamar wrote the "Apology" as the introductory poem in the
album of his daughter, Rebecca Ann. In his Verse Memorials
he placed it immediately before the rhymed introduction. It
was reprinted in Library of Southern Literature *(VII, 2993),*
probably because it expresses most clearly Lamar's attitude to-
ward his own verse.

1843   1857

I never hoped in life to claim
A passport to exalted fame;
'Tis not for this I sometimes frame
        The simple song—
Contented still, with humble name,
        To move along.

I write because there's joy in rhyme;
It cheers an evening's idle time;
And though my verse the true sublime
        May never reach,
Yet Heaven will never call it crime,
        If truth it teach.

The labor steals the heart from wo;
It makes it oft with rapture glow;

216

And always teaches to forego
Each low desire;
Then why on those our blame bestow
Who strike the lyre?

If virtue in the song be blent,
I know no reason to repent
My hours of studious content,
And lettered joy;
'Twere well if leisure ne'er was spent
In worse employ.

LINES
To a Lady on Presenting Her with a Book

*Lamar sent the lines, in their present form, to Anna Truesdell
of Brooklyn, whom he met during his visit to New York in
1845. That he had written the verses at an earlier date for a
different occasion is proved by the fact that they appear in
Rebecca Ann Lamar's album (1843). Here lines 1 and 3 have
been erased and altered.*

1843   1937

To thee, sweet mistress of the shell,
This Book—a New-Year's gift—I send,
And humbly hope that Brooklyn's belle
Will rank me as her warmest friend.

Alas! I have no minstrel art,
To grace the off'ring with a lay;
The best bright feelings of the heart,
I give, instead of fancy's ray.

217

'Tis vain for me to court the Muse,
  And vainer still, the girls to woo;
They both alike their gifts refuse,
  And laughing, say, " 'Twill never do."

Yet, lady fair, at beauty's shrine,
  No bard with more devotion kneels,
And all that others feign in rhyme,
  My heart, alas! too truly feels.

As chance directs, I widely wend,
  By random breezes borne along;
Yet ever in my heart shall blend
  The memory of the child of song.

THE JENNY LIND OF GEORGIA

Lamar's visits to Georgia before 1843 had been hurried, restricted by the demands of business. And he would not have had it otherwise, for energetic activity, like a bright fire, seemed to keep the darkness of his grief from creeping in upon him. But in 1843, freed of all official obligations, he found ample opportunity to revisit the old scenes and renew old acquaintances. Time had so softened the bitterness of his loss— now thirteen years in the past—that he dared relax and revive some of the sweet memories of former days.

The "Jenny Lind of Georgia" was Irene Nisbet, daughter of James A. Nisbet, a lawyer of Macon. A quarter of a century before writing this poem Lamar had met her at the home of her cousins in Eatonton, and had made frequent visits to Macon to listen to her sing "at Lanier's" hotel (see p. 16).

Lamar heard Jenny Lind sing in New Orleans in 1851, and added the allusion to her as the sub-title when he prepared the poem for Verse Memorials.

1843   1857

I

> I've seen the belles of many lands,
>   Pure gems of living light—
> Their native climes illumining
>   As stars illumine night;
> And yet in Beauty's gorgeous sky,
>   No planet have I seen
> With Georgia's sparkling gem to vie—
>   The beautiful IRENE.

II

She is the incarnation bright
   Of some angelic thought;
She is the poetry of heaven
   In human figure wrought;
And never yet was writ or read
   So sweet a book, I ween,
As that fair volume of delight—
   The beautiful IRENE.

III

Her close alliance to the skies
   Is seen in all her ways;
We know it by her gentleness,
   We feel it in her lays;
And who can tell how bright and blest—
   How ever fresh and green—
This world would be, if all were like
   The beautiful IRENE!

IV

There is no winter where she smiles,
   No darkness where she dwells;
She is a morning on the hills,
   A May among the dells.
The groves and valleys know their spring,
   The roses know their queen,
And all the wild-birds sing in tune
   To beautiful IRENE.

V

I well remember all the songs
 She sang me at Lanier's;
They fell upon my melting heart
 Like music from the spheres:
And still as sweet as silver bells
 O'er waters heard at e'en,
The siren-notes are sounding on,
 Of beautiful IRENE.

VI

Oh, let me wander where I may,
 From Georgia's valleys bright,
To where the Brazos rolls its waves
 In musical delight—
Fond Memory still will turn to hail,
 Through every changing scene,
The gem that decks her native land—
 The beautiful IRENE.

VII

Sweet mistress of the tuneful art,
 Bright child of melody,
My star, my poem, and my spring,
 All happiness to thee!
May sorrow never reach thy heart,
 No shadows intervene,
To dim the Eden blooming there,
 Sweet, beautiful IRENE.

VIII

And when thy bright career is o'er
Of loveliness and grace,
And thou art called among the stars,
To take thy shining place—
Oh, mayst thou to that higher home
Ascend in all thy sheen,
And be the morning planet there,
Sweet, beautiful IRENE!

ANNA COWLES

"Anna Cowles," another poem of reminiscence, turns back the years a quarter of a century to the days when the brothers Lamar at Fairfield called on the belles of the surrounding counties. Anna Cowles was the daughter of Jeremiah Cowles, Macon's railway pioneer.

1843   1857

I

I wish I could revive the past,
I wish I could recall
The happy days that fled so fast—
The most beloved of all—
When first I wandered by thy side,
Where bright Oconee rolls,
And thou went'st forth in beauty's pride,
My lovely ANNA COWLES.

II

Long years since then have disappeared,
  In shadows overcast,
Yet deeply in my heart endeared,
  I've borne thee to the last.
Of all the gay, enchanting throng,
  Fond Memory sacred holds,
Thou art the best-remembered one,
  My lovely ANNA COWLES.

III

The light of other days I see
  Still beaming on thy brow;
And never didst thou seem to me
  More beautiful than now.
Though younger belles are blooming by—
  Gay girls with happy souls—
With thine their beauties may not vie,
  My lovely ANNA COWLES.

IV

I marvel if thy heart remains
  Unaltered as thy face.
I marvel if it still retains
  For me a kindly place.
Thou needst not speak—that cheerful air
  The welcome truth unfolds,
That time has wrought no changes there,
  My lovely ANNA COWLES.

V

Then wherefore feel myself forlorn—
  Why should the spirit grieve,
Since the same star that lit its morn
  Returns to gem its eve?
In thee, for ever pure and fair,
  The minstrel still beholds
His morning and his evening star,
  My lovely ANNA COWLES.

VI

I may not feel as once I felt,
  For Passion's reign is o'er;
The shrines of Beauty where I knelt
  Can hear my vows no more;
Yet Friendship's hallowed flame is mine—
  My heart it still controls,
And binds me on to thee and thine,
  My lovely ANNA COWLES.

VII

I soon shall seek my home afar—
  The region of the rose—
The land where Freedom's new-born Star
  Its glorious lustre throws;
Yet even there, where all is bright,
  Amid his evening strolls
The bard will miss his purer light,
  My lovely ANNA COWLES.

VIII

Adieu, adieu!—where'er I rove,
　One bliss will still attend—
That she who was mine early love,
　Will be my latest friend;
And safely anchored in thy heart,
　No storm that ever rolls
Can wreck my spirit's buoyant bark,
　My lovely ANNA COWLES.

SALLY RILEY
Canto II

On his visit to Georgia during the early months of 1843, "for old affection's sake" Lamar resumed his writing of "Sally Riley," abruptly discontinued almost twenty years before. (For Canto I, see p. 143.) The second canto, begun in the spirit of recalling the happiness of "life's tumultuous hour," changes to an elegy for his lost Tabitha, dead now thirteen years, whose memory the scenes of former days made doubly poignant. The entire poem was published in Verse Memorials.

1843　　　　　　　　　　　　　　　　*1857*

I

Some eighteen years ago, when I was young,
　And life was one continued vernal day,
I then my harp to Sally Riley strung,
　And to its music framed a merry lay—
But left it incomplete.—I now rewake
The slumbering chords for old affection's sake.

II

My former canto closed with Sally's [1] praise;
  To honor Sally was my great, high aim;
And I had hoped, in more exalted lays,
  To place her on the Teneriffe of fame:—
But from some cause, to me quite unexpected,
She ridiculed my verse, and love rejected.

III

This made me angry, and I dropped the theme,
  And left her beauties unimmortalized;
"A change came o'er the spirit of my dream," [2]
  And she who was so once beloved and prized,
Now o'er my altered nature lost her power,
And Sally was to me as any other flower.

IV

"Of chance and change, Oh let not man complain;
  Else never, never will he cease to wail." [2]
Thus sang the minstrel in his truthful strain,
  Knowing full well how fickle and how frail
Are all things here below, and prone to vex—
Especially in reference to the softer sex.

V

There's no stability in all creation—
  No permanence in matter or in mind;

[1] Sarah Rossetter; p. 16.
[2] See Byron, "The Dream," Stanza 3; Thomas Moore, *Works* (London, 1912), II, 348.

226

E'en rocks themselves are subject to mutation.
   In every earthly thing some change we find—
Except my purse—there is no change in that—
Not e'en enough to buy a *Roram* hat.

VI

But woman is—of all this shifting sphere—
   The most unstable, fluctuating ray;
Fair Cynthia changes thirteen times a year,
   But woman changes oftener every day;
And yet, like Cynthia too, I must confess,
No change destroys her light of loveliness.

VII

Forever varying, and forever bright,
   She circles in an orbit wild and wide,
Yet scatters blessings in her wayward flight
   That makes us feel she is to Heaven allied—
A bright embodiment of fascinations,
In spite of all her devilish vacillations.

VIII

'Twas so with Sally—once she was, indeed,
   As true to me as needle to the pole;—
Although I sometimes deemed the Turkish creed
   Was half-way true—that women have no soul—
A jealous thought, that rose like visions wild,
But always vanished when my fair one smiled.

IX

But, like her sex, she changed.—The verse divine
   She bade me build, she called it *Namby-Pamby;*

And took my rival's hand instead of mine,
    Which made me take at Ware's a glass of brandy;
Yet wit and sweetness lingered round her still,
And won my praise, despite of every ill.

X

Nor will I now that lovely one upbraid,
    Nor wound her spirit by a word unkind;
She was, in sooth, a very gentle maid,
    In manners, taste, and feelings, all refined,
And never erred but once—but let that rest—
She doubtless meant it kindly for the best.

XI

And how I bore my sufferings at that time,
    It little boots the reader now to know;
Perchance I drowned them in a flood of rhyme,
    Or in the goblet's more oblivious flow;
There's one thing certain—that I did not choose
To terminate them in a running noose.

XII

Oh, Love to me may be a welcome guest,
    But never can it mar my summer day;
The warrior's steel may penetrate my breast,
    But woman's scorn and coldness can not slay;
The spells of beauty and the tricks of art
May chain awhile, but can not crush the heart.

XIII

I love no longer, when I love in vain;
    I leave the chary for the smiling maid—

And she who treats my passion with disdain,
　Her scorn shall be with tenfold scorn repaid;
Proud Beauty can not triumph in her whims,
Unless the lamp of hope she duly trims.

XIV

My love for Sally was an honest glow,
　And seemed inflexible as Fate's decree.
"Wilt thou be mine?"—the gipsy answered, "No!"—
　Which set at once my captive spirit free;
That word dissolved the force of Beauty's spell,
And Love, insulted, bade a long farewell.

XV

O Sally Riley—Sally Riley O!—
　Some eighteen years have passed since last we met,
And I have felt the weight of many a wo;
　But never could, in all my griefs, forget
The happy days, when o'er my spirit bright,
Thy beauty poured a luminous delight.

XVI

I still behold thee in thine early pride,
　In all the brightness of thy morning ray;
And thoughts and feelings through my bosom glide
　That make our parting seem like yesterday.
Mild planet of my youth's idolatry,
Thou beamest on me still—a star of memory.

XVII

Thy smile, as brilliant as the rainbow's hues;
　Thy voice as pleasant as the laughing streams;

229

Thy step, that scarcely shook the morning dews;
   Thy song, that flowed like music in my dreams—
Are all to me as palpable as when,
In youthful days, we frolicked down the glen.

XVIII

The tricks you played me, and your saucy ways;
   The wild-goose chases into which you lured me;
The ridicule you threw upon my lays;
   And, finally, the *jilt,* that fairly cured me
Of love and madness, and my rhymes absurd,
Are all forgotten now;—they are, upon my word!

XIX

I know thee only as an ornament
   Of womankind—a star of light and truth—
My best, bright friend, whose name is blent
   With all that was delightful in my youth,
When pleasures thronged apace, without alloy,
And thou the light and life, the soul of every joy.

XX

But every earthly pleasure hath its bane,
   And darkness follows Fancy's vivid rays;
The power that bids thy beauties bloom again,
   Revives the pangs of long-departed days,
And makes me pour afresh affliction's tears
For the beloved and lost of other years.

XXI

Oh, where are now those fair, enchanting maids,
   Who used to circle round thy father's hearth?

Or, lightly sporting in Oconee's shades,
    Made hills and valleys echo with their mirth?—
Alas! along the margin of those waves,
Sweet roses, like themselves, are blooming o'er their
    graves.

XXII

I'll name them not—the theme is one of grief—
    And who will now with me their doom deplore?
And yet I sometimes think 'twould bring relief
    To many of my woes, if I could pour
My love and gratitude, in one full song,
To those whose memories I have cherished long.

XXIII

But this may never be—for though my heart
    May feel the fervor of poetic fires,
Yet Nature has denied the pleasing art
    To clothe in words the feelings she inspires;
And I must still in silence bear my cares,
Which have no voice, except the voice of tears.

XXIV

Then fare ye well, ye once-delightful train—
    Sweet listeners to, and laughers at, my lays;
When I contrast the glories of your reign
    With all the evil of these after-days,
I wish that mine had been your early doom,
Instead of lingering here to weep o'er Beauty's tomb.

XXV

I met a Rose in life's tumultuous hour,
　As bright as ever bloomed on Sharon's field;
But when I went to pluck the shining flower,
　I felt the thorn beneath its charms concealed:—
Oh, Sally Riley was that rose and thorn—
I wooed her beauties and received her scorn.

XXVI

I then beheld a Lily in the Vale,[3]
　And loved it dearly from the day I found it;
It blushed to hear my warm, impassioned tale,
　But sweetly smiled when to my heart I bound it.
That thornless flower was one whose cherished name
I hold too sacred for the songs I frame.

XXVII

But how can I of her unmindful prove,
　Who blest me with the light of her blue eyes,
And gave me all she had—life, soul, and love,
　And now is smiling on me from the skies?
Oh, that I had the gift of deathless song,
That I might sing of her, and not her memory wrong!

XXVIII

She was all beauty, melody, and mirth—
　A spirit bright, that gladdened soul and eye;
But as the fair and cherished things of earth,
　Whose sweetness links them to their kindred sky,

---

[3] Tabitha Jordan, whom Lamar had married in 1826.

Are always first to wither and to fall—
So perished she, the loveliest of them all.

XXIX

Brief was the space—a few enchanting years,
  Between her bridal and her burial day;
With soul serene, and eye undimmed by tears,
  She smiled upon her friends and passed away,
Like some bright star that blendeth with the morn—
A welcome one to realms where she was born.

XXX

To yonder valley's dark and lonely shade,
  Where winds and streams and birds their music
    blend,
As if they sought my silence to upbraid,
  By pouring requiems which myself should send,
Her cold remains were borne, and buried there,
Beneath the willow sad, that shareth my despair.

XXXI

But Oh, her spirit from this world of wo
  Was borne by angels to her home above;
And she who was my Lily here below,
  Is now a Seraph in the land of love;
And I am left abandoned and forlorn—
My life a long, long night, without the hope of morn.

XXXII

At random driven by the stormy breeze,
  With breakers roaring round him wild and hoarse,

Behold the mariner on rocky seas,
　　Without his polar star to point his course:—
So am I sweeping now o'er life's dark tide,
Without my planet bright, which might in safety
　　　guide.

XXXIII

O Memory, thou art no friend to me;
　　For though my life has flowed in Honor's ways,
By crimes untarnished and from falsehood free,
　　Still on the gloomy past I may not gaze
With rapture or delight—I there behold
Unnumbered woes, and sorrows yet untold.

XXXIV

And thou, fair Hope, with bright, fallacious smile—
　　To me thy promises are vainly made;
No more canst thou my weary soul beguile,
　　Which thou so oft hast flattered and betrayed;
Still gloomy as the past, my coming years
Must darkly roll in solitude and tears.

XXXV

If, in the social hour, I sometimes seem
　　To wear the smile of youth's enchanting prime,
'Tis but a borealis light—a gleam
　　That springeth from a dark and frozen clime;
And only serves my sufferings to conceal—
To hide the wounds which Time can never heal.

XXXVI

And if along the sacred dells and plains,
   Where, with my early friends, I used to stray,
I sometimes pour my rude, unpolished strains,
   As I am pouring now this lowly lay—
I court no purpose, but the peace that springs
From contemplation and the sounding strings.

XXXVII

For fame and fortune let me not contend—
   They bring no rapture to the tortured mind;
But thou, sweet Poesy—affliction's friend—
   Thine is the power the bleeding heart to bind;
E'en songs like mine, though all devoid of skill,
May soften wo, and fortify an ill.

XXXVIII

Then who shall blame me, though I fail to please
   The polished ear, familiar to the Nine?
'Tis meet that he on every source should seize,
   To soothe his heart whose sorrows are like mine—
Whose sorrows may not cease till life shall close,
And I may find in heaven my long-desired repose.

XXXIX

And, like my life, behold my present lay—
   Begun in gayety, to close in gloom.
Then let me pause awhile—some happier day
   I may, perhaps, my humble harp resume,
And with its lighter tones thy praises blend,
O Sally Riley dear, my unforgotten friend!

ON THE DEATH OF MY DAUGHTER

Rebecca Ann, Lamar's sixteen-year-old daughter, died in Macon, Georgia July 29, 1843, while her father was in Richmond, Texas (see p. 66). Three months later his old friend and ex-secretary, Edward Fontaine, wrote Lamar a consolatory letter, enclosing some sympathetic verses (for letter and lines, see notes, p. 309). Lamar replied with "On the Death of My Daughter," which in Mrs. Fontaine's scrap-book is dated Richmond, December 25, 1843.

The poem was first published in The Southern Literary Messenger *for July, 1849 (XV, 398-99), to which Lamar's friend, A. B. Meek, had sent it with a letter of high praise, calling it "almost the very tears of love crystallized into poetry by the spell of genius" (see notes, p. 310). It appears also in Lamar's manuscript album, in the Sandusky Manuscript, in Mrs. Rebecca Chappell's scrap-book, in* Verse Memorials *(1857), and in* The Houston Post *for July 8, 1894.*

1843   1849

I

All honor to thy minstrel skill,
   Dear friend of happier days;
Thy notes are sweet, but sweeter still
   The love that prompts thy lays.
From sorrows deep, and cherished long,
   Thou fain wouldst free my heart—
Thou wouldst, by thine enchanting song,
   New hopes and joys impart.

II

But vain it is thy harp to strike;
   My woes thou canst not drown,

Unless thy notes, Cecilia's like,
　Can draw an angel down.
Until I meet my daughter fair,
　Lost Pleiad of my soul,
The burning tears of my despair
　Must ever, ever roll.

III

Nor would I, if I could, revive
　From my distraction wild;
I love the grief that keeps alive
　The memory of my child;
And if again, by hope betrayed,
　My soul should court repose,
How poorly would the guilt be paid,
　By all that earth bestows!

IV

The morning star that fades from sight
　Still beams upon the mind;
So doth her beauty leave the light
　Of memory behind.
Though lost to earth—too early gone—
　By others seen no more,
She is to me still shining on,
　And brighter than before.

V

The smile she wore when last we met,
　The tear she shed at parting,

The kiss upon mine eyelids set
  To keep mine own from starting,
Like bright remembered dreams of bliss,
  Are lingering with me yet—
That smile, and tear, and parting kiss,
  Oh, how can I forget?

VI

And you, my friend, who knew her worth,
  And loved that worth to praise,
And how amid the ills of earth
  She walked in beauty's ways,
Will not condemn the grateful tears—
  The ever-flowing stream—
That keeps a loveliness like hers
  In memory fresh and green.

VII

No—let me still in silence keep
  My vigils o'er her tomb,
And with my tears forever steep
  The flowers that o'er it bloom.
Though all the world should pass it by,
  A place remembered not,
'Tis meet that I should linger nigh,
  And bless the hallowed spot.

VIII

The sacred love, the holy woes,
  Awakened by the dead,

Are like the fragrance of the rose
  When all its hues are fled;
And as beside the grave we stand,
  The mournful thoughts that rise
Are whispers from the Spirit-Land—
  Sweet voices from the skies.

IX

Then leave, Oh leave me to my grief,
  Too wedded now to part;
'Twill duly work its own relief,
  By eating out the heart;
But till my daughter, pure and bright,
  To me shall reappear,
My life must be a sleepless night,
  Without a star to cheer.

X

You tell me that my grief is vain,
  My child will not return;
No earthly tears can wake again
  The ashes of the urn;
You tell me too that she is gone
  To regions blest and fair—
And wrong it is her loss to mourn,
  Since she's an angel there.

XI

I know it all—I know it all;
  Yet still with grief opprest,

My spirit sighs for her recall,
   And will not be at rest.
I can not, can not give her up—
   I am not reconciled;
Oh take away the bitter cup,
   And bring me back my child!

XII

She was the last enchanting ray
   That cheered me here below—
The only star that lit my way
   Through this dark world of wo;
And now, bereft of that sweet light,
   Oh, how shall I sustain
The shadows of that awful night
   Which must with me remain!

XIII

Like him upon the rocky peak,
   In wrath and vengeance doomed
A victim to the vulture's beak,
   To suffer unconsumed—
So am I doomed in darkness deep,
   All desolate and chill,
To bear a pang that will not sleep—
   A death that will not kill.

XIV

Then be it so—all silently
   I'll bear the adverse weight;

But He I hope in yonder sky,
   Who dooms me to my fate,
Will, in his own good way and time,
   My lovely one restore—
If not on earth, in that blest clime
   Where parting is no more.

XV

I know He will—for even now,
   On Faith's enraptured eye
He breaketh, like his own bright bow
   Of promise from on high.
Amid my deep despondency,
   He whispers in my ear—
"Thy daughter may not come to thee,
   But thou canst go to her."

XVI

Enough, enough—I ask no more—
   A light has flashed within;
My child from earth He only bore,
   To lure me on to him.
Then let him keep the jewel bright,
   Oh, let him wear the gem;
I would not snatch so pure a light
   From his bright diadem.

XVII

The only boon, O God, I crave,
   Is soon thy face to see;

I long to pass the dull, cold grave,
And wing my way to thee—
To thee, O God, and all my friends
In thine eternal sphere,
Where I may make some poor amends
For all my errors here.

BEHOLD UPON YON BENDING LIMB
To the Minstrel Maiden of Mobile

During his visit (1844) in the home of A. B. Meek on Government Street in Mobile, Lamar met Miss Julia Harris (see p. 68). Her verses, published in the newspapers of the city, had gained for her the title "the minstrel maiden of Mobile." Lamar's poem—his happiest reference to the mockingbird— was published only in Verse Memorials.

1844   1857

I

Behold upon yon bending limb
The bird of jest and jibe,
And hark with what enchanting skill
It mocks the warbling tribe!
Were mine the art, its varied notes
To bind in silver words,
I'd frame a song to one whose own
Is sweeter than that bird's.

II

A glowing mind, by taste refined,
A soul sublimely cast;

A loveliness that wins all hearts,
   And truth that holds them fast;—
Oh, these—sweet minstrel maiden—these
   My pleasing themes should be;
And, with my heart in every line,
   The song should flow to thee.

III

And oh, what bard so blest as I,
   Howe'er with laurels crowned,
If through thy pure and rosy lips
   My numbers might resound!
The song approved and sung by thee,
   Were more than golden store—
And rapture for my living years,
   And fame when these are o'er.

I HAVE WEPT O'ER BEAUTY'S DOOM

*Before leaving Washington for Georgia in the spring of 1845,
Lamar wrote these lines as a note of thanks to Bettie Morsell,
a locally popular concert singer in the Capital City. The Rose
of Stanza III was Tabitha, Lamar's wife, who had died fifteen
years before.*

1845   1857

I

Oh, I have wept o'er Beauty's doom,
   So very loud and long,
I did not think my heart again
   Could wake to love and song;

243

Yet, lady fair, thy notes this night
  Have lightened my distress,
And made me feel that woman's voice
  Has still the power to bless.

II

When first upon my spirit fell
  Thy soft, enchanting tone,
It seemed to be direct from heaven,
  And meant for me alone;
For oh, I thought it was the voice
  That charmed me long ago—
And, in the dear delusion lost,
  My tears began to flow.

III

Forgive, forgive this dewy proof
  Of thy o'erpowering art;
For where's the melody but thine
  To melt so cold a heart?—
A heart that has not dared to smile,
  Nor felt one throb of love,
Since she who was my Rose below
  Became a Star above.

IV

O'er loved Laredo's blooming plains
  I soon shall wander free,
And I shall hear the Bravo roll
  In music to the sea;

But where, or where will be thy songs?—
　My soul will pine in vain
To drink once more their golden light,
　And happy be again.

V

Adieu, adieu, thou tuneful one!
　My gratitude I owe
To her who touched my frozen heart,
　And made its fountains flow.
Where'er she wanders through this world,
　May blessings ever throng
Around the bright and beautiful
　Embodiment of song!

MY GEM OF DELIGHT

In 1845 the petite, dark-haired Cassandra Flint (Macon, Georgia) and Lamar were engaged to be married. She was very sensitive because her parents kept a boarding house (Poplar and First streets); and when she heard that the social difference between her and her fiancé was the subject of remark, deeply hurt, she at once returned his ring—a cluster of nine diamonds. Instead of accepting it Lamar wrote for her "My Gem of Delight," both a tribute and an invitation (see p. 73). The poem was sung to the tune of "Flow Gently, Sweet Afton" in the Flint home long after Lamar returned to Texas—alone.[1] The oncoming Mexican War is responsible for the martial tone of the piece.

In accordance with Cassandra's wishes, "My Gem of Delight" was not printed until seven years later, when it was published anonymously in the Southwestern American *(Austin), December 29, 1852, and a month later, with Lamar's name, in* The Northern Standard *(Clarksville), January 15, 1853. In* Verse Memorials *it carries the dedication, "To a Fair Friend, Macon, Georgia," though at that time Cassandra Flint had twice married (see p. 73, note).*

1845   *1852*

I

Oh, bright is the maiden who wakens my sighs,
No planet can equal the light of her eyes;
Her form is elastic—her spirit elate—
The spring of the willow is seen in her gait;
The tones of her laughter are dulcimer-sounds,
And gladness is scattered wherever she bounds.

[1] Letter to the present editor from Mrs. Louisa Flint Reynolds, Cassa's youngest sister.

246

Oh, thou art—my Cassa—that maiden so bright,
Sweet spirit of beauty, and *Gem of Delight*.

II

What gift shall I bring thee to merit thy love—
Some pearl from the ocean, or star from above?
What wreath shall I twine thee to soften thy scorn—
The laurels of battle, or myrtles of song?
Thy will shall be law, and the lofty shall bend;
My harp it shall praise thee, my sword shall defend;
Then tell me, fair Cassa—Oh, tell me tonight,
The best way to woo thee, my *Gem of Delight*.

III

Too cold is this climate for beauty like thine;
No heart can adore thee so warmly as mine;
I laugh at all peril when woman's the prize—
The stars of my banner are love-lighted eyes!
As swift as a falcon the steed that I ride,
And sharp is the sabre that hangs by my side;
Then fly with me, Cassa—there's bliss in the flight,
And glory shall circle my *Gem of Delight*.

IV

But Oh, if my fair one can never be mine,
To silence forever my harp I consign;
Undrawn in its scabbard my sabre shall rust,
And glory and honors I trample in dust.
How cold is all glory by Beauty unblest!
Like Erebus's shadows it falls on my breast;
But Oh, it is sunshine to soul and to sight,
When kindled by Cassa, my *Gem of Delight*.

And should he be, as I have been,
Still true to love and duty,
Then be the minstrel's high reward
The hand and heart of beauty.

CARMELITA

"Carmelita" was written near Monterey, Mexico, a few days before the action at that place, where Lamar rendered valiant service (see p. 75). The lady addressed was a beautiful Mexican girl whose identity has been lost.

The poem appears in none of the Lamar manuscripts, the result of its being composed in camp. After its publication in Verse Memorials *(1857) it was copied widely, appearing in the* Tri-weekly Intelligencer *(Austin), October 3, 1857; in the* Southern Intelligencer *(Austin), October 7, 1857; in the* Northern Standard *(Clarksville), December 26, 1857; in* The Library of Southern Literature *(Atlanta, 1907), VII, 2996; in Mabel Major's* The Southwest in Literature *(New York, 1929).*

1846   *1857*

I

O Carmelita, know ye not
For whom all hearts are pining?
And know ye not, in Beauty's sky,
The brightest planet shining?—
Then learn it now—for thou art she,
Thy nation's jewel, born to be
By all beloved, but most by me—
O Donna Carmelita!

250

II

But wo is me thy love to lose,
  Apart from thee abiding;
Between us roars a gloomy stream,
  Our destiny dividing.
That stream with blood incarnadined
Flows from thy nation's erring mind,
And rolls with ruin to thy kind,
      O Donna Carmelita.

III

'Tis mine, while floating on the tide,
  To stick to love and duty;
I draw my sabre on the foe,
  I strike my harp to beauty;
And who shall say the soldier's wrong,
Who, while he battles with the strong,
Still softens war with gentle song,
      O Donna Carmelita?

IV

I soon shall seek the battle-field,
  Where Freedom's flag is waving—
My Texas comrades by my side,
  All perils madly braving;
I only grieve to think each blow,
That vengeance bids the steel bestow,
Must make thee mine eternal foe,
      O Donna Carmelita.

251

V

Full well I know thy pride will spurn
　　The brightest wreaths I bring thee;
Full well I know thou wilt not heed
　　The sweetest songs I sing thee;
Yet, all despite thy scorn and hate,
Despite the thousand ills of fate,
I still my soul must dedicate—
　　　　To Donna Carmelita.

VI

Then fare thee well, dear, lovely one—
　　May happiness attend thee;
Ten thousand harps exalt thy name,
　　Ten thousand swords defend thee:—
And when the sod is on my breast,
My harp and sabre both at rest,
May thou and thine be greatly blest,
　　　　O Donna Carmelita!

GAY SPRING

*After retiring from office, Lamar when in Austin was fre-
quently a guest at Belle Monte, the home of James Webb,
northwest of the city, and also in the near-by home of Thomas
Duval, who did much of Lamar's legal business. Florence, one
of the five Duval children, was six years old when Lamar wrote
"Gay Spring" to her while he was at Belle Monte in March,
1846. Lamar believed that the lisping melody of the little girl
was an unconscious echo of the birds she had listened to, and
sought to catch in his poem the same lilting music.*

*Inspired perhaps by Lamar's compliment, Florence (later
the wife of Judge C. S. West) herself published a volume,* The
Marble Lily and Other Poems.[1]

"Gay Spring" was reprinted in D. F. Eagleton's Writers and
Writings of Texas *(New York, 1913).*

1846   1857

I

Gay Spring, with her beautiful flowers,
   Is robing the valleys and hills;
Sweet music is heard in the bowers,
   And laughter is sent from the rills.
Oh, let me, while kindled by these,
   The feelings of childhood recall,
And frame a soft sonnet to please
   The fair little FLORENCE DUVAL.

II

The rose may be proud of its red,
   The lily be proud of its white,

---

[1] *Lamar Papers,* Nos. 2212 (IV, 127) and 2376 (VI, 163); *Quarterly* of
the Texas Historical Association, I (1897), 80, 62; Elizabeth Brooks,
Prominent Women of Texas, p. 113.

And sweet-scented jessamines shed
   Their treasures of fragrant delight;
Yet brighter and sweeter than these,
   And far more enchanting to all,
Is the beautiful pink of Bellemont,
   The fair little FLORENCE DUVAL.

III

Her locks are as white as the lint,
   Her eyes are as blue as the sky;
Her cheeks have a magical tint—
   A rainbow which never should die.
Oh, surely there's no living thing,
   That dwelleth in cottage or hall,
Can vie with the Peri I sing—
   The fair little FLORENCE DUVAL.

IV

But why is she resting from play—
   And why is that tear in her eye?
Alas! a bright bird on the spray
   Is pouring its carols hard by;
Her spirit is drinking the song—
   She weeps at the notes as they fall;
For genius and feelings belong
   To fair little FLORENCE DUVAL.

V

Oh, long may the Peri bloom on,
   Still ever in gladness and love,
And blend with her genius for song
   The feelings that light us above.

254

That life may be lengthened and blest,
And sorrows may never enthrall,
Must still be the prayer of each breast
For fair little FLORENCE DUVAL.

LOVELY FANNY MYER

Fanny Myer was Henrietta Maffitt, three years later Lamar's wife, whom he knew in Galveston as early as 1846 (Lamar Papers, No. 2216 [IV, 130]), when "first, on Galvez isle," he "walked in the rainbow" of her smile ("Home on the Brazos," X). During the interval between the writing of this poem (1848) and their marriage (1851), their friendship was almost forgotten until they met again in the home of Mrs. John Settle, New Orleans (see p. 78).

Lamar named his heroine Fanny also in his short story, "The Parting Kiss." The poem appears only in Lamar's manuscript album.

1848   *1937*

I

I can't tell why, but so it is,
    When with her I am walking,
Or snugly seated by her side,
    Beneath the moonlight talking,
I always feel as if my veins
    Were filled with flowing fire,
And think some angel hath assumed
    The form of *Fanny Myer*.

II

She surely is the sweetest flower
This sunny Isle adorning;

She is in Beauty's firmament
The golden Star of morning;
And he who wins her for his bride
May ask no raptures higher;
For home becomes a paradise
When blest with *Fanny Myer*.

III

But what are her charms to me?
For me they are not shining;
Some gayer bard will pluck the rose,
And leave my soul repining.
Her beauty only kindles hopes,
Which must too soon expire;
And woe will follow, when I lose
My lovely *Fanny Myer*.

IV

I know she never can be mine;
No arts have I to win her;
She will not listen to my songs,
Nor wear the flowers I bring her;
And yet the homage of my heart,
O, how can I deny her;
Whilst life shall last, I still must love
My lovely *Fanny Myer*.

A PUN

In collecting historical matter concerning the Austin family, Lamar made a record of the marriage of John W. Honey to Miss Mary S. Austin, niece of Moses Austin. On the back of the document (Lamar Papers, No. 2407 [VI, 176]) he wrote these verses.

1849?   1927

> From sweetest flow'rs the busy bee
> Can scarce a drop of honey gather;
> But oh how sweet a flower is she
> Who turns to Honey altogether.

IN DEATHLESS BEAUTY

Lamar carefully penned "In Deathless Beauty" to Miss Henrietta Maffitt during the courtship in the home of Mrs. John Settle, New Orleans (facsimile, p. 98). The poem appears in Lamar's manuscript album under the title "To Miss ——," and in the Verse Memorials *(text here printed) with the first line as title.*

1851   1857

I

> O Lady, if the stars so bright
>   Were diamond worlds bequeathed to me,
> I would resign them all this night,
>   To frame one song befitting thee;
> For thou art dearer to my heart
>   Than all the gems of earth and sky;

257

And he that sings thee as thou art,
   May boast a song that can not die.

II

But how shall I the task essay?—
   Can I rejoin the tuneful throng,
No longer cheered by beauty's ray,
   The only light that kindles song?
No, no—my harp, in darkness bound,
   Can never more my soul beguile;
Its spirit fled when Henrie frowned—
   It hath no voice without her smile.

III

Then blame me not—my skill is gone;
   I have no welcome song to give;
But thou shalt be my fav'rite one
   To love and worship while I live
Wher'er I wander sad and long,
   I will thine angel-image bear
Upon my heart, as on a stone,
   In deathless beauty sculptured there.

THE SHADY SIDE OF FIFTY-THREE
To a Young Lady in Milledgeville

*When Lamar and Henrietta on their wedding tour in 1851
reached Milledgeville, Georgia, the scene of many of Lamar's
earlier adventures, his wife demanded "a poem of reassur-
ance." Lamar, half in jest, produced these verses. He was fifty-
three, his wife twenty-four.*

*The poem appears in the scrap-book of Mrs. Rebecca Jordan
Curry (misdated ten years); it was published in* Verse Memorials, *with the first line as title.*

1851   1857

I

Oh, is it not a pity, now,
  That I am growing old;
That Time has written on my brow,
  So legibly and bold,
What every glancing eye may see,
  And folly can not hide—
That I am now, of fifty-three,
  Upon the shady side?

II

The happy days, so gay and bright,
  I never can recall,
When beauty was a great delight,
  And love was all in all.
The spring of life is quickly fled—
  And when it hath declined,
A wintry heart and hoary head
  Are all it leaves behind.

259

III

Yet, lady fair, to whom I pour
   This light and laughing lay,
If guilty Time could but restore
   The gifts he bore away,
I then might breathe a softer tale,
   A more devoted strain;
And oh, if passion might prevail,
   I should not sing in vain.

IV

Behold imbedded in thy ring
   That gem of sparkling dye,
Thy fairy hand illumining
   With lustre like thine eye;—
So should my heart encircle thee,
   And thou, implanted there,
My pure and sparkling gem shouldst be,
   To light me everywhere.

LAMENT FOR LORETTO

*The Hardman family lived on North Orange Street, Eufaula,
Alabama, neighbors to Mrs. Mary Ann Moreland, Lamar's
sister. Loretto Hardman, who had been named after Lamar's
youngest sister, died at the age of seven, in 1852, when Lamar
was visiting in Georgia and Alabama (see p. 80).*

*The "Lament," published in the Eufaula Times and News
of May 23, 1852, appears also in Mrs. Rebecca Dollie Chappell's scrap-book. In Verse Memorials it was dedicated to
Loretto's mother.*

1852   1852

I

Mild, blue-eyed queen—enchanting Spring!
   O'er mountain, dell, and plain,
Thou scatter'st with a liberal hand
   The blessings of thy reign;
Ten thousand happy, happy hearts
   Thy glad return will hail,
And who should love thee more than we,
   Of bright Eufaula's vale?

II

And yet, sweet Spring, although thou com'st
   In radiant beauty drest,
Thou bring'st no solace to our woes—
   No sunshine to the breast.
'Tis ours to mourn the early dead,
   A child of beauty rare,
Whose presence made all seasons bright—
   A spring-time everywhere.

III

We find her not in dale nor dell,
　We miss her by the hearth;
We hear no more her joyous laugh,
　The music of her mirth.
The bower she built is blooming yet,
　The flowers are fresh and fair,
But she who was its life and light
　Is seen no longer there.

IV

She was a joy to every heart,
　A light to every eye,
And sadness found no resting-place
　When she was sporting nigh.
Unless thou canst that flower restore—
　Bring back its bloom again,
Sweet Spring, we hail not thy return—
　Thou com'st to us in vain.

V

O blest LORETTO, beauteous one,
　Mild flow'ret of thy race,
No vernal joys nor vain delights
　Can fill thy ruined place.
Around the parent-stem may cling
　The tendrils of the vine,
Yet closer still around the heart
　Our grief for thee must twine.

VI

How bright and brief was thy career,
  How like the star of eve—
The fairest of the shining train,
  And first to take its leave!—
And as that planet, pure and bright,
  Goes gladd'ning down the west,
So didst thou sink, in all the light
  Of loveliness, to rest.

VII

Mild evening star! we may not grieve
  To see thy light decline,
For thou wilt come to-morrow eve,
  And just as brightly shine;
But how can we our grief restrain,
  Or cease our tears to pour,
For that sweet star that set so soon,
  And comes to us no more!

VIII

And is it thus?—is loveliness
  A perishable light—
A blessing lent us for a day,
  To close in endless night?
No, lost one, no—thou art not dead—
  Thy beauty can not die;
And we shall meet again, fair child,
  In thy blest home on high.

263

IX

The hope of this—the pleasing hope
　　Our parting is but brief—
Is all that now remains to us,
　　Our only balm of grief.
Then let us cease our loud lament,
　　Nor dare our GOD upbraid—
The hand, in time, that dealt the blow,
　　Will heal the wound it made.

TO MARION
On Hearing Her Sing

*Lamar and his wife spent several weeks of the summer of 1852
in the home of Harmong Lamar, of Glenville, Alabama. Here
he listened to the singing of Mrs. Marion Harwell, the kins-
woman of Mrs. Harmong Lamar. One year before at New
Orleans, Lamar and Henrietta had heard Jenny Lind, the
great Swedish soprano, referred to in Stanza I. The poem appears only in* Verse Memorials.

1852　　　　　　　　　　　　　　　　　　　　1857

I

What heavenly souls are those I hear—
　　From what blest regions brought?
Some angel must be hovering near,
　　With melody o'erfraught.
Sing on—sing on, sweet child of light,
　　And cheer thy listener's heart;
More welcome are thy strains to-night
　　Than Jenny's highest art.

II

There is a brightness in thine eye,
    A pathos in thy lay—
A light that marks thee from the sky,
    And not of human clay.
I can not think such songs of love
    From earthly lips can flow;
And if thou wert not born above,
    Thy notes are surely so.

III

Blest rival of the tuneful Nine,
    Enchantress of the soul,
As sweet to other hearts as mine—
    Long may thy numbers roll;
And I thy friend, when far away,
    Will bear with fond delight
The memory of each golden lay,
    And bless the minstrel bright.

NORA

Nicholas Lookup left Ireland in 1854 with the promise of a position as governess in Galveston, Texas. When she presented herself at the door of her prospective employers, with the brogue of the homeland fresh upon her tongue, she was refused admittance, and was left, weeping and penniless, at the gate. Here Mrs. Lamar, shopping in the city, found her, and took her to the Richmond plantation. Lamar called her Nora, insisting that he could not live with such a name as hers. She became a favorite with the whole family, and remained until she secured both a position and a suitable husband—as prophesied in Stanza V.

"Nora" is an expansion and adaptation of "Desultory," published in The Columbus Enquirer *of February 8, 1834 (see notes, p. 311).*

1834
1854

1834
1857

I

NORA, cease that lively lay;
    Vain to me its numbers flow;
Sing it to the light and gay,
    Not to him oppressed with wo.
Flowery songs that bind to earth,
Songs of unreflecting mirth,
Sweet to others though they be,
No fond raptures bring to me.

II

Give me in thy gathered breath,
    Gushing songs of days gone by—

Solemn requiems of death,
  Wringing tear-drops from the eye.
O'er the dead I love to weep,
All my thoughts are where they sleep,
And I may not brook the glee,
Mindless of their memory.

III

If thou canst, O lady fair,
  Charm the buried back again,
Breathe, Oh breathe the magic air—
  Bless me with the heavenly strain;
And the forms so purely bright,
While they break upon my sight,
Thou, with them beloved so well,
Ever in my heart shalt dwell.

IV

Songs thou hast of siren flow,
  Gloom or gladness to impart—
Soothing to the mourner's wo,
  Cheering to the youthful heart.
Give the sad ones to the grave,
To the young the merry stave—
Binding thus by melody,
Youth and age alike to thee.

V

And in life's enchanting pride,
  When to Hymen's rosy bowers,
Thou art led a blushing bride,
  Brighter than thy crowning flowers,

267

I, thy friend, will joy to see
One so excellent as thee,
Blest with all that's good on earth—
Blest according to thy worth.

MARY BELL

Mrs. Mary E. Bell, known far and wide for her hospitality, was the soldier's friend during the days of the Republic of Texas. She had married Josiah Bell of South Carolina in 1819, and settled in Washington County, Texas. By the time of her husband's death (1838), she was comparatively wealthy, and was living near Columbia, where Lamar knew her. With the exception of Lamar himself, she, more than any other Texan, helped soldiers to return to their homes in the United States. Tradition says that no worthy man ever asked her for food, clothing, or money and turned away empty-handed.

1854   1857

I

There is a name whose tones once heard,
　Becomes a constant spell;
A musical and magic word,
By which all gentle hearts are stirred—
　That name is MARY BELL.

II

The sunlight of our quiet hearth,
　Which knows her presence well,
Is oft enlivened by her mirth—
And ever cherished is the worth
　Of lovely MARY BELL.

III

Her beauties are the stars above,
  Her heart a living well;
And as for gentleness and love,
Where will you find so sweet a dove
  As lovely MARY BELL?

IV

I can not, in this little lay,
  Her many virtues tell;
But this I know and well may say,
She grows upon us every day—
  The lovely MARY BELL.

THE ROSE, THE MOON, AND NIGHTINGALE

To the Belle of the Brazos

The Belle of the Brazos, to whom the verses were addressed, was Eliza Maffitt, the sister of Lamar's wife, Henrietta. She retained the appellation even after she became Mrs. Budd.[1] At the time of Lamar's marriage to Henrietta, Eliza was a widow, and before they returned to Richmond, Lamar was sending her thirty dollars a month. After their return she became a member of their household. She was a gifted musician and singer.

The poem appears as "Compliment" in Lamar's manuscript album, without the third stanza as here printed (Verse Memorials, text and title).

1854   1857

I

Many a flower of beauty rare
   May blossom on the plain;
But none, however sweet and fair,
   Have reason to be vain—
For all are passed neglected by,
When Sharon's Rose is blooming nigh.

II

Many a star that gems the night,
   In seeming gladness glows,

[1] Emma M. Maffitt, *The Life and Services of John Newland Maffitt,* p. 28.

As if it sought to match the light
    The dazzling diamond throws;
Yet e'en the Evening Star declines
Whene'er the Moon in glory shines.

III

Many a bird may carol loud,
    In sadness or in glee;
But none have reason to be proud,
    Though sweet their music be—
For what can all their notes avail,
Compared with thine, sweet Nightingale?

IV

As reigns the Rose, the queen of flowers,
    The Moon, the queen of night—
As Philomel's melodious powers
    Excel in rich delight—
So reigns my fair o'er Virtue's throng—
The queen of Beauty, Light, and Song.

MY LILY, STAR, AND PEACEFUL DOVE
To the Pride of the Village

Tradition says that Henrietta was piqued that her husband should compliment the "Belle of the Brazos," to whom he had written "The Rose, the Moon, and Nightingale." To make amends Lamar addressed "My Lily, Star, and Peaceful Dove" to his wife. The two poems are companion pieces, parallel in title and structure. The village of the inscription is Richmond, Texas. The poem was published only in Verse Memorials.

1854   *1857*

I

The Rose, in gorgeous dyes arrayed,
   May queen it on the throne;
But more beloved, in yonder shade,
   The Lily blooms alone;—
For who can hesitate between
Her modest worth and beauty's sheen?

II

The Moon may dim the stars above,
   With cold, unkindling light;
But more the golden beams I love
   Of yonder planet bright—
The Star that shines a queenly gem
In dewy Evening's diadem.

III

The Nightingale may strain its throat,
   Ambitious songs to pour;

272

But there's a bird of mournful note,
   Whose pathos pleases more—
The bird that bore, o'er waters dark,
The welcome olive to the ark.

IV

Let others, then, the splendors hail
   Of Brazos' shining belle;
The Rose—the Moon—the Nightingale,
   May suit her glories well;
But more than these, by far, I love
My Lily, Star, and peaceful Dove.

HOME ON THE BRAZOS

Lamar wrote "Home on the Brazos" as a rhymed introduction to his Verse Memorials—a fact that explains the opening lines. The first half of the poem (I-VIII) is a tribute to womanhood; the second (IX-XVIII), a description of the Lamar household at the Richmond plantation on the Brazos, with a recurring at the close of the poem to the first theme.

In 1857 the household consisted of four others besides Lamar: Henrietta, his wife, "the lily of the dell"; Loretto (Lola), Lamar's six-year-old daughter, "with cold black eye and sunny hair"; Mrs. Eliza Budd, Henrietta's older sister, the musician of the group; and Mrs. Budd's daughter, Carrie. A contemporary reviewer of the poem wrote: "An abidance of many months as a stranger guest under the hospitable roof of one of the most happy and harmonious of families enables the writer to bear testimony that the picture which the poet has drawn of his delightful home, in spite of its exceeding beauty, is not altogether equal to its theme." (Lamar Papers, No. 2565 [VI, 356]).

One section of the poem (XII) was reprinted in the Texas Sentinel *(October 31, 1857), and a garbled fragment—probably part of an early version—is among the* Lamar Papers *(No. 2464 [VI, 312]).*

1857   1857

I

O Gentle ladies, gay and bright,
For you—and you alone—I write;
And if my verse should fail to please,
For want of your own native ease,
You must your faithful bard forgive,
Whose songs are not designed to live;

Who only cons a cheerful lay—
Light ditty of a summer's day—
To share, like flowers, a transient while
The light of Beauty's gracious smile,
And then be idly thrown aside—
For ever lost in Lethe's tide!

II

It grieves me, gentle friends, to know
That ye, from whom our comforts flow,
Should not in just proportion share
The brilliant joys you scatter here:
Yet so it is—'Tis yours, the while
All earth is lighted by your smile,
To see your virtues unrepaid,
Your wit despised, your love betrayed;
Nor feel one bliss your charms impart,
Reflected back upon the heart.

III

Proud man may take the morning's wing
And fly wherever dwells the Spring;
The world of passion lies before him,
And Beauty's light is shining o'er him;
And though he may not realize
The highest objects of his sighs,
He still at least retains the right
To chase the phantoms of delight.
But such is not fair woman's doom—
The world she decks is but her tomb!
She must not after pleasure rove,
She must not read the Paphian grove;

She can not play the warrior bold,
She can not delve in mines for gold;
Denied to her the helm of state—
She dares in nothing to be great:
The only bliss that she can know
Must from domestic comforts flow;
And should these blessings ne'er attend,
Then welcome Death, her only friend.

IV

Restricted thus—forbid to roam—
Chained like a captive to her home—
How more than cruel must it be,
If he, who rules her destiny,
Should make that home the home of tears—
A dungeon of despairing years!
Yet this has been, and still must be,
While woman's bound and man is free.
To Beauty's sacred rights unjust,
Sad recreant to his troth and trust,
The husband ceases soon to prize
The one bright angel of his sighs;
Beholds unmoved her falling tears;
And, turning from her cheerful beauty,
Despising truth, and loathing duty,
Seeks in the horrid dens of vice
The madd'ning cup—the treach'rous dice—
And all those joys, debased and vain,
That bring destruction in their train;
While she, who once, with soul elate,
Entwined with his, her hope and fate,
And fondly deemed her home would prove

276

An Eden-world of light and love,
Now finds that home all wo and strife—
A dark entombment of her life—
Where no sweet ray of hope can come,
To light the deep, sepulchral gloom.
The wretch that blights, with serpent-art,
The paradise of woman's heart,
Should, serpent-like, be doomed to feel
The iron crush of every heel.

V

There lies in Fancy's fairy clime,
Like Eden in its early prime,
A lovely landscape, fresh and green,
With fragrant flowers and waters sheen,
And gentle birds of plumage gay,
Pouring their songs from every spray.
Fond woman thinks, if she could dwell,
Embowered with love, in that fair dell
Her life like some bright stream would be,
Flowing in light and melody.
But when she seeks with hasty feet
The blessings of that green retreat,
The luring lawn is scarcely passed,
Ere darkness over all is cast;
And soon she finds her fairy ground
A dreary waste with ruin crowned.
The verdure green has disappeared,
The birds are flown—no music heard—
The turbid waters scarcely flow,
And every flower has lost its glow:
All, all are changed—the vision flies,

And hope, without fruition, dies.—
O woman fair, that landscape green
Is married life at distance seen;
The dreary waste it proves to be,
Is married life as found by thee.

VI

Now, if this realm were mine to-day,
And I a king of boundless sway,
Fair woman soon, from every wo,
Should leap exulting like the doe,
And no presumptuous man should dare
To build his bliss on her despair.
All tyrant-laws I would explode—
I'd purge the statutes—change the code—
And by some system, just and true,
Secure the rights to Beauty due.
But since the world is prone to slight
The wisdom of a rhyming wight,
And falsely deem the tuneful tribe
Unfit for aught but jest and jibe,
I must content me with my lays,
To sing in Truth and Virtue's praise,
And humbly lay the wreath I twine,
An offering frail at Beauty's shrine.
I can not brook the soulless bard,
Who lacks for woman due regard—
Who sees no heaven within her eyes,
And all her world of worth denies.
To me she is a planet bright,
And ever-faithful beacon-light—

The star I seek to guide my way,
Whose lustre never leads astray;
And he, the minstrel mean and vile,
Who would her sacred name defile,
Should ne'er in life those raptures know
Which fame and beauty can bestow.
O may his songs remain unread,
No honors crown his recreant head,
And woman's love, like morning light,
Ne'er dawn on his distracted night!

VII

Ungrateful man! by Beauty blessed,
Too fondly cherished and caressed,
When will you learn the boon to prize—
The blessing sent you from the skies—
An angel with the name of Wife—
Bright rainbow of your stormy life?
Oh, soothe her by each gentle art,
Allay the anguish of her heart,
And leave her not, beneath your scorn,
To sink like some sweet bloom of morn;
But wear her as the priceless gem
That decks a monarch's diadem.
She is the jewel of your youth,
Your manhood's talisman of truth,
And still will be, in life's decline,
Your shelt'ring and sustaining vine.
Then be to her as she to you,
For ever kind—for ever true;
And while her daily smiles you share,
Fond object of her constant care,

Oh, let it be your highest pride
Through life to linger by her side;
And feel and know that, come what will,
One star is beaming o'er you still!

VIII

The sweetest wife, and most beloved,
May be to transient anger moved,
As quiet lakes and tranquil seas
Are ruffled by the passing breeze;
But who for this shall love her less,
Or slacken in his fond caress?
If sometimes, mid her thousand cares,
She should her husband chide in tears—
Rebuke him for some fault forgot,
Some error best remembered not—
Perchance a something undesigned,
A word or look she deemed unkind,
Or, hurtful more to woman's pride,
Some boon demanded and denied—
Oh, let him not, with angry flash,
Retort in language rude and rash;
But, folding in a warm embrace,
Her lovely form of perfect grace,
Inflict upon the rosy *pout*,
Some fifty kisses long drawn out,
And thus a sweet revenge impose—
The only one that honor knows.

IX

And does my Henrietta say—
"I like the precepts of your lay,

But more it would my soul delight
To see you practice what you write?"—
Nay, say not so—nor e'en in jest,
Disturb the halcyon of that breast,
In which thy image lies enshrined,
Like pearl in Ocean's caves confined.
I may, indeed, have often erred,
And deeply wronged my bonny bird;
But, dearest one, as down we go
Life's chequered scenes of joy and wo,
'Tis wisdom's part to cull the rose,
And leave the nightshade where it grows.
If e'er, by angry word or deed,
I've caused thy gentle heart to bleed,
And left thee sorrowing by the hearth,
Neglectful of thy matchless worth,
A due repentance now is mine,
And sweet forgiveness must be thine.
E'en while my passions went astray,
My heart still loved the better way;
And oft in deep contrition longed
To kneel before the shrine I wronged;
For how could I forget the bride
I wooed and won in beauty's pride—
And, dearer still, the faithful wife
Whose love has blessed my troubled life?
The needle, forced by some rude jar,
Forsakes awhile its polar star;
Yet feeling still its secret sway,
It always settles to that ray:
So doth my spirit, tempest-tost,
Too oft its helm of reason lost,

Still turn to thee, its polar light—
The star that ever guides aright.
Then cease, my Henrie—cease to chide—
Look only on the brighter side;
And when around our humble hearth
We meet again in joy and mirth,
Oh, bend on me thine eye of light,
In token sweet that all is right—
As I shall cast me on thy breast,
My only home of peace and rest!

X

Full soon I hope in Texan shades—
Fair land of flowers and blooming maids—
To roam enraptured by thy side,
As blessed with thee on Brazos' tide
As when I first, on Galvez' isle,
Walked in the rainbow of thy smile.
We'll rise, my love, at early dawn,
We'll ramble down the dewy lawn,
We'll drink the freshness of the breeze
We'll wake the wild-birds in the trees;
And as we go through glen and glade,
Culling bright flowers thy locks to braid,
Thy voice, in converse soft and clear,
Shall be my spirit's dulcimer.
No bodings dark shall intervene,
No shadows dim the blissful scene;
But pleasant thoughts—sweet, peaceful dove—
Thoughts born of beauty, truth, and love—
Shall in thy Eden-bosom rise,
And send their moonlight through thine eyes;

282

Or, breathing inward quietness,
Shall silent dwell in their recess,
Like hoarded stores of rich perfume,
Locked in the rose-bud ere it bloom.
The lark's first carol in the morn
Will find us in the field of corn—
The distant field far down the dell,
Whose lively green thou lov'st so well;
And ere Aurora's beams shall mar
The lustre of the Morning Star,
We'll seek again our peaceful cot,
When thine shall be the cheerful lot
Thy household duties to resume;
And mine the task—the sterner doom—
To drive the ploughshare through the soil,
Or mingle in the world's turmoil.
But what is labor—what is strife—
And what are all the ills of life—
If man but meet them undeterred,
By God sustained and beauty cheered?

XI

When duty's claims no longer press,
And labor grants us sweet recess,
Oft will we roam, in frolic-mood,
Through valleys wide and tangled wood,
And reap the joy that Nature yields
To all who love her open fields.
For thee, my love, will Spring unfold
Her gorgeous robes of green and gold;
And, like a troop of rural maids,
The flowery children of her shades

283

Their welcome guest will smiling greet,
And look their best to look as sweet.
The rose will blush with deeper red,
The lily hold a higher head,
The trees assume a livelier green,
The waters roll in brighter sheen;
And all things pleasing, all things bright,
Whate'er inspires a gay delight,
Shall lend their soft, enchanting powers,
To gild and bless the flying hours
And to thy pure and gentle heart
A radiant glow of joy impart.

XII

What God designs for our delight,
It is ingratitude to slight;
And, baser still, with selfish pride,
To seize the joys, and not divide.
Poor worth, indeed, the happiest lot,
If kindred love can share it not!
So, dearest one, as forth we wend,
The good and lovely shall attend—
And hand in hand, and side by side,
We'll frolic all till eventide.
With sparkling eye and spirit gay,
Your sister, love, shall lead the way,
And, with her sweet Euterpean art,
Awake bright joy in every heart.
Her daughter, too—celestial born—
Bright rising star of early morn—
Shall o'er the flowery path we tread,
The sunshine of her beauty shed.

284

Her fairy feet, where'er she goes,
Shall fall so lightly on the rose,
As not to shake the sparkling dews
That hang like diamonds on its hues.
Lola, sweet Lola, shall be there,
With coal-black eye and sunny hair;
An elfin-sprite—a fairy thing—
Light as a swallow on the wing,
Rich as the rose's crimson flush,
And laughing like the fountain's gush,
As o'er the flowery mead she hies,
In chase of rainbow butterflies.
And many a lovely one beside,
In youthful bloom and beauty's pride,
Shall mingle in the gay parade—
Themselves a sunlight without shade.
Nor shall the sprightly lassies lack
Attendants on their shining track;
For round their beauty's dazzling rays,
Like moths around the taper's blaze,
The beaux shall flock—a chosen band,
The best and noblest of the land—
Gay, gallant youths, from vices free,
Of lofty truth and chivalry;
For such alone, and not the vile,
Should share the light of Beauty's smile.
So bright, my love, the train shall be,
So linked by social harmony,
That all who shall behold the sight
Will say with wonder and delight—
"Oh, what a garland have you wove,
Of living beauty, light, and love!"

XIII

And where is she, our beauteous friend,
The boasted flower of "Old Fort Bend"?
Oh, she shall in our sports unite,
Sweet queen of beauty, love, and light.
I name her not—but well opine
That all will know her by this sign—
The lady of cerulean eye,
Of aspect sweet and mild reply.
By those who know and love her well,
She's styled "The Lily of the Dell."
Her fairy form is light and free,
As flexible as the willow-tree,
And, like that tree, though ne'er at rest,
Is still with graceful motion blest.
From Rio Bravo to Sabine,
A fairer face may not be seen—
All radiant with happy thought,
And yet like Grecian sculpture wrought.
The wedded roses on her cheek
A thousand modest virtues speak;
For, like the fragrance of the rose,
Sweet truth in all her language flows.
Her honeyed lips of vermil dye,
Whose breath with Eden-gales might vie,
Are all too pure, too free from guile,
To harshly speak, or falsely smile;
Nor can her bright and sparkling eyes,
In which the light of genius lies,
Direct against a sister's heart,
Malignity's envenomed dart.

No—she is good as she is fair,
A sunny blessing everywhere;
An angel to the suffering poor,
Dispensing kindness evermore;
But most the friend of modest worth,
The unregarded good of earth,
Who pine neglected in the shade,
Where Pride would blush to tender aid.
At home, where woman best appears,
She's mindful of her household cares;
The ever cheerful, faithful wife,
Bright jewel of her husband's life;
And more beloved by all, I ween,
For charms like these—too rarely seen—
Than flaunting dames in rich brocade,
To folly wed, and vice betrayed.
How sweet to hear her flowing words,
Soft as the song of summer birds!
Her lute-like voice, with truth combined,
Is music married to the mind,
Still changing with unlabored grace
To suit the purpose, time, and place.
As subjects grave or gay provoke,
To sober thought or merry joke,
That voice flows on like honeyed streams
Of melody in morning dreams.
When leisure leaves her to be gay,
And all is bright as rosy May,
Behold her in the dance's maze,
A floating star of dazzling rays,
The glory of the festal hall,
The light, the life, the soul of all—
Dispensing, like Euphrosyne,

The joy of motion—light of glee
Until the gazer almost deems
Himself involved in golden dreams,
Or thinks some form of heavenly birth
Has come in rainbows to the earth,
To show this world how purely bright
The creatures of supernal light.
She is—but stay!—I find, my dear,
I'm painting *you* instead of *her;*
For on my soul, and sense, and sight,
Is stamped so deep your image bright,
I can no other charms review,
But those that live and breathe in you:—
So let me change to sable dye,
The azure of that sparkling eye—
And lo! the "Lily of the Dell"
Is but my own sweet Nonpareil!

XIV

The day is spent. At evening hour,
We'll sit and sing in Lola's bower,
Or frolic on the velvet green,
Beneath the moon's inviting sheen;
Nor shall one thought or passion rude
Upon the peaceful scene intrude;
But friendship, love, and gay good-will,
Shall triumph over every ill.
Thus will we many a summer day
Devote to pleasures light and gay—
Sweet pastimes of the cheerful mind,
And of that pure and guiltless kind,

That Memory often will restore
With fond delight when all is o'er.

XV

O ye, who may by chance peruse
These gathered products of my muse,
Remember that my songs were writ
To show my love, and not my wit;
And hard it were by rigid rule
To judge the bard of such a school.
My verse may want the torrent's force,
And some may scorn its quiet course;
Yet there is many a bosom still,
That echoes to the rippling rill.
What though no vivid lightnings shine
Along my loose and careless line,
Yet welcome still in summer night
May be the fire-fly's glancing light.
The bard whom love alone beguiles,
Who only sings for beauty's smiles—
To wake in souls of gentle tone
The tenderness that thrills his own—
May never gain, by lofty thought
And daring speech, the purpose sought;
For gentle woman, pure of heart,
Is won by nature, not by art;
And welcome more than florid lies
Is truth to her in homely guise.
Such is the nature of my lays—
Plain, simple strains in Beauty's praise;
Designed at first for those fair friends
Whose memory with my being blends,

And now sent forth to find their way
To minds congenial, grave or gay.
Oh, could their simple tones impart
One throb of joy to woman's heart,
The bard would find, for all his toil,
An over-payment in her smile.

XVI

It would my spirit deeply grieve
If any song of mine should leave
A stain upon the tender mind,
Or tempt to pleasures unrefined.
I sometimes write in merry style,
To wake the gay, good-natured smile—
To cast a gleam, a flitting ray
Of sunshine o'er a cloudy day;
But not for all Australia's gold
Would I one evil thought unfold,
Or over Guilt's abhorrent mien
Extend a veil of silver sheen.
No—rather let me gently show
The goodly way the world should go;
Inspire the young, unsullied mind
With love of God and humankind,
And teach the beautiful of heart
That blended piety and mirth
Can brighten all things here below,
And save the heart from many a wo.
If, after all, should sorrows rude
Disturb the bosom's quietude,
Be mine the gentle task to dry
The tear that darkens Beauty's eye,

And taste the joy which all must feel
Who shall the wounded spirit heal.

XVII

And now ye damsels sweet and shy,
One friendly word, and then good-by.—
Youth is the season of delight,
And pleasure too is Beauty's right;
But wo betide the maid that strays
From Virtue's pure and sacred ways,
To gather on forbidden ground
The joys which never yet were found!
The wicked may not hope for rest;
The good and wise alone are blest;
And those who think that rapture dwells
In Error's dark, secluded dells,
Will find—when Vice has sent his dart
Envenomed to the bleeding heart—
A disappointment dark and deep,
A dread remorse that will not sleep,
A deathless pang, a foul disgrace
Which time and tears can ne'er efface.
Then fly, ye ever-smiling throng,
Sweet listeners to my careless song—
For ever fly the Upas-shade,
Where all that's beautiful must fade,
And seek those valleys pure and bright,
Fair, smiling vales of love and light,
Where sacred Truth has built her shrine,
And made the landscape half divine.

XVIII

I would not have you over-sage,
Nor prisoned in a golden cage,
But free to roam, to sport and sing
With lightsome heart, like birds of spring;
And, dancing with the smiling hours,
Throw sunshine over fields and flowers.
Yet, lassies, let me say again,
Nor deem reiteration vain,
That virtue is the joy of youth—
There is no peace apart from truth;
And every pleasure wrongly bought
Will be revenged in sober thought.·
If, in your frolics light and gay,
Ye quite forget the coming day,
And have no moral wealth prepared
To bless ye when ye're silver-haired,
Your fate will be like thoughtless bees,
That widely sport in bower and breeze,
Yet gather from the rose's bloom
No honeyed stores for winter's gloom.
Where'er ye go, what'er ye do,
This useful lesson keep in view—
That peace below, and bliss above,
Are only won by truth and love.

O LADY, WHILE A NATION POURS
To Mrs. Ann Stephens

Among the many celebrities whom Lamar met in New York in 1845 was Mrs. Ann Sophia Stephens, wife of Edward Stephens. She had achieved a reputation as a poetess and as editor of The Ladies' Companion, Graham's Magazine, *and* The Ladies' World. *She was destined to write America's first dime-novel,* Malaeska: the Indian Wife of the White Hunter *(New York, 1860).*

During Lamar's stay in New York Mrs. Stephens named a son after him, and published a poem to him in The Knickerbocker Magazine *(notes, p. 312). Lamar returned the compliment with "O Lady, While a Nation Pours," written at New York, April, 1857, for publication in* Verse Memorials.

1857   1857

I

O Lady, while a nation pours
    Its praises in thine ear,
Wilt thou the lay that Friendship weaves,
    A moment deign to hear?
I bring no wreath to flatter pride,
    No gem to brighten fame;
My only gift's a grateful heart,
    And this thou well mayst claim.

II

The world may laud thy genius rare—
    Its triumphs high proclaim;
But there are loftier honors still,
    In-woven with thy name.

293

They are the moral gems, that form
  Thy life's enchanting light—
Unsullied truth—unwavering light—
  And fervor for the right.

III

The cheering smile—sustaining word—
  The ready aid at call—
The active love that worries not
  In working good to all:—
To make another's wrong thine own,
  To vindicate the poor,
To never turn uncomforted
  The wretched from thy door—

IV

These, these are bright, enduring bays,
  That with thy glories blend;
And while they win the world's applause,
  Still make me more thy friend.
The author's fame may pass away,
  The woman's can not die—
The flash of genius is of earth,
  But love is from the sky.

V

Oh, could I snatch, Prometheus-like,
  From Love's celestial throne,
The fire of life—to give my lyre
  The spirit of thine own—

How sweet, in Friendship's sacred name,
  A wreath of song to twine,
Whose kindred fragrance might embalm
  My name and fame with thine!

VI

What though my lyre may only breathe
  Affection's simple tone;
What though no robes of starry light
  Are round its numbers thrown—
Yet ever welcome to the good
  The artless song must prove,
That pours the heart-felt homage due
  To genius, truth, and love.

ROSES AND LAURELS
To Mrs. Caroline Sawyer

Mrs. Caroline M. Sawyer, the wife of a Presbyterian minister in New York, was one of the literati *whose companionship Lamar enjoyed during his visit to the East in 1845 (see p. 70). Upon that occasion she wrote the tribute "To General Mirabeau Lamar" (notes, p. 314). Lamar repaid the compliment with "Roses and Laurels," written May 4, 1857, the night before he left New York for Washington.*

The text here printed is a revision made by Lamar after the publication of Verse Memorials *(notes, p. 313).*

1857   1857
                                                          1937

I

Oh had I, dear lady, the power
  To fashion thy destiny here,
Thy life would be sunshine and blossoms,
  And glory should crown thy career.
No cloud should e'er darken thy heaven,
  No sorrow thy spirit depress,
But all that is lovely and loving
  Should gather around thee to bless.

II

Of roses and laurels united,
  Combining their crimson and green,
Should Fame a rich garland entwine thee,
  And Piety hallow its sheen.
Already such garland thou wearest—
  How pure and bright are its rays!

Its lustre is caught from affection,
　　Its fragrance, the breath of thy lays.

III

O loveliest daughter of morning,
　　Bright gem of thy radiant race,
With goodness illumin'd by genius,
　　And purity heightened by grace,
The minstrel may prize a perfection
　　He ne'er can describe in his lay,
As the beauty that dwells in the rainbow—
　　We feel it—but can not portray.

IV

Though I bid thee farewell on the morrow,
　　My heart is not severed from thee;
For the light of thy loveliness still
　　My companion shall be;
And purer by far than yon planet,
　　That sparkles so bright in the west,
Thine image will rise every evening,
　　And dwell a sweet star in my breast.

FLOWERS FROM THE HEART
To Mrs. Mary Roberts

Lamar wrote "Flowers from the Heart" especially for publication in Verse Memorials. *The verses are a tribute to the wife of Alexander Roberts, the son of Lamar's lifelong friend, Willis Roberts. On his seventeen trips over the Georgia-Texas route, Lamar had been a frequent guest in the Roberts home in Mobile.*

1857   1857

I

Dear, genial friend, enchanting one!
   Though parted many a long, long year,
Still like the bright, returning sun,
   Thy mem'ry rises calm and clear,
And calls me back to those blest days,
   When, seated by your social hearth,
I drank with rapture all your lays,
   And mingled in your children's mirth.

II

There's Laura with her footsteps light,
   Her sparkling eye and ringing laugh;
There's Willis with his flying kite,
   And Eber on his grandpa's staff.
I see them all in merry mood,
   As if they still were by my side—
A noisy crew—but never rude—
   Their parents' pleasure and their pride.

298

III

Fair scions of a generous race!
   Their high inheritance shall be
Their father's worth—their mother's grace—
   Instruction pure, and spirit free.
How sweet to see their virtues blow,
   Like buds expanding in the air,
And in their parents' likeness grow—
   The sons all brave—the daughters fair!

IV

Oh, blest beyond the common lot,
   Have flown my years since last we met,
With every trouble long forgot,
   And scarce a boon to sigh for yet.
Like yon declining sun, my life
   Is going down all calm and mild,
Illumined by an angel-wife,
   And sweetened by a cherub-child.

V

Yet still I oft recall your worth,
   And oft your mirth and music miss;
Old friendship takes a second birth,
   And links the past with present bliss.
I'm happy, too, to know that Time
   Is strewing still thy path with bloom,
And life's best fruit, in richer prime,
   Swells from the blossom's brief perfume.

299

VI

I could not think, dear friend, to close
    This volume of memorial lays,
Nor frame one song to her who glows
    So brightly in departed days.
The wreath I twine can bring no fame—
    Frail garland wove with little art;
And yet it may this merit claim—
    The flowers are gathered from the heart.

THE BELLE OF NINDIRI

The belle was Señorita Maria Martinez, daughter of Tomas Martinez, whose country place was near the little village of Nindiri, eleven miles southeast of the capital, Managua, where Lamar resided when in Nicaragua. Lamar had visited in the Martinez home en route to Costa Rica, and upon his arrival at his destination, like the old Scotch minstrels, paid for his entertainment with a song—a compliment to the daughter of the house. It was written November 7, 1858.

*   The poem was published as No. 2694 (VI, 393) of the* Lamar Papers. *Its similarity to "The Daughter of Mendoza" suggests that it is an earlier form of that poem.*

1858   1927

I

Adieu ye Belles of colder climes
    With all your snowy whiteness;
Your beauty is a Northern-light,
    That chills amidst its brightness;

But welcome to the gay brunette,
With soul of fire and eye of jet,
Light dancing to the castanet—
        The Belle of Nindiri.

II

How sweet to hear at summer eve,
  Her song among the mangoes,
And see her glance like fire-flies
  Along the gay fandangoes.
Her form is light—her spirit bright,
To all a sunbeam of delight,
A rose by day, and star by night—
        The Belle of Nindiri.

III

O, lend to me, Sweet Nightingale,
  Your music by the fountains;
And lend to me your cadences,
  O, rivers of the mountains.
I fain in song would eternize
A brighter light than Helen's eyes,
A jewel dropp'd us from the skies—
        The Belle of Nindiri.

IV

Behold the rosy dawn of day,
  Whose light the lark is hailing;
And mark the universal smile
  Of joy, o'er all prevailing.

Such is the day-break of her face
Diffusing joy in every place—
The bright aurora of her race—
     The Belle of Nindiri.

V

O, lovely maid of Nindiri,
   Bewildering and beguiling;
The lute is in thy silver tones,
   The rainbow in thy smiling;
And thine is, too, o'er hill and dell,
The bounding of the young gazelle—
The swallow's flight and ocean's swell—
     The Belle of Nindiri.

VI

What though we part to meet no more,
   O, Spirit pure and tender,
The bard will bear in distant lands
   The memory of thy splendor;
He'll ne'er forget his gay brunette,
The diamond spark in coral set—
Gem for a prince's coronet—
     The Belle of Nindiri.

THE DAUGHTER OF MENDOZA

Lamar sent "The Daughter of Mendoza" to Señorita Josefa Ana Mendoza, the daughter of José Mendoza, of the village of Pueblo Nuevo, Nicaragua, thirty miles northwest of Managua, where Lamar was living. In her own district she was known as the Belle of Pusada, and considered rarely beautiful. With the poem Lamar sent this note, written in his best Spanish:

Be pleased to accept the following lines in compliance with the promise which I made of writing you a poem. They are not worthy of the pleasing subject which has inspired them; but I can not make them better in so short a time. I regret that I was not able to write them in your language. But the task of translating them can serve as an exercise for one of your admirers . . . (Lamar Papers, No. 2721 [VI, 408]).

The poem was published in The Macon (Georgia) Daily Telegraph *of May 6, 1861 (the text here printed), with the explanation that a wanderer had found it in Nicaragua. The last of Lamar's poems, it has been the favorite of anthology-makers (notes, p. 315).*

1858   1861

I

O lend to me, sweet nightingale,
Your music by the fountain;
And lend to me your cadences,
O river of the mountain!
That I may sing my gay brunette,
A diamond spark in coral set,
Gem for a prince's coronet—
The daughter of Mendoza.

II

How brilliant is the morning star;
The evening star—how tender:

303

The light of both is in her eye—
Their softness and their splendor.
But for the lash that shades their light,
They were too dazzling for the sight,
And when she shuts them, all is night—
The daughter of Mendoza.

III

O! ever bright and beauteous one,
Bewildering and beguiling,
The lute is in thy silver tone,
The rainbow in thy smiling;
And thine is, too, o'er hill and dell,
The bounding of the young gazelle—
The arrow's flight and ocean's swell—
Sweet daughter of Mendoza.

IV

What though, perchance, we meet no more;
What though too soon we sever;
Thy form will float like emerald light,
Before my vision ever;
For who can see and then forget
The glories of my gay brunette—
Thou art too bright a star to set,
Sweet daughter of Mendoza.

NOTES

Page 82. When Lamar returned to Richmond from Mobile in 1855, he brought to his wife a copy of The Knickerbocker Gallery, *a gift from A. B. Meek. The fly-leaf bore this tribute from the Mobile poet:*

Fair daughter of a gifted sire,
Whose lips were touched with hallowed fire,
And glowed with light and thought intense,
The very soul of eloquence;
And, happier still, the cherished bride
Of one who is his country's pride—
To whom the blended wreaths belong
Of valor, statesmanship, and song;
Fair lady, unto thee so blest,
    And worthy of such noble love—
So doubly honored, so caressed,
    So prized all other forms above—
To thee, whose sweetly-cultured mind
By every virtue is refined—
This wreath of kindred thoughts I send,
A tribute from thy husband's friend.

"THE MAIDEN'S REMONSTRANCE"

Page 131. The revisions for the Verse Memorials, *which affected more than half the original lines, tended toward the smoothing of the rhythm. The last four lines of the* Enquirer *version read:*

And he who woos and will not wed
    Is viper in the roses,
And many a tear the maid may shed
    Who on his faith reposes.

"ARM FOR THE SOUTHERN LAND"

Page 169. The Texas Republican (October 10, 1835) printed the following version, revised by Lamar to apply to the Texas struggle:

Arm for your injured land;
   Where will you find a braver?
Low lay the tyrant hand
   Uplifted to enslave her.

Each hero draws
In freedom's cause,
   And meets the foe with bravery;
The servile race
Will turn their face,
   And safety seek in slavery.

Chains for the dastard slave:
   Recreant limbs should wear them.
But blessings on the brave
   Whose valor will not bear them.

Charge, charge my braves on Cos,
   And let no feuds divide you;
Behold the tyrant toss
   His banner to deride you.

The foe should feel
Proud freemen's steel,
   For freemen's rights contending;
Where e'er they die,
There let them lie,
   To dust in shame descending.

Thus may each traitor fall,
Who dare as foe invade us;
Eternal fame to all
Who shall in battle aid us.
Z.

"SUNSET SKIES"

Page 172. Though the Verse Memorials *text presents many differences as compared with that of the* Enquirer, *most of the variants are merely verbal. The most important difference occurs at the last of the fourth stanza, where the early text reads:*

As if they fain would have me ride
In those bright regions by their side.

"THE HARP I DARE NOT WAKE"

Page 176. The last twelve lines as printed in The Columbus Enquirer *(Nov. 15, 1834), differ from later versions. They are:*

And should I touch its chords again
    To gladden other ears,
O who would prize the empty strain
    When all the soul was hers?

Then let me still the song deny
    That beauty sweetly claims.
I have no heart—I have no sigh
    To offer with my strains.

And well I know proud beauty spurns
    The minstrel and his rhymes
Who sings to one, yet fondly turns
    To bow at other shrines.

307

"WOMAN"

Page 189. The first stanza, as printed in the Enquirer *(April 17, 1835), is as follows:*

O, I have left a sunny clime
Where every face was fair,
And many a one did sweetly shine
To banish my despair;

But why regret the friends I leave,
Since everywhere I find
That love and beauty still abide
With all a woman-kind.

What appears to be a revision of the last stanza follows (Lamar Papers, *No. 2212a [VI, 16]):*

Thou art indeed the poor man's friend,
The rich man's brightest gem,
Through weal and woe, the brightest light
In night's rich diadem.
Thou art indeed a sister star
To Judah's gem on high;
A lovely light that guides aright,
For all to wander by.

"ON THE DEATH OF MY DAUGHTER"

Page 236. The letter and lines from Edward Fontaine to Lamar are (Lamar Papers, *No. 2159 [V, 505]):*

My Dear Friend:
It was not until a few days ago that I heard of your overwhelming affliction. Knowing the deep anguish you must have suffered and are still suffering and being acquainted with your

capacity for mental agony, I am filled with uneasiness on your account. Do let me beg you, my dear General, to pray fervently that you may be enabled to bear your irreparable loss with the firmness of an Aemilius, and the resignation of a Christian. I read today in my wife's Album those touching lines addressed to your daughter, commencing with

> O do not ask me now for rhyme,
> For I am lonely-hearted,

and catching something of the inspiration of your own sorrow, I penned the enclosed lines which you will please accept as an effort to do what none but Omnipotence can perform. It is vain to forbid the "reft bosom to grieve." Yet it is an abortive attempt which sympathizing friendship ever makes. Your own opinion of rhyming being "the labor steals the heart from woe," this must be my excuse for this innocent endeavor to soothe the bitterness of my own feelings.

> She is gone from our path like a Heavenly strain
> Of music that floats o'er the moonlit plain;
> Which, though the lulled ear would court its stay,
> Soon passes and dies to deep stillness away.

> O that the power to soothe thy pain
>   Were given to a friend,
> My plaintive lyre would breathe a strain
>   Thy sorrows all to end.
> Its notes would lift thine aching eyes
>   Above the sacred shrine
> Where broken now that Casket lies,
>   So late a form divine.

> 'Twould show thy fond parental gaze
>   The Gem it once confined
> Now bright amid the brightest blaze
>   Of Seraph's charms combined.

That Jewel bright from Heaven's height
 To earth can never fall;
Its lustre pure is now secure
 From Nature's dismal pall.

O do not deem that river's side
 (Chattahoochee's Water)
Now coldly wraps thy spirit's Bride
 Or thy lovely Daughter.
Above that cherished river's wave
 Their blest forms are shining.
Then look not on that silent grave,
 Cheerlessly repining.

Brilliant stars in Heaven's sky
 Ever beaming on thee,
They now invite thy soul to fly
 Above earth's misery.
Guardian Spirits, they hover near
 Thy heart's deep agony;
Friend of my soul, do not fear—
 Angel friends are with thee.

My wife joins me in fervent prayers for your temporal and
eternal happiness.
                              Your friend,
                                Edw. Fontaine.

*A B. Meek sent Lamar's "On the Death of My Daughter" to
J. R. Thompson, editor of* The Southern Literary Messenger,
*with the following letter, printed with the poem in that peri-
odical, XV (July, 1849), 398:*

My Dear Sir:—Herewith I send you a poem, from the pen of
a friend, which he has consented to have published at my

instance. Were I at liberty to communicate his name, you would find it highly distinguished at the South, in many departments, both of Thought and Action. Like the young German, Körner, the author has twined the brightest laurels of the Muses around the crimson splendors of the sword,—with the super-added distinctions of the Statesman. These verses will speak their own praise. They are a touching tribute of paternal affection, and seem almost the very tears of love crystallized into poetry, by the spell of genius. Since the Monody of Mason, on the death of his wife, I know nothing of the kind more beautiful or pathetic. Thus much you can say from me.

Very truly, your friend,

A. B. Meek.

"NORA"

Page 266. "Desultory," the early form of "Nora," appeared as follows in The Columbus Enquirer (February 8, 1834):

> Fair Lady, cease that lively lay,
> Ill suited to that deep distress;
> It may delight the young and gay,
> But not the heart of loneliness.
> Thy angel voice is soft and clear
> Like music from a distant sphere;
> But when to sprightly warbling lent,
> It wakes unwelcome merriment.
>
> With gladsome heart I may not greet
> The flow'ry songs that bind to earth;
> They fall like some forbidden sweet,
> The music of untimely mirth.
> My heart lies buried with the dead;
> I live with those whose souls have fled,
> And cannot bear the Lethean strains
> That bring oblivion of their names.

311

O give me in thy gathered breath
    A gushing song of days gone by;
Some solemn requiem of death
    That brings the tear-drop in the eye.
I love o'er buried friends to weep,
My mind still lingers where they sleep;
And if thou canst their forms restore,
I'll love the song—the minstrel more.

"O LADY, WHILE A NATION POURS"

Page 293. Mrs. Ann Stephens published the following poem—
"To General Mirabeau B. Lamar"—in The Knickerbocker
Magazine *for March, 1845 (reprinted in* The Georgia Tele-
graph, *Macon, April 1, 1845):*

The sands have all been golden sparks
    Which measured out the time
Since thou, brave friend! hast been a guest
    In our chilly northern clime:
The sweet and dreamy summer's sun,
    That kindles half the year
The blossoms of thy prairie-land,
    We can not give thee here.

Our eaves are hung with icicles,
    Our mountains clad in snow;
And the jewelry of Winter chains
    The brooklet's silvery flow.
But the sunshine of thy own bright deeds
    Its genial warmth imparts;
And blossoms are surrounding thee,
    From a thousand friendly hearts.

High deeds, high thoughts enkindle still
    Our Northern patriot blood;

312

No frost can reach its sparkling thrill,
  Or check its ruby flood.
Our love will ever linger round
  That bright and fragrant land,
Which owes its wealth and freedom
  To thy strong and willing hand!

To a wilderness of blushing flowers
  Thy sword and lute have given
High Freedom, and the voice of song—
  Those two best gifts of Heaven.
And thou hast won the pale Lone Star
  Its brightest golden beam;
And from our own dear home afar,
  We joy to watch its gleam.

"ROSES AND LAURELS"

Page 296. In Verse Memorials *(September, 1857) the third
stanza reads:*

O beautiful daughter of Morning,
  Were mine but the alchemist's art,
How soon should this world be transmuted
  To all that could gladden thy heart!
Fame, Fortune, and Friendship—blest trio!
  Like spirits should come at my call,
And crown thee a queen among women—
  The brilliant Aurora of all.

Lamar revised the stanza in a letter of December 1, 1857, to C. C. Savage, Washington, D. C. (Dienst Collection).
Mrs. Caroline Sawyer wrote the following verses, entitled "To General Mirabeau Lamar" (Lamar Papers, Nos. 342 [I, 343] and 2181 [IV, 101]):

How shall I wake the farewell strain, and weave
    The simple lay that may my theme befit?
For thou has bid me sing, and I would leave
    Some echo in thy soul, to linger yet
        When thou art far away!

High song should greet the gallant and the brave,
    And lofty numbers swell the proud refrain;
Yet, o'er thy brow though verdant laurels wave,
    And mine is but a woman's faltering strain,
        Thou wilt accept the lay.

By the glad gatherings round the social hearth;
    The thoughtful mingling, mind with kindred mind;
The quiet converse and the gentle mirth;
    The generous glow and sentiment refined—
        I shall remember thee!

So, in thy home where fadeless beauty dwells—
    Where broad savannas drink the torrid ray—
When in thy breast some pleasant memory swells
    Of by-gone scenes and friends far, far away—
        May I remembered be!

Yet think of me as thou wouldst think of one
    For whom 'twere well that earth's vain dreams were o'er;
Whose troubled journey may be nearly done,
    Whose spirit yearns to seek the better shore—
        The beautiful and far!

314

But fare thee well!—thy country calls thee back;
Lone and in peril, she hath need of thee;
Go—and, in all your proud and shining track
May thou and she alike victorious be!—
Adieu to thee—Lamar!

"THE DAUGHTER OF MENDOZA"

*Page 303. For a few of the many republications of the poem
see: J. C. Kyger,* Texas Gems *(Denison, 1885), p. 20; S. H.
Dixon,* The Poets and Poetry of Texas *(Austin, 1885), p. 178;
S. H. Dixon,* Memoirs of Georgia *(Atlanta, 1895), II, 25;
Edward Mayes,* Lucius Q. C. Lamar *(Nashville, 1896), p. 17;
E. C. Stedman,* An American Anthology *(New York, 1900),
p. 88; E. C. Stedman and E. M. Hutchinson,* A Library of Ameri-
can Literature *(New York), I, 478; L. L. Knight,* Reminiscences
of Famous Georgians *(Atlanta, 1907), I, 174;* Library of South-
ern Literature *(Atlanta, 1907), VII, 2993; Mildred Rutherford,*
The South in History and Literature *(Atlanta, 1907), p. 130;
Louise Manley,* Southern Literature *(Richmond, Virginia,
1907), p. 223; Carl Holliday,* Three Centuries of Southern
Poetry *(Nashville, 1908), p. 53; W. P. Trent,* Southern Writers
(New York, 1910), p. 159; D. F. Eagleton, Writers of Texas
(New York, 1913), p. 42; L. W. Payne, Southern Literary Read-
ings *(Chicago, 1913), p. 126; Jennie Clarke,* Songs of the South
(London, 1914), p. 17; M. G. Fulton, Southern Life in Southern
Literature *(New York, 1917), p. 197;* Kind Words *(Nashville),
February 22, 1920; W. L. Weber,* Selections from the Southern
Poets *(New York, 1921), p. 209; H. R. Greer,* Voices of the South-
west *(New York, 1923), p. 3;* Pan-American Magazine *(New
Orleans), October, 1923; L. W. Payne,* A Survey of Texas
Literature *(New York, 1928), p. 20; Mabel Major,* The South-
west in Literature *(New York, 1929), p. 27; East Texas Maga-
zine (Longview, Texas), July, 1929.*

SELECTED BIBLIOGRAPHY

MANUSCRIPT SOURCES

Dienst Collection. Certain letters to and from Lamar, especially during the years 1850–1857. Now in the possession of Dr. Alex Dienst (Temple, Texas) and the University of Texas.

Lamar, Mirabeau B. Album of twenty-three poems in his own handwriting. Now in the possession of Lamar's family (Galveston, Houston, and League City, Texas).

———. "Journal of My Travels." A sixty-eight-page account of his journey from Georgia to Texas in 1835. Now in the possession of Lamar's grandchildren (Houston, Texas).

———. Private unpublished correspondence, in the possession of the Lamar family.

Lamar, Rebecca Ann. Album containing forty-seven of Lamar's poems in his handwriting. Now in the possession of a branch of the Lamar family at Columbus, Georgia.

———. "Diary." Lamar's daughter's account of her visit from Georgia to Texas in 1838.

Sandusky, William. Manuscripts of twelve of Lamar's poems in Sandusky's handwriting. Now in possession of the Sandusky descendants (Wascom, Texas).

BOOKS AND ARTICLES

Baker, D. *A Texas Scrap-Book.* New York, 1875.

Barker, Eugene C. "Mirabeau Bonaparte Lamar," University of Texas *Record*, V, No. 2 (Aug., 1903), 146-60.

Binkley, William C. *The Expansionist Movement in Texas* (University of California *Studies*). Berkeley, 1925.

Brooks, Elizabeth. *Prominent Women of Texas.* Akron, Ohio, 1896.

Brown, John Henry. *History of Texas.* 2 vols., St. Louis, 1893.

Buckley, W. J. "Speech before the Texas House of Representatives, Jan. 3, 1860." *State Gazette Appendix,* IV, 92-94.

Burnet, David G. "Death of Gen. Lamar," *The Northern Standard* (Clarksville, Texas), Jan. 14, 1860.

Caldwell, Robert G. "Mirabeau Buonaparte Lamar," *Dictionary of American Biography* (New York, 1933), X, 553-54.

Cate, Wirt A. *Lucius Q. C. Lamar.* Chapel Hill, 1935.

Cazneau, Mrs. W. L. ("Cora Montgomery"). *Texas and Her Presidents.* New York, 1845.

———. "The Presidents of Texas," *The Democratic Review* (N. Y.), XVI (March, 1845), 282-91.

Christian, Asa K. *Mirabeau Buonaparte Lamar.* Austin, 1923.

Cooke, F. J. "Brigham and I," *Educational Free Press* (Austin), I (March, 1902), 7.

Copcutt, Francis. "Mirabeau B. Lamar," *The Knickerbocker,* XXV (May, 1845), 377-87.

Croffut, W. A. "How They Did It," *The Galveston Daily News,* April 10, 1885; reprinted from *Detroit Free Press,* April 4, 1885.

Daniell, L. E. *Personnel of the Texas Government.* San Antonio, 1892.

DeCordova, Jacob. *Texas: Her Resources and Her Public Men.* Philadelphia, 1858.

Dienst, Alex. "Mirabeau B. Lamar, Patron of Education," *East Texas* Magazine (Longview, Texas), July, 1929.

Dixon, Sam H. *The Poets and Poetry of Texas.* Austin, 1885.

———, and Louis W. Kemp. *Heroes of San Jacinto.* Houston, 1932.

Eagleton, Davis F. *Writers of Texas.* New York, 1913.

Elsemore, Moses. *An Impartial Account of the Rev. John N. Maffitt.* New York, 1848.

Fontaine, Edward. "Mirabeau B. Lamar," Richardson's *The Texas Almanac* for 1858. Galveston, 1857. (For authorship, see *Lamar Papers,* No. 2591.)

Foote, H. S. *Texas and Texans.* Philadelphia, 1841. (A reprint of the account in the Houston *Telegraph,* April 14, 1838.)

Fry, Anna M. G. *Memories of Old Cahaba.* Nashville, 1908.

Gambrell, Herbert P. *Mirabeau Buonaparte Lamar.* Dallas, 1934.

Gibson, F. M. *"Verse Memorials," The Texas Sentinel,* Oct. 31, 1857. (A review.)

Graham, Philip. "An Unsigned Poem by Lamar," University of Texas *Studies in English,* No. 13 (July 8, 1933), 113.

———. "Mirabeau Lamar's First Trip to Texas," *The Southwest Review* (Dallas), XXI (1936), 369-89.

Gulick, Charles; Allen, Winnie; and Smither, Harriet, eds. *The Papers of Mirabeau Buonaparte Lamar,* 6 vols. Austin, 1920–1927.

Harden, Edward J. *The Life of George M. Troup.* Savannah (Georgia), 1859.

Hobby, A. M. *Life and Times of David G. Burnet.* Galveston, 1871.

James, Marquis. *The Raven.* Indianapolis, 1929.

Johnson, Frank W. *History of Texas and Texans,* vol. V. New York, 1914.

Johnston, William P. *The Life of Gen. Albert Sidney Johnston.* New York, 1878.

Jones, Anson. *Memoranda.* New York, 1859.

Kendall, George W. *Narrative of the Texan Santa Fe Expedition,* 2 vols. New York, 1844.

Kennedy, William. *Texas,* vols. II and III. London, 1841.

Knight, Lucian Lamar. *Georgia and Georgians,* 6 vols. Chicago, 1917.

———. *Georgia's Landmarks, Memorials, and Legends,* 2 vols. Atlanta, 1914.

———. *Reminiscences of Famous Georgians.* Atlanta, 1907.

Lamar, Mirabeau B. *Letter, Telegraph* (Houston), June 23, 1838.

———. *Letter on Annexation.* Macon, 1844.

Lamar, Mirabeau B. *Verse Memorials.* New York, 1857.

Lamar, William H. "Thomas Lamar . . . Descendants," *Publications* of the Southern Historical Association, I (1897), 203-10.

Lamar Papers. See Gulick, Charles.

"Lamar's Inauguration," *Niles National Register,* LV (Dec. 29, 1838), 274.

Lane, Walter P. *Adventures and Recollections.* Marshall, Texas, 1928.

Leclerc, Frederick. *Le Texas et sa Revolution.* Paris, 1840. This is dedicated to Lamar. English translation in *Southern Literary Messenger,* VII (May-June, 1841), 398-421.

Levasseur, A. *Lafayette en Amerique,* vol. II. Paris, 1829.

Lubbock, Francis R. *Six Decades in Texas.* Austin, 1900.

Maffitt, Emma M. *The Life and Services of John Newland Maffitt [Jr.].* New York, 1906.

Martin, John H. *Columbus, Georgia.* Columbus, 1874.

Mayes, Edward. *Lucius Q. C. Lamar.* Nashville, 1896.

Meek, Alexander B. Letter in *The Southern Literary Messenger,* XV (July, 1849), 398.

Miller, S. F. *The Bench and Bar in Georgia.* Philadelphia, 1858.

Peareson, P. E. "Reminiscences of Judge Edwin Waller," *Quarterly* of the Texas State Historical Association, IV (July, 1900), 33-53.

Quintero, J. A. Review of *Verse Memorials* in *Lamar Papers,* No. 2565 (VI, 356).

Raht, Arda T. "The House of Lamar," *San Antonio Express,* March 22, 1936.

Reese, Ruth Sara. "Mirabeau B. Lamar, Father of Texas Education," *The Texas Outlook,* XIX (Nov., 1935), 34.

Rutland, J. R. "The Artistic Side of Lamar," *Dallas News,* Nov. 26, 1936.

Smith, Sol. *The Theatrical Apprenticeship and Anecdotical*

Recollections of. Philadelphia, 1846. This book is dedicated to Lamar.

———. *Theatrical Journey-Work.* Philadelphia, 1854.

———. *Theatrical Management.* Philadelphia, 1868.

Sowell, A. J. *History of Fort Bend County.* Houston, 1904.

Sparks, W. H. *The Memories of Fifty Years.* Philadelphia, 1870.

Strong, Samuel M. "Gen. Mirabeau B. Lamar," *The Republic* (Macon), Jan. 15, 1845.

Sullivan, J. S. "Death of Ex-Pres. Lamar," *Galveston Weekly News,* Dec. 27, 1859.

Telfair, Nancy. *Columbus, Georgia.* Columbus, 1929.

Terrell, Alex. W. "The City of Austin from 1839 to 1865," *Quarterly* of the Texas State Historical Association, XIV (Oct., 1910), 113-28.

———. "Mirabeau B. Lamar," *Library of Southern Literature,* VII, 2987-3002.

———. "Recollections of General Sam Houston," *Southwestern Historical Quarterly,* XVI (Oct., 1912), 113-36.

West, Decca Lamar. "Mirabeau B. Lamar," *Houston Chronicle,* Jan. 27, 1929.

Willson, Marcus. *American History,* Bk. III, Pt. III. Cincinnati, 1847.

Yoakum, H. *History of Texas,* vol. II. New York, 1856.

INDEX

323